Miracles . . .
And Other Ordinary Things

Lana J. Ford, Ph.D.

I0891949

Temple Golden Publications
P.O. Box 10501
Sedona, Arizona 86339

Published by
Temple Golden Publications
P.O. Box 10501
Sedona, Arizona 86339

Cover design by Lana J. Ford
Cover Photo by Gene Falk
Illustrations by Lana J. Ford
Computer Graphics by Karla Mullennix

First Printing October, 1995

Bibliography: p. 400
1. Miracles 2. Health 3. Psychology 4. Spiritual 5. Self-Help

ISBN 0-929686-04-7

Dedication

To my children Michael and Jennifer. For their continuous and unconditional love, and gentle guidance in teaching me to love.

Acknowledgments

This text would not have been possible had I not been gifted with life-long masters and teachers, too numerous to mention. I am most indebted to Marlene Myhre, my publisher, for her gentle and patient guidance in editing, preparing for publication, and making all the connections that birthed my text into print. I thank Karla Mullennix for her incredible perseverance and loyalty as she transformed my sketches into computer illustrations.

I share great cosmic joy with Gayle Watts and Ingrid Muller for their willingness to play, as we each unfolded at the same time, in different ways. I offer heartfelt thanks to Margaret Dwyer for helping me focus the purpose for my being on the planet; to Saivahni Sharma Singh for her spiritual guidance; and to Jean Houston for her assistance in awakening me to the deeper meaning for being through Mystery School of 1991.

I acknowledge Ned Herrmann for his support and Peter Fenner, for his patience and gentle prodding as I completed my doctoral studies. A deep heartfelt acknowledgement to Barbara Rider, Joane Wyrick and Lou Carmona, long-time professional colleagues who offered support while I was pursuing a professional career. For my students at the University of Kansas during the years of 1972–1974, I am particularly grateful for their wisdom in teaching me how people learn.

Special thanks goes to Robert Ford, who provided the strength for the initiation of this journey. I am forever grateful to J. Lawton Smith, M.D. for awakening me to the meaning of my illness.

For their patience, nurturing, and extraordinary love, I am grateful to my children Michael and Jennifer Ford, who have shared this journey with me since the beginning. Finally, for the genetic stuff of which I am made, and for their continual support, I offer my gratitude to my biological parents Lawrence and Velma Young.

L.J.F.

Introduction

I have a story to tell -- it's about miracles and other ordinary things. You see, miracles happen all the time when you know how to look for them, when you understand that you create them. And in my heart, I know that miracles and love are really the same thing; they both come from the heart. They alter our sense of reality, they go beyond what we think and what we feel.

The first part of this book is a story about my experience which began twenty-two years ago. At that time, I was informed I had a brain tumor and that it was terminal. As a result I spent nearly two years being partially blind. But I didn't die. Then my diagnosis was changed to Multiple Sclerosis. So I went "shopping" for cures, for treatment, and for understanding. That was when I recognized that all my efforts were outwardly directed. I began going inward, not even knowing what I was doing -- just trusting the internal guidance. Then I became aware that what I was doing was working, my body began healing. Still I found no logical answers to my nagging questions, my insatiable curiosity regarding why I had the problems in the first place.

Once I regained my sight and my physical body was restored, I continued to look even deeper into the meaning of the illness, into the wisdom of the body. I pursued formal education thinking that I would find the answers to my experience if only I *knew* more. I began looking into other cultures, religions and philosophies. I explored the ancient and esoteric literature. I read and studied everything I could find -- from physics to astrology, psychology to cosmology. But it wasn't until I began the committed journey inward and realized that we are God–seeded, that it is Spirit which heals; therein lie the miracles.

Now we can journey together. For this is no longer just my story. This is a book about the way in which our consciousness is encoded in the language we speak, the thoughts we think, and the emotions we feel. This book is beyond the mind/body connection; it is about spiritual beings having a human experience. Having a healthy body doesn't mean that health is a physical issue. We live in a holographic body in an interactive universe.

It is time now for all of us to be pioneers into health for it is my belief that we have never experienced "real" health. My sense is that health is not the absence of disease, it is not the opposite of illness. Health is joy and bliss. It is a sense of exuberance that we can hold no matter what opportunities or challenges are presented to us. Health is an awareness of our Divine Heritage, but it does not exist until we are willing to call it forth, until we are able to recognize our responsibilities. We begin the journey into health by turning adjectives into verbs. We turn descriptors into action. And in that action there is "response–ability" –– the ability of the body to respond. We do this by opening up ourselves to the deeper meaning for being here.

Healthy body, Heal–thy body. Heal thy body!

L.J.F.

Contents

Miracles . . .
And Other Ordinary Things

Chapter 1 My Story

In the Beginning

I was married and had just given birth to my son Michael. Actually he was born in February and my experience started in following September. It was 1972. I had just returned to teaching at the University of Kansas following several years of private practice as an occupational therapist in California. My husband had left a navy career, largely at my request, and was a graduate student in law school at the University of Kansas. It was a busy time for the both of us. In addition to teaching classes in the Occupational Therapy Department, and acting as a liaison to the University Affiliated Facility serving handicapped children, I was also in graduate school working on a masters degree in special education. It wasn't that I was so much interested in special education, as I was in the course work related to "How is it that we learn?" It seems I have had a lifetime interest -- actually more than interest -- a lifetime curiosity about learning. At the time I was intrigued by the differences in how normal and retarded children learn. I thought perhaps a degree in special education would give me insight into how it was that I learned. You see, for as long as I can remember, I have had the unspoken feeling that I was somehow different, as if I wasn't from here. Well of course, I was from here in the sense that I was born in this country. But there was a deeper part of me that didn't seem tied to time or space.

There were things that I knew for which I had no way of accounting. I just *knew* them. I knew that ghosts, goblins and "goolies" were not just things that went bump in the night. They were real to me, as real as my other imaginary playmates. Oh, I know there is that "grown up" notion about children creating imaginary playmates out of a traumatic childhood. But my childhood was not traumatic. My parents were loving and supportive. I had a twin brother whom I thought then, and still do, was some sort of guide for how to do life on planet Earth. So while my upbringing was pretty normal, I also grew up learning to ignore the little inklings of insight about "other world" stuff. But then I am getting ahead of my story.

I was writing about being a wife and mother at the University of Kansas. And there was that book I was writing about retarded children. It seems funny now that I would focus a book on children, writing of diagnoses, disease, and treatment when I was about to embark on a journey that would challenge my understanding of limitations. Yes, it was a busy time, and I suppose my experiences could be just those of stress. As a new mother, a college instructor, as well as a student, I could have let myself off the hook, so to speak, by suggesting that the symptoms I was about to experience were related to that stress. I know better now, and I suspect I did then.

I remember sitting on the couch ready to go to a party several of my students were hosting. Suddenly, I began having a strange experience. I noticed that all the objects in the room were loosing their color. It was sort of like watching an old black and white movie. I was fascinated more than anything. Then objects began to fade in color, almost as if I were looking at negative images. I could see through them as if they were transparent. Not only were objects transparent, they were shimmering, with little sparkly threads touching the adjacent objects -- as if they were all connected by some imaginary web. Then they began moving, circling and circling. I had the strange sensation the world was closing in on me. I was in a fog that was getting thicker and thicker. I was spinning, as if I was going into a tunnel. Then my world disappeared.

As I sat on the little rose colored couch I had upholstered myself, I quietly began exploring all my sensations. I could hear the water running upstairs where my husband was showering. But it seemed so far away -- a world away. My son Michael must have dropped off to sleep because I could no longer hear the squeaking of the crib, which happened as he gently rocked himself, just before dozing off to sleep. As I began to experience those initial symptoms, I remember talking to myself as I had never done before. I was doing a body scan like a co-pilot readying the aircraft. Hearing O.K. Speaking O.K. I pinched myself and took note that feeling was O.K. Mostly I was curious. I felt no pain, no sense of panic. I scanned my memory for all the medical symptoms I could think of but came up with nothing. *No-thing!* I just couldn't see.

I remember my husband coming down the stairs and asking: "Are you ready?"

"No", I replied.

"Well what else do you have to do?"

"Nothing" *(No-thing!)* It's not that I have any thing to do. I just can't see you. I can't even see my hand in front of my face! And I am feeling very weird, like the world has just become a psychedelic panorama." Then I began to cry. It wasn't from fear. But for the events over which I had no logical explanation.

With that, we called our local physician. "You probably are experiencing hypoglycemia", he reported. "Low blood sugar. I suggest you eat some oranges and if you are still having problems in the morning give me a call."

I ate oranges. In fact, I ate a whole bag of them until I could feel the acid peeling off the layers of tissue on the inside of my mouth. But still I couldn't see. Just blankness. It didn't matter if my eyes were open or closed. As I crawled into bed, I wondered if I would be able to tell when I was awake or asleep.

I must have gone to sleep, because I remember waking up. Waking up and being able to see just fine. But by the time of my first scheduled appointment in the early afternoon, the fog had begun to settle in. Yet in some bizarre manner, it felt familiar, cozy, like it does when you are all snuggled inside, looking at the fog outside. It was then that I began having the strange sensation, for which I had no way to describe, that there was another "me," looking at the me who was having the experience. The scheduled appointment revealed nothing *(no–thing).* Yet it was my first step into the vast incredible maze of the medical world, only this time I was the patient.

As I have mentioned, at the time of these initial symptoms, I was teaching a course on mental retardation. I remember reflecting on reading material which suggested that with any traumatic health issue, it seems that one of the first reactions we have is to go shopping for a different diagnosis. And I found that I was behaving like the subject of one of the case studies selected for use in class. I could hear in my memory my telling students about the urge to shop for a different diagnosis. I remember stating, "We make it seem soph- isticated by saying to ourselves, we are getting a second opinion!" Now I know that a diagnosis doesn't mean that it is real, unless of course, we determine for ourselves that we need the diagnosis, or that kind of information. Information, *in-form-ation;* how different our world would be, if at those moments, we were to first seek inspiration, *in-spirit-on.* And again, I get ahead of my story.

But before I continue, I really do think we have this "shopping" well camouflaged. I know that was the case for me. I didn't want to accept what the medical community offered me. The shopping wasn't for a better bargain, a diagnosis of lesser effect, it was an attempt to forestall the possibility of determining for myself, the meaning of the illness. My reality at that time, was that I was not sick. Not ill as we would ordinarily define it. I didn't have any real symptoms. No headache, no vomiting, no change in blood pressure. Urine was clear, pulse rate normal. I wasn't hallucinating; I knew who I was and where I was. There was nothing *(no-thing)* wrong with me. I just couldn't see.

That first visit produced the diagnosis of hypoglycemia, but the blood work and the urinalysis were negative. Yet, probably because it was expected of me by friends and family, I did indeed go from physician to physician, from specialist to specialist. Interestingly enough, I discovered that if I saw ten different doctors, I had ten different opinions. Some were close to agreement, others were worlds apart. So

I begin to entertain the notion that perhaps the physicians didn't have all the answers. After all, their training is directed towards finding a diagnosis based on the description of symptoms. And each probably did precisely that. But their diagnoses did not fit my reality. I felt as though they were just speculating, like the stock market. One day it was up, the next it was . . . .

Besides, no one at that time could define for me what I was experiencing that made any sense to me. I mean, find some sort of reasonable, or even unreasonable explanation for all the internal stuff. I wasn't acting normally! I should have been scared or worried or something! I should have been less curious. I began to question why it was that the medical community just wanted to label my symptoms, not understand them; or understand me. How was it, I asked myself countless times, that I lived in this body and hadn't the faintest idea of how it really worked? Oh, I knew the superficial anatomy and physiology as a health practitioner, but what made me really tick? In my case, at the time, what made me *not* tick? My only recourse was to go inward, to find as I had in my childhood, the wisdom from inside. . . those little inklings of truth. . . those intuitive impulses. . . that state of being in which I *knew.*

The Blessings

Then the blessings. If I was to view my experience using a different lens I might have said, "then the tragedy struck." I was informed by my neuropthalmologist that I had a brain tumor. It was at the back of my head, the occipital area where we process sight. It also spanned the optic chiasm, the particular nerve tracts which link the right and left hemispheres of the brain together. It was believed to be terminal.

Terminal. *Terminal!* Ending my life -- at age thirty-one as a mother of a year old child? As wife of a man who purposely left a career because I was not cut out to be a "Navy Wife?" What did I feel? The enormity of those words engulfed me. I felt cast into a place that had no meaning, no time and no space. Even the words didn't make sense. All there was, was a profound sense of something unfolding, a feeling not of dying but being birthed, a knowing of nothing, *no-thing!* And I surrendered to it all.

I have vivid memories of those times. My reaction was not anger. I had a strange sensation of being blessed. I felt that it was a blessing that I had trained as an occupational therapist. I had worked with many persons of different diagnoses. I began to remember all sorts of encounters -- the parents who were angry to learn their child was retarded. The guilt felt by the sweet lady in the nursing home as she lay whispering that she knew how bad she was and how she had to be punished by God. I remembered working with a mother of a cerebral palsy child who refused to cooperate on a feeding program. She used to shout at me, "If this is God's will that my child is this way, I am going to feed him the same as the rest of my children." And she did. She fed him fried chicken on which he continuously gagged, suffering in the end from malnutrition. This, despite my shouting back at her, "But God made occupational therapists who help children with feeding problems."

I don't know how many times I sat quietly and reviewed in my mind, all the encounters with all the patients I ever had. I think I responded most to the remembrances of their feelings. The feelings of fear, anger and guilt, feelings full of judgment about the injustice of illness. I remember wondering a lot about God. For me, God was in a separate category called "religion," something I dealt with in church choir on Sunday mornings. I didn't think I was religious but something was happening -- something beyond the world of the five senses, beyond seeing with my physical eyes. Were these experiences a clue that things unseen and suspected of being subtle are more important than the world we construct from our five senses?

I couldn't ignore the truth that was yearning to pour forth. This truth seemingly bottled up for centuries, and like a wave, wanted to burst forth, to flood my waking moments. I knew I was not angry, and I was not afraid. I attended to the experience that there was another "me" inside of me, monitoring my reactions. There was that "me" watching my conversations and my fumbling that sometimes resulting in falling. There was that "me" who lived inside me who could sometimes look out and see the world taking on a different meaning. But mostly, day in and day out, I knew that I was not going to die. The words haunt me still. I remember telling a physician, "I will not die because I have not yet done what I came to do on this planet! I don't know what it is I have to do, but I know that the terminal diagnosis has no meaning for me." The unaware me, seemed startled by the words coming from my own mouth. I didn't seem to have control over them, as if I were listening to someone else's dialogue. These incidents, I was to discover in the intervening years, were the real gifting. My unshakable faith that I had something important to do. . . was this a miracle in the making?

Often I would come home in the evening and sit rocking in my favorite old wooden rocker, holding Michael. I had created in my head a world that was timeless. I could move forward and backward on a line of thought. I began to wonder "what if" I would die. What would it be like for my son to grow up without a mommy? What would my husband do? If I died, would he find another wife? And if I didn't die, but wasted, would he find a mistress? And what if it was all some kind of cosmic joke, some sort of semantic language game? It seemed I could make an entire movie with different outcomes. I could review my life in a forward rather than a backward direction. I was often struck by the funny notion that maybe memory included the future as well as the past. I mean, how could one tell if he or she were taping into a future memory or just day dreaming? Was there any real difference? Yet, despite my mental gymnastics, I wanted to pretend that I could be as quiet as possible. A being stuck in no time and no space, with no past and no future. A creature who only held her son in her arms, the only creatures in the world, rocking, rocking, rocking.

And there were those times when the internal dialogue was so loud as to assure me that others around me could hear the madness of my internal ravings. I had a hard time letting go of wondering what it would be like to die. Where would I go? I asked these questions of the "me" that was inside as well as the "real" me. I contemplated these things with a great deal of curiosity. My life became filled with internal dialogue -- the only conversations which made any sense. I began reflecting on each day, each hour, then urgently noticing that I could reflect on my feelings from minute to minute. It was as if I was wanting to change my life from a moving picture to a slide show, then examine the slides frame by frame.

In the speeded up version of my life, I reviewed my memories countless times, searching always for a deeper meaning. I paid particular attention to the repeated memory of the visit to the physician in which I was told I had a terminal condition. I remember that at one moment I was sitting in the doctor's office, wanting to talk with the doctor. Then I walked through the door to his office. Within minutes he told me I would die. Not just die, but soon! Terminal. I got up, walked through the door and returned to the waiting room for my husband to pick me up. But in those minutes, those infinitesimal moments between the slides, what happened to me? I asked if in that space could it be possible that my pictures of reality changed? And if they changed, could I redirect the change in another direction? Was it possible that in those moments of believing a diagnosis, I gave up all belief in myself? And did I give up control of my life to someone else because I thought they knew more than I did? Could it be possible that illnesses are created in these moments . . in the space between the events? Could it be that a medical diagnosis works like a placebo? That when an idea is planted, it begins to grow, only if I have provided the right environment for it, an environment of doubt, fear, need, lack and limitation. But did I have the courage to change my own meaning? I mean, could I just ignore the medical diagnosis? Could I create an environment in which a seed of dying could not live?

Over the next six months or so my vision came and went, sometimes it would slowly fade, as in the shower. As the hot water poured down my backside, my body began to disappear from the feet upward. I felt like the disappearing woman, except it was a phenomenon over which I had little control. It gave me the illusion that I was not here. And it made me ponder. If I am here when it seems I am not, then where am I? Am I only here when I give my attention to me? Is this the same as waking, sleeping, waking, sleeping? A constant going and coming out of different states of consciousness? If so, then where do I go when I am not attending to me? Where am I when I am not here?

As often as I tried to make sense of these experiences, the meandering of my mind, I found there were no answers. I couldn't find anything that fit into a logical, rational, organized world. These thoughts, these feelings, were in the realm of experience. And I even wondered if these were the thoughts that people thought as they were about to go mad, or insane, or have a psychotic episode. No matter how many people I told my story to, there were few who could really share my experience. After a while people didn't want to listen, and were perhaps perplexed because I ceased asking for advice from anyone. While I asked the hardest of questions, at the same time there was that *knowing* that I was not crazy. It was as if I was growing inside, expanding, while looking none-the-less unchanged on the outside. Not only was I having strange experiences, but I was learning to trust them, as a part of something that was "normal" for me. These experiences began to give me a sense of being "multi–dimensional," of having an awareness of me that was not bound by time and space, but as a being who was limitless, eternal. It was this part of me that was eavesdropping on the me who was having the experience.

I began developing a sense that sometimes I was actually "in" my body and sometimes I was not, well, not completely. A portion of me was in my body that could make it move and walk and talk. Another portion was out wandering the universe, playing with angels, using imaginary filaments of light to draw people to me. It seemed that I could draw people to me and while I was talking with them, I was simultaneously *knowing* exactly what they were about to say. This was sort of like having two me's, one slightly out of step, a cog ahead, relaying information back through milliseconds of time, to a me casually standing in place having a conversation. Perhaps that was why I felt no fear and no anger. I was truly having fun and I thought that it was perfectly "normal." It was as if I were watching a play, a script in which I was both the main actor and the director.

It's hard to explain the experiences of being "expanded," of knowing about events before they would happen. Like the experience of suddenly loosing my vision when I was driving. As an example, I share with you that particular event.

On the morning I am remembering, I got up at the usual time. As an aside, awakening was always interesting because it became a conscious process. As soon as I was aware that I was no longer sleeping, I did what I call a "body scan." I mentally scanned my body. I noticed I could feel the sheets and had the funny sense the sheets could feel me. That was how I knew I was still here. I listened and noted that I could hear. I breathed and noted that indeed, I was alive. Then would come the moment of truth. I opened my eyes. Sometimes the world was there in full living color. Other times it was foggy and devoid of color. Sometimes it was transparent, with the shimmery web–like projections connecting everything. Sometimes there was no difference whether my eyes were open or closed. I would have to use my hand to feel my eyelids. And sometimes it was just white -- the most awesome all encompassing white you can imagine.

On the particular day I am remembering, I awoke, did the body scan and with a deep breath opened my eyes. To my delight, the world was there in full living color. I loved those days so much. It was such a treat for me to see that the grass was green and the sky was blue. I didn't take those simple things for granted anymore. It seemed the simple things took on so much more meaning. How I treasured those moments. And each morning that I created with sight indicated to me that nothing, *no–thing,* was really wrong.

The Making of Miracles

That particular morning was important. I was eager to greet my day as I had an appointment with the neurologist. I assured my husband that I was just fine and that it really was O.K. for me to be driving. I jumped into my car and proceeded down the street humming softly to myself. I remember the toll road and I specifically remember contemplating if the toll gate would take twenty five cents in pennies rather than a quarter. Then I reasoned that by the time I played this little game and dug out all my pennies, I would be late for my appointment. But the thought of the little scenario made me giggle.

I proceeded across the bridge that spans the James River in Jacksonville, Florida, marveling at the bridge construction although I had crossed the bridge many times before. As I neared the hospital, I moved into the left lane as the road dead-ended into a park. I remember wondering why I had never walked in the park. In taking that moment of contemplation, I noticed two young men walking on the sidewalk. Then suddenly the world disappeared! Blank. White. In the blink of an eye (literally), the world I was musing was no longer there.

I could hear the cars honking behind me. It seemed then as if my perception stretched way beyond my physical space. There was that part of me out away from my body. In that millisecond I sensed that to my right there was a space between two cars in a right lane of cars that were also turning left. My choices seemed limited in that millisecond. Stop? Go forward? I chose the latter. I gently pressed on the accelerator knowing that by going straight I would cross two lanes of traffic turning left in front of me.

The curb jolted me into remembering to put on the brake. I remember breathing. I was not hit by the turning traffic. I was just sitting in my car that jumped the curb by the park, unable to see.

Just then I heard a male voice ask: "Are you O.K. miss?" It was the voice of a young man. It was the voice of one of the two men I had seen walking on the sidewalk just moments before. I listened not with my ears, but with my heart. I could feel the fear in his voice, but it was a question of genuine concern. I reasoned, it meant I could trust him.

"AAAA," I breathed, "I am not hurt. But I am not O.K. I know this sounds bizarre, but I can't see."

"You can't see?"

"She must have hit her head or something," another male voice offered.

"No, I didn't hit my head. I am on my way to see the neurologist. I have a visual problem and sometimes I can see and sometimes I can't. Seems I just found one of those times I can't."

I remember joking to deal with my own trembling. From somewhere outside of me I had the strange sensation that all of this really sounded pretty bizarre. Yet again, it was as though that other part of me was watching the scenario between me and two strangers. I mean, if a lady can't see then why is she driving a car? I know that I didn't dare go into an explanation of my symptoms for them. What would I say? Besides, my symptoms changed all the time. And then, there was that part of me who checked out those two young men before I decided to jump my car over the curb. Of course I checked them out! Why else would I have a conscious memory after all these years of that tiny incident? Some part of me knew they would offer help.

And indeed they did. The two young men offered to drive me to the doctor. They parked the car, and acting as if I were frail as well as fragile, walked me to the doctor's office. One of them offered to call my husband. In those moments of waiting with them in the waiting room, I had a profound sense of knowing them, although I could not see them with my physical eyes. And we had never met before. Yet I knew something about them -- as if this was not the first time they had been my caretakers!

I had started writing about the gifting. From this point, it will take me the rest of the book to explain why I feel a terminal diagnosis was a blessing, a gift. And it may take me some time to share my feelings about extra-sensory perception, seeing the young men as important caretakers before the incident of jumping my car over the curb. But let me return to my story. On that day there was another gifting which has long served me well. It has been a guiding perspective for the way in which I interact with patients.

It was strange sitting in the doctor's office. It seemed as if the top of my visual field was all foggy, but I could see forms and shapes out of the lower part of my eyes. As near as I can describe it, I had an awareness of "self" and "not self." (At least a "self" that was not of this world). It was a sensation that made me feel strangely vulnerable. I could sense the neurologist looking at me. And I could sense him moving around the room. Suddenly I felt his hand resting on my knee. I think he meant it for reassurance, but he could have told me he was going to touch me. It made me furious, a kind of anger bordering on rage, which I stifled.

He performed several of the standard neurological examinations. I had done many of them before. Yes, I could touch my fingers to my nose without wavering. And yes, I could walk an imaginary straight line. I didn't tell him that was the easy part. I just imagined the line, then as if I were really seeing it, I could walk it. But it wasn't imaginary, to me, it was real. My knee jerk reflexes were intact. So were my foot reflexes. Regardless, he made the recommendation that I have a myelogram.

I remember thinking that was the test to determine the electrical potential of specific nerves, so I agreed. Still, there was that part of me that knew this was a waste of time. I wanted to ask for whose benefit was I having the tests? Was it for me? Or was it to satisfy the physician who wanted to have his diagnosis confirmed?

Thoughts like this wasn't really bothersome for me because I have had them for such a long time. Not just since the advent of my initial diagnosis, but I have had them for my entire life. The only thing that was bothersome was having few friends who were willing to examine their own experiences. The year was 1972. There was no evidence to support a mind–body–spirit connection, but then, there was little information about the mind–body connection. There was no public acceptance that the mind controls the body. There was little awareness that the brain functions like a computer. The brain is not the originator of thought, that comes from the Mind that is non–local, not tied to time and space, a field of eternal energy. No, there were only bio–mechanical views of the body. Then there was the physician who was, for the most part, the representative of scientific "truth" about the body. The skeptic in me got triggered. Why didn't anyone ask if I had an understanding of what was happening to me? Why didn't anyone act as if my experience was important?

I remember the myelogram as being a painful experience for me. It certainly made no sense to do all that poking and prodding. The doctor inserted a needle then put an electrical charge through it and moved it around. All the while asking me in a calm voice if I could feel it. The audacity! I was again outraged! I wanted to scream; I wanted to cry. Not just out of a sense of my personal pain, but a pain that came from the very archetype of the female form. I was outraged at the violation of MY body!

As an occupational therapist, I knew something about the electrical potential of peripheral nerves. I knew about the sensory system and the nervous system. Tests of light touch, pressure and two point discrimination could have been done first which would have ruled out the need for a myelogram. I could feel hot and cold, there was no disruption of sensation in any of the nerve tracts. Proprioception and kinesthesia were intact (abilities to identify location of a body part in space and to identify movement of an extremity up or down). I thought it was dumb to have tests ordered when all my sensory input seemed intact, at least to me. But mostly I think the anger was about the way I was treated, the way I was reduced to a set of symptoms.

"The test results show no abnormalities. The results were negative."

"I know," I replied. I knew my comment was sarcastic. And I *knew* from the outset that there would be no "medical evidence," just an X-ray with a big white spot in the middle of my head.

"So we are going to treat you as if you have Multiple Sclerosis."

"AS IF!" echoed in my head.

"I like the other option better," I countered. "The terminal one."

And again, the memories came flooding back. I

remembered a neighbor who had Multiple Sclerosis and how sad it seemed to me that she lived in a body that deteriorated although her mental faculties remained intact. Me, with Multiple Sclerosis? Yet over the course of several months, the visual problems became amplified. I began having moments when my speech became slurred. Sometimes I had to catch myself before I stumbled.

I know now, these were the miracles in the making. They happen in the time and space of *"no-thing-ness".* They are the stuff of the universe. They are found in the "ordinariness" of our daily lives. A terminal illness, from which I did not die. Two men who assisted me when I jumped the car over the curb. My awareness that my experience and the interpretation of it were more important than the diagnosis. My playing with paying a toll in pennies instead of a quarter. My beginning glimpses of the "self" and the "not self" (except I didn't have the understanding right in those days). I came to understand that coincidence and serendipity may be the anonymous face of God. But this understanding could be found only if I went inside, only if I looked for the deeper meaning. It lies there, waiting to be called forth.

Then there was another miracle. I found myself again pregnant. While that is certainly a miracle in itself, it is not the one to which I refer. But then, I am getting ahead of myself. I suspect with all my energy directed toward my internal dialogue and carrying on with "business as usual" -- teaching, going to classes, being wife and mother -- I neglected (or did I?) to resume birth control.

By the second month of my pregnancy, my

physician suggested I give serious consideration to abortion as pregnancy exacerbates symptoms of Multiple Sclerosis. I remember following that suggestion, standing in my kitchen and making an outrageous statement to the universe. "Come on lady, (the "eternal me" talking to me), this is not personal! This is not as tough as it seems. I have already gone through the death and dying stuff! And I will do terminal things no more!

Always backward in time, I reflected. I wondered why I was so careless about getting pregnant the second time. Then I remembered. About eight months or so after Michael was born, my physician asked me if I had resumed taking birth control pills.

"No," I remember replying.

"Do you want to get pregnant again so soon? Your son is not yet two years old."

Again, "No."

"Then I suggest you get started back on the pill." With that, he gave me a sample of orthonovum and a prescription. I had it filled on the way home. But, by the middle of the month, I had to call my doctor again. "I am bleeding in the middle of my cycle. I just started the pills and already I am having a period."

"That's just break-through bleeding. It's nothing serious. It probably means that the prescription is not strong enough. Come by and I will get you some more samples and a stronger prescription."

I remember sitting and rocking, always rocking . . . rocking . . . thinking about the *"no-thing"* that was wrong with me with another child squirming inside. I began again reflecting on my medical history. The constant change of diagnosis. When did it all start?

Was the blindness part of the terminal diagnosis or related to the Multiple Sclerosis? Was this a progression or just a series of events? What if they were separate? That I was blind, but it was not terminal. Period. Then I "got" the Multiple Sclerosis. So I asked myself: Did I have the symptoms of Multiple Sclerosis before or after the diagnosis?

From my own medical training I knew the diagnosis of Multiple Sclerosis was based solely on symptomatology. There are no laboratory or definitive tests for the diagnosis. Yet I knew about the disease. I learned about it in school and I had seen it in the patients with whom I worked. But what if . . . what if . . . ?

What if I entertained an outrageous proposition? Suppose I created the illness. Not because I necessarily wanted to. I don't believe it was a willful act. I was aware of the psychological gains that are experienced by people who have chronic conditions. But I didn't feel that I needed or particularly wanted to be taken care of. I didn't view myself as dependent. So if there were no secondary gains . . . then what?

Always inward. Reflecting, asking, sorting, analyzing, searching, seeking, speculating, wondering. Wherein was the truth, *my* truth? Was I creating the chaos just to then create order? I had some tough questions. Yet I wondered if I really created the symptoms? I knew that the tumor held no truth for me despite the X-ray. And the dying had no immediate meaning. Maybe I only needed to learn about living. And beyond that, living exceptionally without limitation. I had to *do* something. "Take responsibility" was the internal command. "Response-ability." Language, meaning, interpretation. I could do it, I had the "ability" to make my body "respond!" It was after all, *my life!*

I went backward on this line of thinking. Then I took a quantum leap. I reasoned that if I created it, I could uncreate it. No judgment. No worry about intent. Just an unbiased observation. So I began by pouring over the medical books, looking at the course of the disease process as well as all the symptoms I had or might expect to have. I started *playing* with my discoveries. "Let's take an outrageous stance here," I remember saying to myself. "This is not personal. It's not me who has the Multiple Sclerosis, it is my body. I am attached to this body, but I AM more than my body." And I knew, or at least my "other self" knew exactly what M.S. was all about. Since part of me knew, somehow that information was getting into my body. But the "me" who was the eternal eavesdropper, the "me" that was in this body was going to run interference. I was stepping into that gap. The space between the slides. I reasoned: "I AM that which is between my mind and my body."

As I would say something that sounded like it was slurred I would stop. I told myself: "Run the movie backward, slow it down. . . frame by frame . . . freeze it! Hold time in that space of *no–thing!* Listen to me say what I just said with perfect clarity. See me saying the words with perfect form of my mouth. Get an image of perfection. Hold the image. Now breathe. And again. Match the image to what I just said. Ready. Go!"

Sometimes my conversations were in the third person, the one who was giving the guidance. Other parts of the conversations were in the first person, that was the "me" in the body. Yet both were the same, there was a oneness. There was no separation of self, rather a multiplicity of self. Yet again, not a warring as one might find with multiple personalities. Even now, I know my experiences were not pathological, they were insightful!

Over and over I practiced the process of guiding my body into the desired sounds needed for speaking. Not at the end of the day, but in each moment when I felt the body was out of balance. In each moment that I was aware that I didn't sound "right." I put all my energy into being totally aware of every utterance I made. Every motion I completed with my body. And I discovered my moment to moment monitoring worked!

It worked not only with my speaking but with my body. As soon as I would reach for something and knock it over or see a shaky response, I would stop. "Back it up lady," was the internal command. "Get an image. Breathe. Match the motion to the image. Slowly. Concentrate. Be present. Be mindful." And as if directed by that part of me which was eternal, I began changing: "I AM graceful, I AM in control of my body. I AM directing and guiding my movements." These words came not so much spilling from my head as from my heart.

It was working! It was working! My symptoms were no longer accelerating with my pregnancy. More reasoning with myself. "If I can fight for my life little one," I would say, as I rocked and rocked, holding the body growing in my belly, "I can fight for yours too." Or maybe, it was the other way around.

The Gifting

The months ticked on. There were times when I really did feel vulnerable. Yet throughout the duration of my "illness," I continued teaching at the University of Kansas. Sometimes when I walked into my classroom I couldn't see any of the students, but I could feel them, I could sense them. The students were truly wonderful. They would escort me to my class if needed. They accepted oral individual exams rather than written tests. On the one hand, it became a time of high creativity for me. I needed to figure out how to be a college professor without benefit of lecture notes, without the traditional tests, papers and assignments ordinarily expected to determine student grades. In this, I discovered there was something marvelous about nontraditional teaching. *I learned that the response of students was based on the clarity of my questions. I began to understand that learning was not meant to be a competitive activity.*

As I learned that learning itself was not competitive, that spilled over into a discovery that living wasn't competitive either. As I made these discoveries, the questions continued on an internal level. I *knew* I wanted to know how it is that we learn and why some things are easier to learn than others. I wanted to explore death and dying and figure out for myself *(my self),* why there was so much sadness involved. I asked if the sadness was because people wouldn't see each other any more? I thought that was sort of funny, because a long time ago I remember coming to the insight that when a living friend of mine was not with me, in a way, he or she still was. Because they "lived" in my head -- in my memory, in my dreams, in my imaginary conversations with them. I asked, when a person dies, why can't they continue to live in the memories, the dreams, the imaginary conversations? I pondered that while the physical reality changes, it simply wasn't a big deal. A deeper truth was emerging. *An awareness that the eternal reality does not change. It comes from a separation of ourselves from the rest of the cosmos.*

I came to discover for myself that the sadness we feel with the death of a loved one or a friend is because of fear of the unknown -- not an unknown of what happens to them after death, but a fear of what happens to *us.* We haven't realized that *no-thing* happens. The person still lives in us, because we have created them. We have created our memories, our dreams . . . our conversations with them.

It seems that during those years that the questions kept coming, but so did the answers. I was often struck by the profound thought that if I wanted answers to difficult questions, I had to first be willing to ask the questions. Then I only had to listen for the answers. The knowledge comes from inside!

How I finished my masters degree while working full time and being a wife and mother seemed a wonder to those who knew me. Yet for me, it was all very ordinary. I didn't feel as if I had changed, yet I know that I made radical changes in my perceptions. My personal experience of the nonseeing part of me held no "real" reality. It was just there. I reasoned that if the nonseeing part was not real, or was at least of little importance to what the experience was really about, then the challenge was to get on with the business of living.

I remember another gift, which could just as easily be called another "blessing." At the time I could not realize the nature of either, but it was somehow different. It was a gift of self. One evening I remember crying. Not so much out of sadness, but out of frustration, the continual coping with the unknown, the *"no-thing-ness,"* my inability to really share what was going on with me. It seems I held a belief that I was supposed to know what was happening. Or, I reasoned if I did know, then I would be better able to cope. I wanted the outcome, before I had fully engaged in the process.

It was during those times that I felt child like. No not child like, but like a child. Later I would realize they were just human needs. I wanted to be held. I wanted someone to wrap their arms around me, brush away my tears, pat the top of my head without being condescending and tell me that everything would be O.K. I didn't want to acknowledge that we all have a child in us, a child who has real needs for security, for love and protection. I didn't want to acknowledge those needs, perhaps out of a fear of being regarded "childish." Somewhere along the way I had a belief that crying was not an acceptable way for an adult to act. I had no understanding at the time, that fears or feelings of vulnerability can be tied not only to events in this lifetime, but to events in other lifetimes.

On the evening I particularly remember, I was crying and feeling vulnerable. I snuggled with my husband. I wanted him to share my experience, my apprehensions, the incessant non-stop dialogue in my head. It was then that he said, "It's your problem kid."

At the time and for many years after, this

statement would be like a branding iron on my heart. I felt abandoned. Yet there was a part of me that knew this was a gift of "self." Perhaps as a guide and teacher, my husband had held a giant mystical mirror in front of my face. My experiences really were my problem. The gift of self was to discover that the strength was within me and not outside me. Yet, it was more than that. The "self" has many aspects. There is the personal self who has the life experiences. Then there is that eternal self or "higher self" (that other "me" I discovered) who guides the experiences of the personal self. It is the Higher Self who is timeless and spaceless . . . connected to all other beings, times and events. It is that Higher Self that yearns to find the connection with the Beloved, to find and have a personal experience with God. Yet it is only in the internal searching that the gift of self can be realized. But then, it would take me nearly fifteen years to realize the preciousness of that gift of those few moments.

As I view that evening from my current perspective, I doubt that the man who was then my husband would even recall the incident I have just described. Even if asked, I imagine he would deny it . . . it would have been forgotten. It was just one of those moments of conversation that he would likely have no reason to recall. And yet as I review the events that unfolded in that time, I have to ask myself if I was really willing to openly talk about dying? Was I really willing to share my fears with him? Did I ever ask for his support in making any kind of transition--either to dying or debilitation? No, for me, time was encapsulated in many moments of space. I explored the void within, the *"no-thing-ness."*

Rather than expanding my world to include him, I retreated into my head, separating myself from him. I had thoughts, insights, revelations I thought I couldn't address which were beyond coping with my symptoms. I wondered that if I would die, how would he continue in a law career and raise a young son? A daughter? Who would "mother" them? Would he go looking for "wife," "mother," or a "mistress."

We never talked about these things. We lived our lives separately together. I imagine he was consumed with his own fear regarding my dying or disability. I am sure he pondered whether he could raise children alone. Certainly, it was not an issue of capability, as he had feelings which ran very deep. He just wasn't any better at expressing them than I. I think now, it was more an issue of our cultural conditioning. Single parents in the 1970's were by far the exception than the rule. I imagine too, he contemplated my diagnosis of Multiple Sclerosis, when it was finally determined that I would not die. Living with a disabled person would certainly have been a long way from what he had envisioned when we were first married. Then too, there was the long period of separation for us when he was in the Navy. By the time we had been married for six years and our son was born, we had spent less than two years living together. A Navy career with long separations is not necessarily conducive to building lasting trust and open communication.

Revelations

In my eighth month of pregnancy with my second child, my husband obtained a job with a law firm in Jacksonville, Florida. I had not particularly thought of moving, having just finished graduate school at the University of Kansas and having the opportunity to really enjoy teaching. He had finished law school and gone on a diving trip with a fellow law student. His friend, also an attorney, had obtained a job in Florida. I thought it wonderful the two of them were taking a much needed vacation after the rigors of finishing law school. But I certainly did not expect that he would obtain a job there.

When he called from Florida, I was surprised, yet, it was just another challenge. Having finished graduate school, I reasoned it didn't really matter where in the country I lived, I would still need to be concerned with my medical condition. Relocating at that time seemed only a minor challenge compared to some of the other things I was experiencing. Also by that time, my visual problems had abated to the extent that I could see well enough to care for myself and my son. Friends were most supportive in helping me get ready to move. The M.S. symptoms were intermittent, as is usual in the "first stages." And despite the medical recommendations, I had not terminated my pregnancy. Still, it was a wary stewardess who let me on the plane to Florida in my obvious eighth-month poorly coordinated pregnant condition.

Upon my arrival in Florida, I made arrangements to see J. Lawton Smith, M.D. I was referred to him by my physician in Kansas. He was at the Bascomb

Palmer Eye Institute in Miami, Florida. Not all of my physicians agreed with the diagnosis of Multiple Sclerosis, nor the brain tumor, yet several continued to focus on the visual problems. I lived in that dual world--daring to believe that none of the diagnoses were right, yet entertaining the possibility that someone out there might have some answers. As the problems were primarily visual, it seemed some likely answers would come from looking again at those symptoms.

When I met J. Lawton Smith, I thought he was the tallest man I had ever seen. I was amused that he hummed during the entire six hour examination. Occasionally he brought in several young residents who peered into my eyes, and for the hundredth time, asked me to look up or down. I felt a little like a guinea pig, yet was continually distracted by the humming of J. Lawton.

At the end of a grueling day, he sat at his desk with his back to me and dictated a lengthy report with me still sitting in the examination chair. My medical background was not nearly adequate for the highly technical report he was making. Yet there was just enough knowledge in my head to spark more than hope in my heart.

As he finished his report, he turned to me and said: "Let's get your husband."

He then looked sternly at me, and in a tone that was more fatherly than physician, he said: "Now, young lady, there are many things I want you to understand. First, you do not have a brain tumor, but I can't say that you never did. That white blotch on the initial X-Ray simply isn't there anymore. A misdiagnosis? Maybe, maybe not. Maybe, it was a miracle. Just know that the problem isn't there anymore. Second, you do not have Multiple Sclerosis, despite the symptoms you experienced. And again, had I seen you six months or so earlier, I may have concurred with that diagnosis. So feel blessed you did not abort that little soul inside. She came to help, you know."

"Third, and I want you to really get this . . . *the reason you were blind is that you could not see."*

I was more than startled.

"I suspect you will begin to understand what this means if you look hard enough. Oh, you think you need some answers? Learn to trust yourself. You may have had a tumor. Yet when that changed, we still needed a diagnosis. That's when it was determined you had Multiple Sclerosis. You may have had M.S., the brain scans seemed to point in that direction. I suspect there is also the possibility that you had an allergic reaction to birth control pills. Funny how the soul sometimes resists the seemingly simple controls we exert on the body. I can't say the allergic reaction was the cause, we do know that visual loss can be a side effect of some of the birth control pills. We do know that birth control pills alter the natural hormonal balance. So the stopping of the pills, in an inverse way, also causes a hormonal imbalance until the body has a chance to adjust. And it was during that adjustment time that you got pregnant."

"So let's bring ourselves current. My suggestion is for you to nurse your baby only for six to eight weeks. By that time, she will have all the colostrum she needs to develop the immune system. Be advised that the continued nursing, in a sense, while it is a natural state, continues, in your case to be a state of imbalance. So stop the nursing and your hormonal system will readjust. This is a key, but it certainly isn't the only one."

"I anticipate that over the next six months after you stop nursing the baby you will have a gradual return of your vision. There may be some permanent loss in the right eye, but likely correctable with lenses. The most important thing is that you continue exactly as you have. As you look deeper into yourself, you will find what it that you need to see."

Then J. Lawton Smith, M.D., perhaps the only true physician I have ever known and whom I know was a Guardian Angel, took my hand and that of my husband and said, "Now we will pray." And in that moment of revelation, a seed was planted. A God-seed that would take twenty years to sprout.

The Incubation Period

The next ten years were years of change, but different from the proceeding three. These years were filled with adjustment and growth. Not so much a time of internal growth, but the manifestation of it in very subtle ways. In my view of the world.

Poetry became my window to view my inner processing. I suspect that it was no different from dream analysis, except that as I wrote, I was fully awake, alert and conscious. It was as if I needed to bring all the thoughts, the questions and the answers into form. To bring the abstract into the concrete.

I feel
Like a model . . .
Trying on life-styles for size.

Each is becoming in its own setting
Each looking strange in displacement.
I wonder
What I would wear
If there were
no one around?

When my children were two and four respectively, my husband and I divorced. After a year of readjustment with a dear friend in Denver, I was again restless to continue on my own. I returned briefly to Jacksonville for a summer job, still hoping to put my former marriage back together. (I hadn't yet learned that experiences are life lessons for our own evolvement of consciousness. And that when lessons are realized, they need not be repeated). When it was apparent that I would not be able to do that, I left Jacksonville with my children, $1,000 in my pocket, and the promise of a job interview. At that time my source of courage was firmly rooted in the knowing that if I could overcome a terminal condition, blindness and Multiple Sclerosis, the business of being a single working mom was a piece of cake! I went forth with a simple statement: "Universe, here I come."

We ended up in Ohio where I obtained a job conducting research with severely retarded children under a government sponsored grant. It was the late 1970's and federal monies were becoming scarce. So after a year in Ohio, I determined it was time to take a "hard line" job rather than work for "soft monies" (money that expired with the decline in federal grants). There were also other things seeded in my awareness. Views about the mysteries of human nature were expressed in my poetry:

I had a miserable night last night
It carried over to work this morning.
But Brian said good morning with his eyes
Mercury brushed my tears away
Beverly ran her fingers through my hair.

Did my boss call me?
Did the lady in charge
Inquire about my health?

Brian and Mercury and Beverly
Live in an institution
They are called retarded.

But who was compassionate?
Who was concerned?
Who reached out and held my hand?

Michael, Jenny and I moved to Virginia in 1978 where I took a position as Assistant Professor of Occupational Therapy at the Medical College of Virginia. It was a time of much professional growth. I consulted with many community agencies and with the Army Medical Specialists Corps. I assisted in formulating a plan whereby dependents of military families could receive intervention services while on overseas assignment.

And it was a time of enjoying my single parenting. We had many friends who assumed surrogate "father" and grandparent roles. I was involved with scouting and T-Ball with Michael. Weekends were spent camping or visiting the numerous museums in Washington D.C. And the poetry continued to be the door to my inner–sanctuary.

Can you enter our world?
The world of Michael G
Jenny Beth
and me?

We make no promises
We share nothing, no–thing
important
Save the kite in the sky,
The crayons on the floor,
The sun–dried clay
hidden from the world in a
pile of toys
marked "for goodwill."

Can you still laugh
And remember
Endless games of chase
when the object was not to
hide or seek
but not to get caught?

Can you remember how funny your
feet feel
When you put your shoes
On the wrong feet?

Can you make a squashy mud pie
And not let your fingers

stick together?

I would wish you could enter
The world of Michael G
Jenny Beth
and me
For it, too, is marked
"for good will."

Throughout that time, my thoughts about my recent "illness" seem to be brewing on a back burner. At times I was reflective and introspective. I joined a Transactional Analysis group and learned about the child, parent and adult roles in each of us and how we communicate from those needs and wants. It became clear to me that during those times when I behaved as a "child", when I cried and wanted to be taken care of, those were "normal" parts of me. We do have child needs even as adults -- the need for comfort, for reassurance, for protection.

I slept in Jenny Beth's bed tonight
She and Michael were away with
their daddy.

A five-year-old's room
complete with fairy tales
and stuffed toys
Makes me feel very small inside
looking out

At a mommy who is maybe not
always patient

Who not always listens well.

I'll try again tomorrow.
Maybe then my tears will have dried
on her pillow and
Jenny Beth will never know
That a mommy is sometimes
a little girl, too.

Still I looked and searched inwardly. I made mental checklists of things that were true for me, and things I no longer believed in. I no longer needed to validate what I was learning from the outside world. I knew that when I needed "proof," it would be there. Yet it would remain on an internal level until I developed the courage and the confidence to release my need to have my experiences validated by anyone outside of me. I knew that what I had learned about the body had not yet been accepted as the current state of knowledge. In 1974, I could hardly go around telling people that it was possible to resurrect the body! That was pretty strong language. I didn't even feel that I could say that it was possible to heal the body. I just yet didn't trust my own level of knowing.

For me, I had discovered that my beliefs and attitudes, my mental and emotional states had a profound impact on my physical body. I knew that feelings and emotions couldn't just be compartmentalized into the "personality" or be stuck off someplace called the "unconscious." I knew there was a causal factor between emotions, thoughts and the breakdown of the body. There was a deeper wisdom growing. *I knew that it no longer made sense for me to seek outside counselors or physicians to interpret for me what was going on inside me.*

I began to feel a need to move on. While I was becoming more and more competent in my teaching, I was becoming less tolerant of those who chose to live life controlled by external boundaries and perceptions. I was aware I challenged my peers and my supervisors. I offended not by action but by attitude. I wanted to tackle many problems, to get rid of the limitations. I wanted to be competent professionally and personally. I wanted to grow in love and connection with my children.

I have a sense now that when we really want to grow, we are either given that opportunity by the universe, or on some unseen level we create it (by calling forth all those shimmering web-like connections?). Sometimes, signals from the universe come in very ordinary ways.

In 1980, I was asked by the American Occupational Therapy Association to represent the Association at the U.S. Senate Subcommittee hearings. It was critical that the practice of Occupational Therapy be recognized as a Related Service under Public Law 94-142 -- the law which entitled handicapped children access to a free public school education. I was so excited that I went running down the hallway to my Chairperson to share the news.

She looked blankly at me and said: "Fill out the travel forms before you go."

I had had a gift like this before, the gift of self of my illness as *my* problem. I let go of the feeling of being crushed. I turned on my heel and charged from her office thinking, "No one, not even you can break this bubble. It is mine for the claiming."

While I did make the presentation before the U.S. Senate Subcommittee, in that instant in time, I also knew that I was no longer supported. I need another challenge. Then, there was within me a curious part which wondered if it is I who creates the chaos in my life, so that I can then make order of it. I mused, that would make me both destructive and creative. And yet, I do not feel this is the case. At least then I never felt that the world "out there" was chaos. I felt there was an explicate order to things, I just couldn't grasp it. I didn't know at the time that both positions are true; in cyclical fashion destruction breeds creativity breeds destruction; implicate order comes from chaos and vise versa. I just remembered the internal propositions that perhaps my life changes were related to my Gemini nature. I liked change. I liked challenge. Perhaps, I reasoned, my soul was working through different layers of reality. Maybe, I was just here for the journey.

I have stopped in my tracks and
taken note of my running,
A constant running to
new places
new people
new jobs.

Upon arriving, I find the people
Look just like the ones I have left.
Only a change of name is made.
What is it run to
if not run from?

In 1982, I again moved the three of us. That time to Kalamazoo, Michigan where I took another teaching position at Western Michigan University. It was a time to put down some roots for the children and I want those roots in the midwest. I liked the seasonal changes and the kids appeared to love the rare snowfall that we had in Virginia.

Several years after my arrival I decided I need to pursue a doctoral degree. I reasoned that if I waited until my daughter graduated from high school, I would be fifty years old and by then, perhaps too old to utilize that education or make a career change. I didn't know it, but even that was belief that I would have to work through.

So I bit the bullet, took out student loans and begin my doctoral work while still employed full time. Fortunately, I selected a graduate school which required that the degree be multidisciplinary, and one that could be completed on my own time. What fun, I mused. I would have an opportunity to combine psychology, neurology and education.

As all doctoral students will report, the degree is not so much an accomplishment in itself, but seems an initiation into the elite world of the scholar. You know -- that person who wears ragged clothes, hangs around "coffee" houses and speaks in very long words to which his or her colleagues nod in serious agreement. At least that was my 1960 image, although I entered the doctoral program in 1985. I had evidently forgotten that the real wisdom was internal. Or perhaps I had not yet learned to fully trust the wisdom from inside. Perhaps I was just eager to learn more. I was, I guess, again searching for evidence to support my own findings. Were there others who held my emerging point of view that we are all connected in some indescribable way? Did others suspect there were no accidents in the physical universe? Did others, besides the religious leaders of our time, believe there was a mind-body-spirit connection? Was there anyone else in the whole world who believed that both the universe and the body function holographically?

I'll spare my out-of-school tales. The highlight is the work I completed was with Ned Herrmann, who was regarded as the "Father of brain technology." I was excited to learn about the brain because I believed that this knowledge would answer many life-long questions. I wanted the information for my clinical practice. I had some patients who would go to great lengths to describe how handicapped they were despite their minimal involvement. There are others with severe involvement who seem to calmly take the illness (terminal or chronic) in stride. Then there was my own experience.

I think spring is coming.
The brown snow reluctant to
Disappear harbors anxious
New blades of grass.

People venture out coatless
Only to appear shivering
On the street corners
at nightfall.

The farm animals show the first signs
Of scratching with their
shedding.

I think spring is coming.
I feel new and fresh
In love with life

After a long life of winter distress
It is time for me
To blossom, too.

Little did I know that by the time I finished my doctoral program, I would come to a point where all my formal education would lose its significance. Nor did I realize that completion of my doctoral degree would serve as springboard into other realms, other perceptions. Little did I know that I was on a journey into the depths of the soul; entry into the *no–thing–ness.*

Chapter 2 The Physical Body

Introductory Comments

In the writing of this book, my challenge has been not only to describe my journey and my personal experiences, but to somehow put my experiences into a framework so that you can share my journey. I don't really know how to do this other than to invite you to go with me through a series of steps, not unlike the revelations which I have had. Then, I suppose there is that consummate teacher part of me, that somehow wants only to offer assistance. I do not wish to tell you what to think or believe, but give you opportunities for making your own discoveries. So in a way, I am only a guide, not because I have all the answers, but because I have had much guidance, much support and much love, which I can in turn, share with you. Not only have I had guidance from friends and family, but from a different place; we'll get to that. I do know that from talking with many, many people, that I am not the only one out there who has had unusual experiences. So for them, perhaps I can serve as a spokesperson. What has worked for me, may not be appropriate for you. On the other hand, I will try to share as much of me as I can, just in case some of my discoveries also work for you. For the most part, I have started with opinions, beliefs, and feelings. Then I have questioned where they came from. In most cases this has been followed by a period of reflection -- searching, asking, sorting, analyzing, intuiting -- always looking for that "other" interpretation, a deeper meaning. I extend to you my hand, and my heart that we may journey together.

Kinesthetic Awareness

It is my opinion that we are not very much in touch with our physical bodies. Can you, for example, sense the outside three toes on your right foot without moving them? Can you sense your fingers without moving them? How about the tip of your ears? Or the backs of your knees? If you are like many people, it is easier to sense your fingers without moving them, than it is to sense your toes. And probably the tips of your ears, rather than the back of your knees. That may be related to distortions in our body image. Somehow over time we continue to take the body for granted without having parts of our physical body in our awareness. As you can well imagine, it gets even harder when we try to contact our stomach or our liver or even our brains.

Why is this so? Well, by evolutionary design, all our senses are directed outward. Sight, hearing, smelling, tasting and touching all tell us something about the world outside our body. Our educational systems and our current medical knowledge has only begun to let us know that we have senses that tell us what is going on inside the physical body. This means that there must be some kind of "invisible" realm that exists in which a deeper understanding can be obtained.

Contacting invisible realms is not so frightening when we recall that even as small children we did not have to know about electricity to turn on a light. We do not have to test gravity each morning when we jump out of bed to know that it is constantly there. So there must be realms that are not detectable through the five senses, but that can be known, explored and understood by other human faculties. We might call this kind of knowing "kinesthetic awareness." It is a kind of knowing that is not related to analytical thinking, but is likely related to intuition -- a kind of knowing that often is not possible through words. This kinesthetic awareness is related to body wisdom. Our bodies already know what is good for them and what they must do in order to work smoothly and efficiently for us. If we can come in contact with the wisdom of the body, that may be the first step in coming in contact with much more of our being which also remains at the invisible level.

As is often the case, one of the ways we come in contact with our physical body is when we become aware that it is NOT working. For example, recall a time when you had a large bundle of clothes or a box that you were carrying downstairs and when you thought you were at the bottom step, your body suddenly went KERPLUNK! It is likely you either assumed you were at the bottom and were not, or thought you had one more step to go. In either case your kinesthetic body was not in contact with your physical body. In a funny sort of way most of us don't contact our kinesthetic awareness directly -- it contacts us!

This then leads us to ask "Why did we loose our body image or our kinesthetic awareness?" Well, quite frankly we haven't had much encouragement to keep track of our body image. Jean Houston, author of *The Possible Human,* 1982, asks us to remember for instance, when you were in first grade in physical education class. Imagine your gym teacher shouting: "Chest out! Belly in! Now march!" All of us sucked in our baby fat, threw out our little chests, held our breaths, turned red in the face and stiffly high-stepped around the play-ground. What we learned from this little exercise a long time ago was not how to love our physical bodies, but if we worked with them it wasn't very much fun. Somewhere deep inside of us we learned that if working with our bodies meant we got stiff necked and pop-eyed then we weren't going to do anything with our bodies anymore. And so began the chain of events that allowed us to begin forgetting about our bodies.

As we grew into teenagers nobody told us how our emotions were tied to our physical bodies so we had to go through that terrible time of adolescence bearing our pimples on our faces that always seemed to pop out the night just before the big date. Girls allowed themselves to get overweight so no one would see that they were developing into women. Males had to endure the change in voice and deal, sometimes it seemed constantly, with the embarrassing wet sheets at night and bulging pants by day. So another layer of forgetting about our bodies occurred.

As we continued into adulthood, some of us took jobs that we didn't want or discovered relationships were not as we imagined they would be. Pretty soon our boss or our "significant other" who was a "real pain in the neck" became, in our bodies, a pain in the neck. Thus, we began a pattern of taking the stresses and strains of life, the negativity, into our physical bodies.

What no one told us however, is that negativity is stored in the body at the cell level, either directly or in association with a memory of something that happened in another time and space when we were disappointed, abandoned, rejected or hurt. The unfortunate trick is that the body never forgot, it turned our aches and pains of living into aches and pains in our bodies. Then as we realize that we are "sick and tired" of life, we begin to experience "disease." We recognize that we are not at ease with ourselves, our lives, our loved ones, or our bodies. We can however, with our awareness begin to heal the body, begin to heal that which we really can see.

We can begin to contact our physical bodies and reconstruct our body image by directing our awareness to our bodies. By awareness, I mean that we talk to our bodies and we listen to them, rather than taking them for granted. Following is a process which allows us to begin paying attention to our bodies. You may wish to record and listen to the process for maximum benefit. However, just by reading your kinesthetic body will respond.

Alignment of the Physical Body

Lie down on the floor . . . and get in touch with your breathing . . . breathe in all the goodness, love, and pleasure that you can . . . and breathe out any negativity, resistance, or tension that you feel . . . breathe in the goodness, love, and pleasure . . . and breathe out the negativity, resistance and tension . . . check to see if the breathing comes from the diaphragm . . . so that as you breathe in, you feel you stomach expanding . . . and as you breathe out you feel it contracting . . . or it may help you to use a number cycle of breathing . . . so that you breathe in to the count of three . . . 1 . . . 2 . . . 3 . . . and slowly exhale to the count of nine . . . 4 . . . 5 . . . 6 . . . 7 . . . 8 . . . 9 . . . do that until you feel comfortable with it . . . in to the count of 3 . . . and out to the count of 9.

Now scan your body . . . beginning with the feet . . . check your toes and relax them . . . notice if you have the same sense of the four smaller toes as you do the big toe . . . allowing yourself to keep them in your awareness as you relax them . . . then relax your ankles . . . noting if the space under the ankle on the right is the same as the space on the left . . . see if you can relax so that the space seems to be the same.

Then relax your muscles on the front and back of the legs . . . feel the contact of the calf muscles on the floor . . . and sense the floor in contact with the calf muscles . . . then relax the muscles on the front and back of the knees . . . checking to see if the space underneath your right knee is the same as your left knee . . . is it the same, greater or lesser than the space under your ankles . . . adjust your body in any way that you can so that the space seems more equal between the two legs . . . and between the back of your knee and your ankles.

Then relax the muscles on the front and the back of your thighs . . . again letting them sense the floor . . . and letting the floor sense them . . . relax your buttocks and your pelvis . . . both the front and the back . . . sensing any differences between your left and your right . . . making whatever adjustments are needed in either your body or your awareness . . . relax the muscles in your lower back . . . sensing if the space under your lumbar area is the same, less than, or greater than the space under your knees . . . or under your ankles . . . if the space seems much greater . . . try bending your knees . . . keeping the feet on the floor and gently rap the pelvis on the floor . . . lifting it up off the floor . . . then back down . . . do this 1 . . . 2 . . . 3 times . . . then 2 times . . . then 3 more . . . then stop this and keeping your knees bent allow your knees to fall from one side then the other . . . letting your top knee slide down the bottom leg . . . do this several times . . . then imagine the same movements but do not move the physical body . . . you will be using your kinesthetic body.

Now just imagine bending your knees . . . keeping the feet on the floor and gently rap the pelvis on the floor . . . 2 . . . 3 . . . then 4 times . . . now imagine letting your knees to fall from one side to the other . . . imagining the top knee sliding down the bottom leg . . . imagine this happening several times . . . then straighten your legs again . . . compare the space under your lumbar spine to see if it is now more similar to the space beneath your knees and your ankles . . . recall what was different in your experience when you actually moved your physical body and when you only imagined moving it . . . you likely will find that there is no difference . . . the conscious mind responds only to thought and your body does not have to actually move to *experience* movement.

Let us continue now . . . continue with deep breathing . . . inhale to the count of 3 . . . (l . . . 2 . . . 3) . . . and exhale to the count of 9 (4 . . . 5 . . . 6 . . . 7 . . . 8 . . . 9) . . . relax the muscles in your stomach and your chest . . . then go to the upper back . . . sensing your shoulder blades on the floor . . . and allowing the floor to sense your shoulder blades . . .

note the shift in your awareness as you concentrate on feeling the floor . . . and allowing the floor to feel your body . . . check to see if contact of your right shoulder blade with the floor is the same as your left shoulder blade . . . if it is not . . . cross your arms so the hands hold the elbows across your chest. . . and bring the elbows up over the head . . . keeping the arms close to the ears . . . moving them as far back toward the floor as you can . . . then back down to your chest . . . . do this several times . . . then imagine the movement several times without actually doing it . . . sensing any difference in your awareness . . . do the imaginary movement again and sense if there is movement up and down in the eyes . . . just putting this in your awareness . . . then place your arms straight out in front of you . . . reaching for the ceiling . . . keeping your elbows straight . . . pushing and pulling with your shoulders . . . pushing upward . . . and relaxing into the floor . . . now imagine this same motion of pushing your arms up toward the ceiling . . . imagine doing this several times . . . note if there are any movements of the tongue as you do this . . . again just placing this extraneous movement in your awareness.

Then place your arms back at your sides with the palms facing up . . . noting how the arms lay next to the sides of the body . . . imagine a straight line running through your body from your head to your toes . . . in relation to this straight line . . . note the angle of your arms . . . and if the angle of your arms at the shoulder is about the same as that of your hips . . . make whatever adjustments you need in your position or in your awareness so that the angles at the shoulder and hip are about the same.

Now relax the front and back muscles of your upper arms . . . and your lower arms . . . check your hands and relax them . . . sensing any differences between your fingers and your thumbs . . . feel the floor with the back of your hand . . . and allow the floor to feel the back of your hand . . . turn your hands over and allow the palm of your hands to feel the floor . . . and the floor to feel the palm of the hands . . . then allow your hands to rest either palm up or down . . . whichever is most comfortable.

Scan your body . . . allowing yourself to relax completely . . . feeling safe and supported . . . sensing both the universe within and the universe without . . . now relax the muscles of your neck . . . and your face . . . letting go of the tension around your mouth . . . your nose . . . your eyes . . . your forehead . . . and the top of your head . . . note if your head is turned more toward the left or the right . . . if it is turned . . . move your head so that it feels like it is in the middle.

Breathe again . . . this time breathing in the Light and breathing out the Love . . . breathing in the Light and breathing out the Love . . . recognizing your completely relaxed physical body as a vehicle of consciousness . . . stay in this place for several minutes. . . then touch the floor or bed with your hands . . . open your eyes . . . and move slowly to an upright position.

After competing this process you may have noted that you really do feel better physically because you have consciously attended to the physical body. You may have discovered that your imaginary movement has nearly the same effect as your real movements. That is because the deep receptors in the body which respond to impulses from the autonomic nervous center, *also respond to thought.* The messages of both real and imagined movement are carried on units of protein called "neuropeptides" that are in every cell, tissue, organ, and muscle in the body. You may have also discovered some extraneous movements, like movements of the eyes when you raised your arms over your head, or movements of the tongue when you pushed your arms toward the ceiling. These are movements our bodies have retained as we have come up the evolutionary cycle. We'll talk about evolutionary effects on our bodies in a moment.

Mindfulness

Before we continue, let us go backward. You know, reflecting and asking questions to see if there is any evidence or any clues about how our bodies are put together. Robert Masters and Jean Houston, both of whom I have had the opportunity to study with, in their 1978 book *Listening to the Body,* offer several insights. They suggest that as people go through life they acquire either random or specialized knowledge about the body. But that knowledge is usually compartmentalized, related to specific events and stored in memory, relative to specific times. You know those little neuropeptides, I just mentioned, not only are they the "messengers" of the body, they are also responsible for transformation, biochemically, of those messages into memory. So ironically, memory is not in the brain, *it is at the cellular level of the body!*

Not only are few people aware of this information,

but few take the time day by day to reflect on their experiences. Even fewer take the time minute by minute to look at a whole host of alternative interpretations that can be made of daily life events. It has been my experience that in the act of reflection, deeper meaning can be achieved. A meaning in which the perceived negative event can be turned into a positive event (and therefore stored at the cell level as a positive memory). Oh, did you just ask "What difference does it make?" Well, the negative information stored at the cell level, is passed on to new cells through the process of mitosis -- you know that cell division process you learned about in high school. So negative cellular memories, in effect get multiplied over and over again. Eventually the cellular membrane is affected and distorted cells emerge, or cells enter a process called entrophy, and die. Dying of cells is not really a problem as every cell will be replaced in the human body in less than a year. The problem is, who is sending out the good news? In other words, if too many cells are sending out negative messages, eventually tissue will be involved, then organs, then entire bodily systems.

For most of us, life events which are perceived as negative are called stressors. Stress is not new to most people living in this country. There are numerous "stress workshops" available in nearly every medium sized city in the Unites States. But so few of us really learn about the management of the stresses of life. To manage unpleasant situations or stress, some learn to relax by thinking pleasant thoughts, some engage in physical exercise, still others engage in biofeedback or meditation. Whatever the method, most people would readily accept, at least on some level, that there is a connection between mind and body or body and mind, even if you were not aware of the function of neuro–peptides. The important thing is that for any of these "techniques" to be beneficial, they cannot be understood through the intellect alone. For real understanding, experience is required.

Through the experience of talking to the body it has been discovered that emotional states trigger diffuse responses in the brain and set off nearby motor responses. As changes are made in states of feeling, there is a resultant change in physical states of being; and both can provide physiological changes as well. Physiological changes may include lowering of blood pressure, slowing of the pulse rate and an increase in the regularity of breathing (thereby getting more oxygen to the brain, causing mental clarity). This suggests that while movement alone is beneficial to the body, as in the case of physical exercise, when a person is able to raise their awareness -- to think and feel the motions in the body, the results are much more effective. In other words, awareness of the body, and dialogue with the body helps establish effective communication between the brain and the parts of the body which may have ceased to respond to voluntary control, or whose responses have become sluggish or poorly coordinated.

I suppose it seems logical to ask what is this *awareness?* Awareness is not effort, it is a kind of "mindfulness." An ancient Buddhist text suggests it is the person's natural state and that awareness is cultivated as a habit. Once attained it is not lost. So how does one get it in the first place? Before I attempt to describe mindfulness, it is easier to describe what it is not -- because it approximates how most of us lead our lives as human beings. It is common place knowledge that we only use about five or ten percent of our mental abilities at any one point in time. And it is likely that, that percentage of mental activity, is most related to conscious effort like thinking about paying bills, planning how to pull the stump from the back yard, or rehearsing what we want to say to our loved one after a recent argument. Our mental activity is rarely concerned with *finding meaning of life events in each moment of time.* Far less mental activity is spent reviewing our feelings, our reactions to events. Even less is spent attempting to understand that in each moment of time we have choices. We have the capacity to make other decisions.

Let me give an example. Let's say that a child truly loves his father, and he wants to emulate him. He wants to copy him and be just like him. He watches and observes him, how he moves, how he uses to tools around the house, and his body postures when he talks with his wife. Out of a strong desire to "be like" his father, the child may begin to imitate those behaviors. Through his play, he matches his body movements to the imaginary model he creates of his father. He may begin to stand with his shoulders drawn back, his strong little chin thrust forward. He may not be aware, even as a young toddler, that eventually, if this posture is practiced over and over, it becomes habituated. In other words, the imitation seems to come from an "uncons–cious" level. Yet, it can lead in several decades to curvature of the spine. As the child observes his father expressing anger, standing tall, and rigid, he may not understand that the restriction in breathing, which he also imitates, will eventually inhibit the freedom of movement of the lower part of the body, the hips and the knees. More importantly, while this young child may not recognize how these habituated patterns will affect his physical body, he is equally unable to recognize how these rigid postures may affect his personality, his view of himself, or his image of himself as he grows into manhood.

Then of course, since we are creatures who make adaptive responses, each of us makes a contribution to the patterns of the body; the patterns of thinking and feeling in response to life events. Let's say that this young child who has already imitated rigid postures of his father by the time he reaches adolescence, now responds in a single instance in time to the yelling of his mother. He may cringe, hunch his shoulders, perhaps even tilt his head to one side. These patterns too may become habituated, in fact, they may become exaggerated in response to anger of other people expressed throughout a life time. Yet through all of these experiences, there is little awareness, little mindfulness. We have been conditioned to believe that all these responses that the body makes over time are unconscious responses, that or they are a "product" of growing old. I have real trouble with the word "unconscious," because it implies that there are things going on in our bodies over which we have little control. We haven't learned that we have a whole history of making responses, responses out of our desires to be lovable, to be loved, to be worthy of love.

It is very difficult to talk about "mindfulness" when we have few role models. We have not had guidance from parents or teachers about any of this. I am not inferring that parents and teachers are not loving or good role models. In our Western traditions, we haven't been raised to live our lives moment by moment . . . to go into that space between the slides, the snapshots of life events. We busy our lives from childhood through adolescence and into early adulthood learning the behaviors of others because we believe they are important. Being pleasant and polite means people will like us and we will get the jobs we want. We cultivate skills around the reinforcements we receive. These skills in turn lead us to acquire jobs. Jobs, in turn, reflecte we will have money to buy not only what we need but what we want. Having what we want, means we will have a tangible measure of "success" as we move into adulthood. But success has little meaning when the job is taken away, either through economic and social change or as a result of the aging process. And all of a sudden, we find ourselves in the later years of our lives reflecting on "what is the meaning of all this?"

Mindfulness requires attention. A willful commitment to be fully engaged in whatever is happening at the moment. I would like to share with you the words of Thich Nhat Hanh author of *The Miracle of Mindfulness,* published in 1987. As chairman of the Vietnamese Buddhist Peace Delegation and a nominee for the Nobel Peace Prize, he speaks of mindfulness more eloquently than I:

> Thirty years ago, when I was still a novice at Tu Hieu Pagoda, washing the dishes was hardly a pleasant task. During the Season of Retreat when all the monks returned to the monastery, two novices had to do all the cooking and wash the dishes for something well

> over one hundred monks. There was no soap. We had only ashes, rice husks, and coconut husks, and that was all. Cleaning such a high stack of bowls was a chore, especially during the winter when the water was freezing cold. Then you had to heat up a big pot of water before you could do any scrubbing. Nowadays one stands in a kitchen equipped with liquid soap, special scrubpads, and even running hot water which makes it all the more agreeable.
>
> While washing the dishes one should only be washing the dishes, which means that while washing the dishes one should be completely aware of the fact that one is washing the dishes. At first glance, this might seem a little silly: why put so much stress on a simple thing? But that is precisely the point. The fact that I am standing there and washing these bowls is a wondrous reality. I'm being completely myself . . . conscious of my presence, and conscious of my thoughts and actions (p. 3).

From this, we gather that "mindfulness" is a state of focused awareness -- aware of the smallest movements of the physical body, aware of the feelings one is having while engaging in the activity. Mindfulness is a vigilance about the body which brings forth wonder and curiosity. In the simple act of washing dishes, how does my hand "know" how to open just the right amount to pick up the plate? What adjustment does my body make when shifting to pick up the heavy pan? Mindfulness is tuning into the wonders of the body. Since I have implied that there is a mind–body link, what is happening in the body is really phenomenal. With each task that we complete which requires a motor act, the brain directs something called "motor planning" which in turn triggers deep tendon responses of proprioception which is the body's response to location of a body part in space. Kinesthetic responses are also called forth, the body's interpretation of whether movement is up or down. Taken together, I lumped motor planning, proprioceptive and kinesthetic responses into what I called "kinesthetic awareness" as presented earlier in this chapter.

Let me expand a little on this. The best example I can give of this is to invite you to remember your first experience driving a car with a stick shift. As a new activity you had to be mindful -- fully present. You had to think about the timing of letting out the clutch while simultaneously pressing on the accelerator. You had to learn, then remember, the pattern on the gear shift, and how each of these speeds were related to what you were also doing with the clutch and accelerator. And on top of it all, you needed to remember to guide the car straight down the road! Imagine the demands you placed on the body when you entered that first turn -- check for traffic, turn the left signal on with the left hand, step on the brake with the right foot, put the clutch in with the left foot, downshift with the right hand, look in the rear view mirror, turn the steering wheel to the left, step on the accelerator to go forward, now use the left foot again to put in the clutch and with the right hand shift into a higher gear. Whew!

It's a wonder any of us learned to drive! We thought it was all a cognitive activity, a learning activity.

But in reality, every movement required getting a sense of how far to reach in shifting, how hard to press on the accelerator or the clutch. Our body was calling forth many microscopic receptors giving us feedback about the body as each part moved through space. Not only were there thousands of neural networks formed, the brain got a picture of this activity *in its entirety* -- and that picture, like a hologram, would be retained in memory as a single motor planned event.

The wonders of the body make this all possible. While learning a new activity requires much brain power over which we are hardly conscious or even mindful, once it is learned we habituate. Our brain remembers the motor patterns so we don't have to go through all these steps over and over. It is a way of managing the system efficiently. Unfortunately, as our bodies assumed more and more control through the neural networks, *we become less and less involved. Our attention drifts. We are no longer in the process of attending.* We begin to think, projecting our awareness into other times and places -- going backward in time to remember the day's events, or going forward in time to think about what we will cook for dinner.

Guided Imagery

Having written a little about mindfulness and focused attention, I want to introduce a few concepts having to do with imagery which we will be using in many processes throughout the book. Jeanne Achterberg, author of *Imagery in Healing,* published in 1987, defines imagery as "the thought processes that invokes and uses the senses: vision, audition (hearing), smell, taste, the senses of movement, position, and touch. It is the communication mechanism between perception (our views of the world), emotion and bodily change." I, like Jeanne, like to call it the "stuff of the imagination." Imagery can be used to call forth the biochemistry of emotion when we remember the scent of a lover. It is used in the mental rehearsal of the marathon runner. Depending on the images we evoke, it can cause the blood pressure to go up or down, the breathing to accelerate or decelerate, the brain waves to change or modulate. Indeed, it is the "stuff of dreams" that I will cover in a later chapter.

However we might try to define imagery, it too, is one of those things best experienced. All of us have a lifetime of experience with imagery. Let's play with this a moment. Imagine a green meadow. That's not hard; all of us have either been in a meadow which was green, or we have seen pictures of them. Only those for whom these experiences are not relevant to the individual's culture or geography would have a difficult time doing this -- say a person who was born and raised in South Africa, where experiences of "green," "meadow," and even these words may have little meaning.

But let's say that I said: "Imagine a place where you feel very safe and supported, a place of great peace, a place where you could experience being profoundly connected to the rest of the world." Ahhhh, now it gets very interesting. Some people will invent or call forth images not unlike those when I specifically asked you to think of a green meadow. Others will bring forth a memory or a vision of sitting on a mountaintop, or perhaps sheltered by a tree next to a rippling brook.

Some may remember actual memories of sitting at night around a campfire holding hands. These images come spilling forth from *experience,* not because I used any of these language cues! This means that we have made individual interpretations of "safety," "being supported," and "being connected."

Where do these come from? Well, it's not really unlike motor planning. Our motor experiences are "chunked" together using tiny elements of a sequential task to create a bigger model. So driving a car, using a stick shift calls forth the "hologram" of that very detailed sequence of movements, that I described previously. Many of these responses are controlled through the left hemisphere of the brain. When we talk about imagery, we are calling forth from the right hemisphere of the brain, the visual spatial images. Usually we are calling forth those images which have an emotional connection, thereby triggering the limbic system which processes emotional content. So the word "peace" brings forth a dual feeling -- both the visual image and the attached emotional response. No, it is more than that. To interpret the meaning of the word "peace" activates the language centers of the left hemisphere of the brain. When we go deeper into the functions of the limbic system where emotions are interpreted, we would encounter a phenomenon wherein there is an accompanying physiological response with each event we would call emotional. The heart palpitates when we are excited, the tears begin to fall when we are sad, the blood pressure elevates when we are anxious. So imagery can be thought of as evoking an entire mind-body response.

Jeanne Achterberg presenting at the 10th Annual

Conference on Common Boundaries in 1991 suggests in her audio tape titled *Imagery in Healing* that "imagery is the vehicle through which mental processes reach deep into cellular structure." Citing Matthew Fox in her presentation, he suggests that "imagery is the midwife that allows inner experiences to be birthed into conscious expression." Citing yet another author, Rachel Naomi Ramon suggests "imagery is the language of the unconscious." As a foremost authority in the medical uses of imagery in healing, Jeanne suggests that image alters the RNA, and the DNA at the cellular level; it alters the *intelligence* of the cell. So powerful can the image be that it "evokes" responses at the cellular level that could not ordinarily be made. The image "evokes" cellular healing, it does not "cause" it, or "trigger" it, but "calls it forth." Mindfulness is much like this. It exists as latent awareness, but is not present until it is "called forth," until it is willed into action.

In her tape series, Jeanne then goes on to cite the example of a young woman in California in the early 1980's who was hitchhiking in the high country. She was picked up by a man, raped and brutalized and left on the side of the road with both arms amputated. Yet this young woman walked for three days in the California heat before getting assistance. When asked several years later how she could possibly have survived the ordeal, she stated she "became" Lindsey Wagner; she literally took on the "persona" of the bionic woman! And the image itself "spoke" deep into her cellular structures evoking the clotting factors within.

Returning to Jeanne's 1987 book *Imagery in Healing,* she tells us of a similar story:

> A physical therapist told me of a time in her life when she was about to finish her master's degree and was suffering from massive uterine hemorrhage. All the usual treatments had been tried: hormones, dilation and curretage, bed rest. The only treatment left was hysterectomy--an unpleasant option since in the first place, it would probably keep her from graduating at her scheduled time; but more important, she was unwilling to face a life of childlessness at her age. She knew that she couldn't continue bleeding so profusely without serious consequences. She begged off her surgery for a week and went into seclusion. During this time she visualized a white light shining its healing rays into her uterus. At the end of the week, the bleeding had stopped completely. That was five years ago, and no similar problems had occurred since. She hadn't told her story to many people, and being in a medical profession, she was just a little embarrassed about the circumstances of her recovery (p. 170–171).

I suppose I mention this particular use of imagery as it seems a little close to home. Since I have been "sitting on this book" since my experiences nearly 22 years ago, I am more than just a little sympathetic about being in a medical profession and sharing my own journey of healing. Perhaps it comes forth now, because there has been such a shift in consciousness as to allow different perspectives. Perhaps it has been the number of people with whom I have spoken, who have had similar experiences. And perhaps, it has to do with the continual personal trust of my own experiences and my willingness to share regardless of the receptivity of my audience.

The Physical Senses

Before we can continue to work with the physical body we must also come to recognize that in some aspects we seem wired all backwards. All our senses are directed outward! Our sight gives us information of where we want to live, in the desert with palm trees or on a mountain side with streams and forests. We use our sight to determine what type of house we want to live in. A colonial house with columns on the front porch and shutters on the windows looks much different than a contemporary house with its angles and skylights and overlooking decks. We use sight to pick the style of clothes we wear and whether they are Hawaiian prints, pastels with little embroidered flowers or bold stripes. We use our sight to give us information as to who looks trustworthy or mean or kind.

We depend heavily on sounds. Have you ever heard the sickening gurgling sound when the water pump on your car goes out? And isn't it a marvel that a mother can walk into a nursery with fifty screaming children and can tell whether or not *her* child is crying? A really good carpenter in large shop can tell if the apprentice is pushing the wood through the saw too fast because he can hear the strain on the saw blade. And most of us, young or old, can easily distinguish the sound of a garbage disposal gobbling up a spoon! So powerful are these experiences that we not only get a visual image, we can get an image of sound, smell and even touch.

Even without auditory or visual imagery have you ever thought or been mindful about taste as giving us real information about the world around us? Would you continue to drink a glass of milk after the first taste lets you know the milk is sour? Would you think that lemon in tea would be perfectly fine but lemon in coffee might be a little strange? And have you noticed that smell is very much tied to what we taste? You have likely had the experience of trying to eat a really lovely meal with a bad cold and have felt like you missed out because you couldn't taste anything. I would also imagine you have had the experience of noticing that a backed-up toilet smells decidedly different from stepping outside after a warm summer rain. And you *know,* though it is hard to describe, the smell of puppy breath.

Certainly not last, the sense of touch gives us an incredible amount of information about our environment -- the difference between hot and cold, differences between soft and hard, rough and smooth, porous and prickly. And we could go on and on, picking and choosing, comparing and contrasting differences in touch, even to the extent that we can discriminate a caring touch from an indifferent touch.

Regardless of how long our list about our senses becomes, either separately or working in combination, they only give us information about the world outside of us. To begin to directly experience that which we cannot see, to develop an internal sense of who we really are, we can use imagery to heighten our awareness, to evoke mindfulness. We could start using our senses to re-experience the world outside us. But for my purposes, I think it more important to move into the world inside.

Let's play! Let's do a process using guided imagery. Caught you by surprise? I know, I do this when lecturing publicly or to a group of students. It usually drives everyone crazy. Throwing caution to the wind, I assure you it is intentional. A rapid change, a quantum leap, requires a rapid adaptive response. Sort of like when the foot slides off the clutch petal in the middle of a turn. To avoid grinding the gears in the middle of shifting, you must quickly depress the clutch and let up on the accelerator. Besides, this keeps our communication more personal, more tied to real time and space, as if we were having dialogue with each other.

Following is a process in which we sit or lie comfortably and allow images to come to us with our eyes closed. You may wish to record this section or have a friend read it to you. If you are working alone, give yourself some closed-eye time between each paragraph. Some images may come from memory of an experience and some may come from intuitive processing. In either case, images lie at the doorway to the unconscious, much like dreams, except that they are experienced in a state of altered awareness. Dreaming and visual imagery allows us an opportunity to begin exploring the invisible parts of our bodies. Visual imagery allows us the opportunity to immediately recall experiences, while dreams are often forgotten when one returns to an awake state. Thus, imagery can be used to assist us as we go deeper and deeper into our journey of discovering the invisible parts of the possible humans that we are.

In this next process, you may encounter information which your mind may want to analyze and question. It is recommended that you just relax and enjoy the process just as you would a movie. The information that is presented will be discussed after you have had an opportunity to experience it. This learning experience may be different from that which you experienced in school wherein you were first given facts, or rules, then expected to interpret the information or play the game. This section is written to first give you an experience then assist in interpreting the experience. It's a little like life, we just do it then begin to make sense of it after we have done it.

Entering the Brain–Body Temple

Lie comfortably on the bed or floor . . . allow yourself to enter into deep breathing . . . breathing in all that is good, pleasurable and loving . . . breathing out whatever negativity, resistance or tension that is present . . . breathing in to the count of 3 . . . and out to the count of 9 . . . relaxing the body.

Imagine now you are taking a walk . . . you may take the walk alone . . . or may bring along a special friend . . . imagine walking into a bright golden field of daisies . . . lie down in this field of golden light . . . breathing in the warm sunshine . . . and blue sky overhead . . . feel the daisies brushing gently against your face . . . and know that you are safe here . . . cradled in the arms of Mother Earth . . . hear the birds as they glide gently over your head . . . speaking to you in their soft whisperings . . . relax and have a sense that you could spend a long, long time here. When you feel it is time to go, imagine rising slowly . . . caressing the flowers with your hand . . . and continue walking until you reach the edge of a forest . . . for now, bid your friend goodby . . . and ask that he or she wait a moment for you.

Journey now into the deep woods . . . noting the canopy of green overhead . . . the soft crush of pine as you gingerly walk through the opening into the heart of the whispering pines . . . see the rabbit as it scurries into shelter on your left . . . and the squirrel as he chatters at you from a treetop . . . pause and still your breathing . . . as a newborn fawn raises his velvety ears still wet from birthing.

Enter now into a clearing . . . where the rays of sunshine make a shaft of light on your special home . . . a home known only to you . . . a home not often shared . . . a home of your own creation . . . take now the golden key from your pocket . . . and enter into your special place . . . you are entering your mind and your senses.

Stop in the entry way and take whatever cleaning supplies you feel you may need for cleaning your mind and senses . . . you may visualize actual mops and brooms . . . or if you wish . . . a special magic wand . . . a crystalline structure that you will carry in your right hand.

Go first to the *blue* room of your left hemisphere . . . this is the place of *analytical and logical thought* thought . . . go to the windows . . . and open them wide . . . letting in the blue of the sky . . . notice the size and shape of this room . . . look around and sense how much time you spend here on a daily basis . . . notice the furnishings . . . know that when you are in this room you gather facts . . . analyze issues . . . problem solve logically . . . measure precisely . . . understand technical elements and consider financial aspects . . . notice too that it is from this room that movement of the physical body takes place . . . check the wiring to ensure the possibilities of smooth coordinated movements . . . see what needs to be cleaned or re–arranged . . . and do it now . . . remember what you need about this room . . . then leaving the door open . . . go down the hallway.

Enter now the *green* room of the left limbic system . . . you may have noticed that you went down a few steps . . . into a deeper structure . . . this is the room of *controlled, sequential, detailed* activity . . . go to the windows in this room . . . and open them . . . letting in the scent of pine from the forest . . . get a sense of the size and shape of this room . . . and how much time you spend here on a daily basis . . . in this room you find overlooked flaws . . . approach problems practically . . . stand firm on issues . . . maintain a standard of consistency . . . provide stable leadership and supervision . . . read fine print in documents . . . organize and keep track of essential data . . . develop detailed plans and procedures . . . implement projects in a timely manner . . . articulate in an orderly way . . . from this place you carry out the sequence of movement . . . notice for yourself if this is not so . . . don't you move at the shoulder before you use your hand . . . don't you move at the hip in order to place your foot in walking . . . see if this room is neat and orderly . . . become aware of the furn–ishings . . . do what you need either with your cleaning tools or your magic wand

. . . to clean or re–arrange this room . . . do it now . . . remember anything you need to take care of in this room . . . then leaving the door open . . . cross the hallway.

Enter now the *red* room of your right limbic system . . . this is the room of *emotions and feelings* . . . it is also the room of kinesthetic awareness . . . or imagining a movement before it is actually made . . . you can get in touch with kinesthetic awareness by remembering having the shivers . . . or sensing someone behind you . . . go to the windows of this room . . . open them . . . letting in the warmth of Mother Earth . . . recall the size and shape of this room . . . and how much time you spend here on a daily basis . . . sense that from this room you also recognize interpersonal difficulties . . . anticipate how others will feel . . . pick up on non–verbal cues . . . relate to others in empathetic ways . . . engender enthusiasm . . . persuade or teach . . . understand emotional elements . . . and consider values . . . look around this room now . . . basking in the warm glow . . . notice if there is anything that you would like to clean up . . . or re–arrange . . . if there is, do it now . . . then leave this room leaving the door open.

Go up the hallway and enter the *yellow* room of the right hemisphere . . . the room of *creativity and intuition* . . . look around this room noting the size and shape . . . recall how much time you spend here on a daily basis . . . go to the windows and open them . . . flooding the room with golden light . . . look around and sense that from here you read signs of coming change . . . you see the big picture . . . and recognize new possibilities . . . you tolerate ambiguity here . . . integrate ideas and concepts . . . sometimes you even bend or challenge established rules . . . and take risks . . . you put unlike things into a new whole . . . and you problem solve in intuitive ways . . . from this room you keep track of movement patterns and spatial relationships . . . with an intimate sense of knowing how far to reach . . . or how high to step as you move through your world . . . look around and see if anything needs cleaning . . . or re–arranging and do it now . . . then remember all that you need from this room . . . leave this room with the door open and go to a central hallway.

Climb up the stairs to the balcony and look below you . . . as there are no floors in your magic house it is easy to see into all the rooms . . . and from this place you can even move walls! . . . scan the rooms now . . . the blue room of analytic thought . . . the green room of detail . . . the red room of feeling . . . and the yellow room of creativity and intuition . . . check the size and shape of these rooms and if any walls need to be moved do it now. Then continue up the stairs to the floor of perception . . . go into the room of *vision* . . . . note the color . . . and size . . . and shape . . . go to the windows and open them . . . look beyond the landscape . . . beyond the forest . . . beyond the Earth . . . look beyond the beyond . . . then place your awareness again back in this room . . . see if there is anything you need to clean up here . . . paying special attention to *illusions* that may need to be swept away . . . use whatever cleaning materials you need . . . or the magic wand . . . when you have finished, leave the door to this room open . . . and walk to the next room.

Enter the room of *hearing* . . . note the sounds . . . and the size . . . and shape of this room . . . go to the windows and open them now . . . listen carefully to the sounds beyond the silence . . . the breathing of Mother Earth . . . the whispers of the angelic choir . . . then place your awareness back in this room . . . see if there is anything you need to clean with your tools . . . or your magic wand . . . pay attention to *voices you may hear* . . . and if they are not from your Highest Good . . . gather them into a balloon . . . and release them out the window . . . transmuting them to the Heavens above . . . then see how comfortable you are in this room . . . when you have finished . . . leave the door to this room open . . . and walk into the next room.

You will find yourself in the room of *sensing* . . . scan the size and shape of this room . . . go the windows and open them . . . feeling the warm breezes touch your face . . . pause for a moment . . . and sense how you process touching . . . allowing your fingertips and toes to feel the walls and the floor . . . and allowing the walls and floor to feel your fingertips and your toes . . . remember making mud pies and having them squish up between your fingers . . . remember walking barefoot . . . on the hot summer sand . . . and skipping through mud puddles after a summer rain . . . remember the first snowfall dropping fluffy soft flakes on your nose . . . and remember how a special mothering person could completely surround you . . . by your just sitting in her lap . . . place your awareness again in this room . . . and note if there is anything you would like to move or remove . . . or if there is anything you need to clean with your tools or your magic wand . . . do it now . . . then go out of this room . . . leaving the door open.

Enter now the room of *taste* . . . look around at the size and shape of this room . . .see if it has any color . . . go to the windows and open them . . . breathing air in through your mouth and nose . . . sense now the most pleasurable tastes you can . . . your favorite fruit . . . crunchy vegetables . . . the amber fireside taste of coffee . . . the tartness of lemonade that makes the back of your mouth almost ache . . . see if there is anything you want to move around or clean up . . . do it now . . . when you are ready, leave the door open and go to an adjoining room.

You have entered the room of *smell* that has a close proximity to the room of taste . . . look around at the size and shape of this room . . . see if it has any color . . . go to the windows and open them . . . imagine smelling fresh baked bread . . . and the pine forest after it rains . . . smell the breath of a newborn puppy . . . and clothes fresh from the clothesline . . . see if there is anything you want to move or arrange . . . and do it now . . . then leave this room with the door open.

Now enter one final room of senses . . . a room you may or may not have visited often . . . the room of *Extrasensory Perception* . . . see if this room feels familiar to you . . . how large it is . . . what the shape or color is . . . go to the windows and open them . . . as you do so remember that you have been here before . . . that sometimes when you have been close to someone it seemed you could tell what they were thinking . . . or sometimes you can sense that someone was behind you . . . before you turn to see them . . . sometimes you have sensed things . . . and said to yourself. . . you were just imagining . . . and have dismissed these senses from your mind . . . allow yourself to remember them now . . . remembering the possible human that you are . . . see if there are veils that need to be removed in this room . . . cobwebs that need to be swept away with your crystalline wand . . . trust that needs to be restored . . . scan this room and see if it needs any other rearranging . . . and do it now . . . then when you are ready . . . leave, keeping the door open.

Move up the stairs to the balcony . . . now as before look down into the rooms of the senses . . . note the relative size of each to the other . . . from this vantage point make any changes in the structures that you choose . . . expanding any of the rooms . . . changing their shape . . . see the secret passages from rooms of thinking that are linked up to rooms of perceiving . . . linking them all together . . . sense that you are much more than seeing . . . hearing . . . touching . . . tasting . . . or smelling . . . you are much greater than analytic thought . . . or concern for detail . . . more than values and emotions . . . more than creativity and intuition . . . see if you can hear what the moon whispers . . . that you but dimly perceive . . . that you are a being who is interactive . . . the sum of all creation . . . an entity who is the mind of nature . . . the soul of the Earth . . . the imagination of the Divine . . . you are a dream not yet dreamed . . . a dream being in which empathy is as fundamental a force as gravity . . . where compassion floods forth with the constancy of sunlight . . . you are part of the universe . . . . you are energy . . . space and all time.

Now breathe in the golden light that you are and blow it down through the rooms of perception . . . inhale again and blow it down through the rooms of thinking . . . descend down the stairs . . . pause on the landing of your senses . . . and notice those rooms are clearer to you than when you started . . . thank these senses for all that they provide you . . . and descend to the rooms of thinking . . . wander through each leaving the doors open . . . observe too that they seem clearer than when you first entered each of them . . . thank yourself for thinking . . . then place your cleaning supplies and magic wand by the doorway . . . and leave your temple . . . making sure to use the golden key to lock your special place . . . and put the key in your pocket . . . move back from your special place and see now how a shaft of Light descends around your home . . . protecting who you are . . . your senses . . . your thoughts . . . your feelings. . . the seen and unseen parts of who you really are.

Breathe in the green of the forest and begin making your way out of the sheltering arms . . . seeing the animals with clearer awareness . . . feeling the bond of love that you hold with all creatures . . . sense too that you are part of the forest as it is part of you . . . and as you soak up the strength of Mother Earth . . . know too that it is important for you to be a part of the greening of the planet . . . and that you can do that with love . . . walk now out of the forest and see your friend waiting for you . . . and taking the outreaching hand of humanity . . . walk back through the golden field of daisies . . . feeling at peace.

Chapter 3 Thinking Styles of the Brain

From the proceeding process you may have discovered that you felt quite comfortable investigating your brain and your thinking processes in this way. So you have had a direct experience with your own brain even before I have begun to explain how the brain operates, functionally, not physiologically or neurologically. Some of you may have noticed that you felt more comfortable in the blue and green rooms, that would indicate that you use those functions in technical careers, primarily the left hemisphere of the brain. Others such as artists and teachers may have felt a clearer sense of who you were in the red and yellow rooms associated with right brain or right hemisphere functioning. For those of you who spend considerable time thinking, using both analytical and intuitive problem solving skills, you were likely more comfortable in the blue and yellow rooms. These rooms or ways of looking at the world have also been associated with what Carl Jung called introverts. Then there were likely some of you with yet another way of processing, those of you who could most clearly relate to the green and red rooms, the rooms of detail and emotion. In my research with Ned Herrmann, author of *The Creative Brain,* 1988, persons feeling "comfortable" in these rooms are likely to be what we call "limbic processors." They are the "doers" with strong feelings, often associated with what we could commonly call extroverts.

There are many, many variations of these combinations which come from combining the quadrants differently, as well as the quality or amount of thinking which originates from these parts of the brain. The important point is that each of us has a particular style of thinking that resulted, in part from our upbringing and from the choices we have made regarding the work we do, the vocations or careers we have chosen.

Let's start by making this simple to understand. If we could neatly divide the brain into four quadrants, it would make discussion easier. In reality, however, the brain works by having energy pass back and forth between the left and right hemispheres of the brain and between the upper and lower portions or the cerebral hemispheres and the limbic system. However, the reason for selecting the four quadrant model will be important as we explore other information in later chapters. It is important to recognize, that like imagery, the model I present is only a metaphorical model. This does not mean it is "real;" only that we have a way in which we can talk about it. Since you have had some experience with me in looking at imagery through some processes, let's now begin to bring images into our discussion. Sometimes visual images can convey meaning in ways that are as powerful as words. (See Figure 1)

The "blue room" you experienced was the metaphor for the left cerebral hemisphere. It is characterized by logical, analytical and quantitative processing. You use this part of your brain when you gather facts, analyze issues, problem solve in logical ways and argue rationally. You also use this part of your brain for measuring precisely and for understanding both technical elements and financial aspects. If you are not a financial wizard, this does not mean you are brain dead! I'll explain in a minute why we use some parts of our brain more than others.

MODEL OF COGNITIVE FUNCTIONING

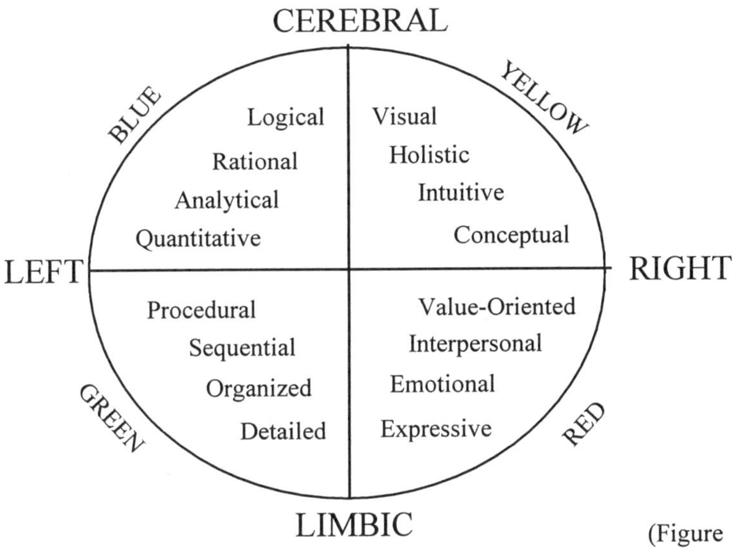

(Figure 1)

The left limbic mode or the "green room" is characterized by planned, organized, detailed and sequential activities. It is from this place in the brain that one develops the abilities to see and implement projects in a timely manner. Further, the ability to organize and keep track of essential data and maintain a standard of consistency comes from the functioning of the left limbic system. A person with a strong left limbic method of solving problems would likely be a good administrator, perhaps a banker, certainly someone I would trust my money to if I were to make conservative investments in the stock market.

The right limbic mode, if we were going around our "house" in a counterclockwise direction, is represented as the "red room." It is characterized by emotional, interpersonal and kinesthetic factors. It is from this place in the brain that one develops the ability to recognize interpersonal difficulties, anticipate how others will feel and intuitively pick up on non-verbal cues. From this site of neural functioning, we develop the ability to relate to others in empathetic ways, engender enthusiasm, persuade and teach.

Finally, the right cerebral mode or the "yellow room," taken by itself is characterized as the site of holistic, intuitive, synthesizing and integrative types of thinking. One who uses thinking patterns dominated by this center will be able to see the "big picture," and "read" signs of coming change. A person with dominant thinking skills which come from this cognitive preference is one whom I would trust to make high risk investments. The ability to tolerate ambiguity and bend or challenge established policies comes from this site in the brain. Unlike the left hemisphere dominated person who problem-solves in rational ways, the right hemisphere dominated person problem-solves in intuitive ways.

If I were to simplify our first model and add concepts of time, our model may add even more insights. (If I had transparent film, I would just keep building the stack higher and higher, but unfortunately I am limited to working in this two-dimensional flat plane method of communicating). (See Figure 2).

In the simplified version, which is easier to remember, the upper left quadrant or the left cerebral hemisphere is that part of the brain which processes *facts.* Because of its neural connections, time is managed in a sequential, step by step fashion. The lower left quadrant or left limbic system is that part which is concerned with *form,* with structure. It serves as the "safekeeping" system and functions in present time. The right limbic or lower right quadrant is that part of the brain which we associate with the processing of *feelings;* it is usually associated with past time. The upper right or cerebral right hemisphere, in simple terms, is where we process information which we might call *fun,* due to the nature of visual spacial processing, and the interpretation of symbols and dreams. The cerebral right is often associated with future time.

ORIENTATION OF THE SPECIALIZED BRAIN

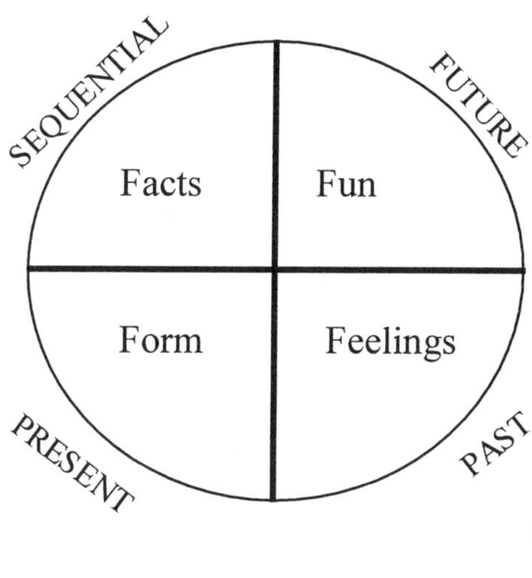

(Figure 2)

Now using the clues provided in Figure 2 with those from Figure 1, we can, when astutely listening to others, figure out the thinking dominance of the speaker. Why bother you ask? Well, for one thing, to see if we are sharing the same point of view. Not that we have to, because diversity can lead to a greater richness in solving problems than one would find with one who thinks just like you do. That we all know, is sort of like having a dialogue with the image in the mirror. It's safe, but not as interesting.

Languages of the Specialized Brain

The *verbal* characteristics associated with the left cerebral system are dominated by logical analysis, often which overpowers, as it were, the "languages" of the other quadrants. This person's language is dominated by both the factual content of an event and the objective analysis of it. Language is often very precise, not unlike that which characterizes a newscaster. In working toward group decisions, the person dominated by the left cerebral hemisphere is likely to focus questions on "What?" For the most part, their concern is with present time.

A person with a dominance in the left limbic system, on the other hand, may speak in complete sentences and be highly articulate, but may be more comfortable with technical information. Dominance in this area is evident by the descriptive organization of materials, and the development of products and procedures. Language clues more often focus on "things" rather than "people." Persons with a dominance in this area are often likely to ask questions concerning "How?" something will be accom-plished. These two "languages" of the left side of the brain, being both rational and orderly, are the languages which dominate Western culture. (See Figure 3).

LANGUAGES OF THE SPECIALIZED BRAIN

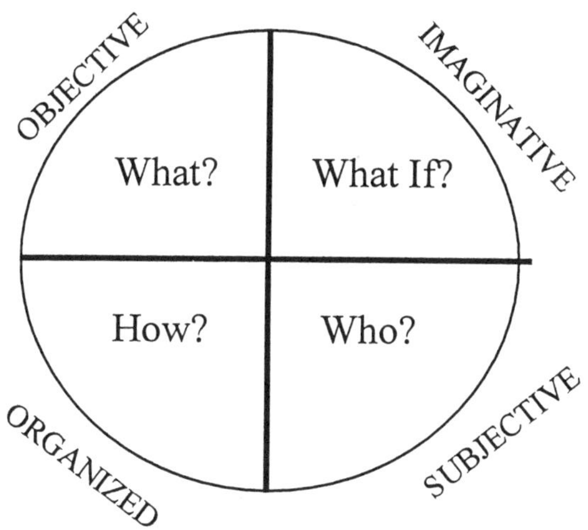

(Figure 3)

Contrast these languages with the verbal characteristics of the right side of the brain. Characteristics of the right limbic system lead to development of a language in which the person is more informal, "chatty," and concerned with personal topics of conversation. Interpretations of events are always subjective in contrast to the objective interpretations made by a person with a left cerebral dominance. You can count on a person with this dominance to ask the

"Who"? type of questions. They will be concerned with values and feelings, often drawing on the past for making interpretations of events.

Then we have the person dominated by the right cerebral hemisphere--his or her communication style is visibly (and audibly) different. The speaker may go off on a tangent or carry on multiple conversations at the same time, frequently loosing words or even entire thoughts in the middle of a statement. In contrast to the left limbic person who likes *procedures,* the right cerebral dominated person likes *process.* The focus is often to ensure that every possible avenue gets covered. This person often prefers to leave the decision making to a left cerebral dominated person. A person with a preference for this mode of processing is concerned with the future and asks the "Why?" or What if?" questions associated with the realm of imagination.

Let's look at some typical phrases which may be helpful for understanding the differences between the processing modes. (See Figure 4). The person with a left cerebral mode of processing, who is characterized by logical and rational processing, wants to understand by "knowing the bottom line.", completing a "critical analysis," wanting to "take it apart" and understand the "key points." It is my opinion, or rather my personal bias, that the medical profession is dominated by this reductionistic method of thinking, reasoning, and speaking. The individual with a left limbic mode of processing is concerned with "law and order," "going by the book," "playing it safe." This person most often wants to avoid "setting a new precedent," preferring the safety of status quo.

Persons with a strong right limbic mode of

processing can be counted on to be concerned with "team work," "personal growth" and may speak of "human resources" and "networking." This person may want events to be "participatory" or "interactive." On the other hand, the right cerebrally dominated person uses typical phrases such as "brain–storming," "getting the big picture," "linkages," "playing with an idea," and being on the "cutting edge."

POSITIVE LANGUAGE ATTRIBUTES

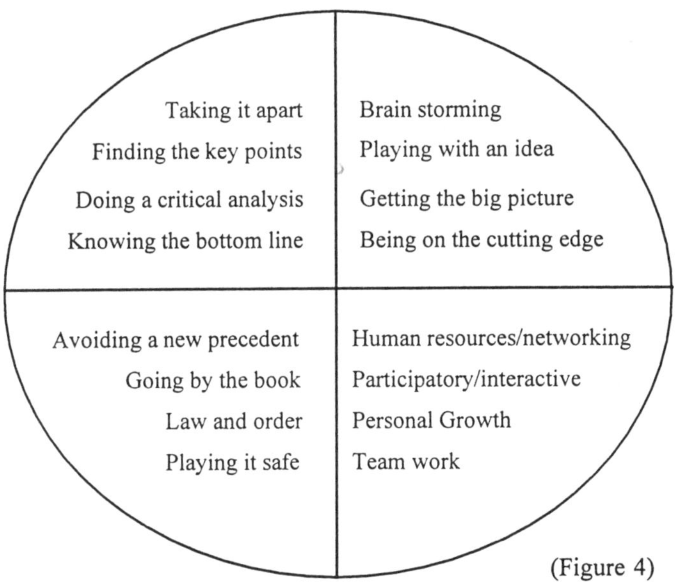

(Figure 4)

Another way of looking at the differences between the processing modes is to examine what Ned Herrmann calls "zingers" or negative comments made by others. (See Figure 5). People may view the person with a strong left cerebral processing preference as "critical," "uncaring," "powerful," or "unemotional." The person with a left limbic preference may be labeled "boring," "non–imaginative," or "a stick–in–the–mud." Those with a right limbic preference may be regarded as "all hearts and flowers," has a "soft touch," "hugs a lot" or "just talks, talks, and talks." Finally, an individual with a right cerebral preference may be regarded as "not realistic," "has her head in the clouds," "dreams a lot," is "just plain weird," or simply "can't seem to get focused, is not grounded."

"ZINGERS"
NEGATIVE LANGUAGE ATTRIBUTES

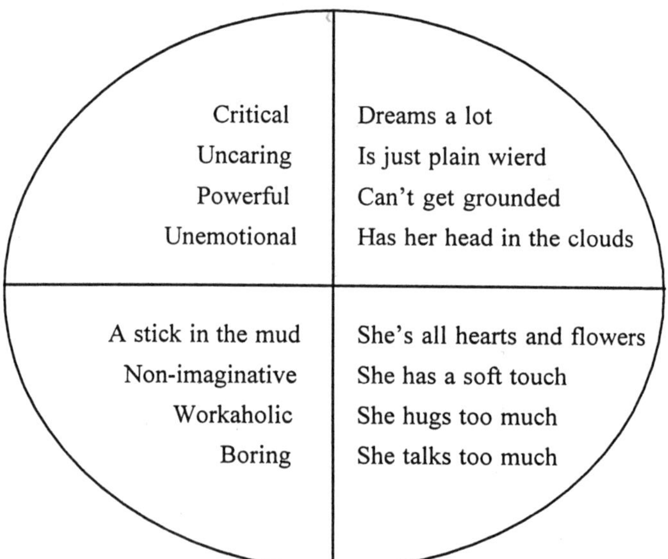

(Figure 5)

It is important as we talk about the characteristics of the brain as reflected in language, that we place no more importance on one style than another. The information is offered here so that we may begin to obtain clues about how to establish effective communication with each other and with ourselves, if we are to have effective internal dialog. The idea of course is to have "whole brain" communication, which means to have equal representation of all four quadrants in group or self decision-making. Because people don't really develop in these nice little boxes as I have described and may have multiple preferences, a couple representing the left and the right mode of processing, would between them have a "whole" brain. Too often, as in this case, the viewpoints are considered too divergent, each wanting to make the other "wrong" in an attempt to justify a personal position. Either that, or each individual develops a co-dependency on the other, thus depriving both of development of full human potential.

Let me give you a fun example to illustrate this point. Consider the word "money." That single word has, according to our model, four different meanings. (See Figure 6).

To the cerebral left person, it means ways to "count" it, to rationally determine ways to multiply it, or diversify the return. To the person with a left limbic dominance, money means ways to "save," to invest not for the purpose to create more abundance, but for the purpose to ensure its safety. The right limbic person, dominated by interpersonal values and feelings, will always look for ways in which money can "help" others, bring them pleasure or joy. Fortunately for many of us, this is the person who uses their money to buy us those birthday cards which no one else seems to remember. Yet the meaning she attributes to money is of no greater important than the one who chooses to save it. The orientation is simply different. The right cerebrally dominated person, looks at money as ways to have fun, ways to "spend."

LINGUISTIC INTERPRETATION OF MONEY

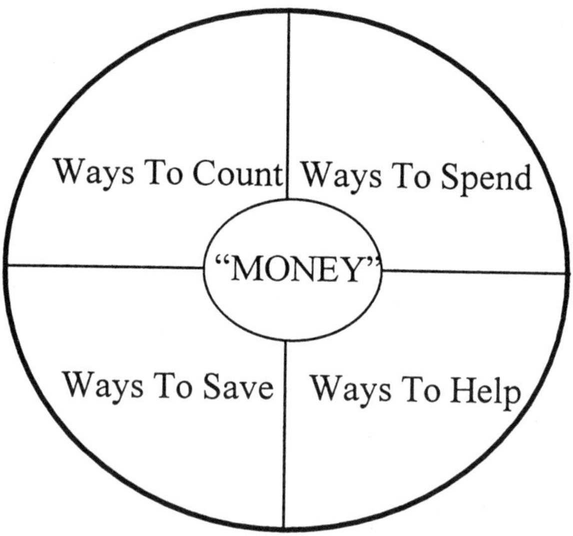

(Figure 6)

I give you now a second example, that of "unfinished business." (See Figure 7). Notice the incredible differences in interpretations that can be made. The left cerebral dominated person thinks in terms of "he owes me money" while the left limbic person may feel "the other hasn't yet completed the plan." The right limbic person may feel that unfinished business relates to "hurt feelings." The right cerebral dominant person may intuit the other "hasn't explained all the possibilities." Interpretations of a single sentence are indeed astronomical.

LINGUISTIC INTERPRETATION OF "UNFINISHED BUSINESS"

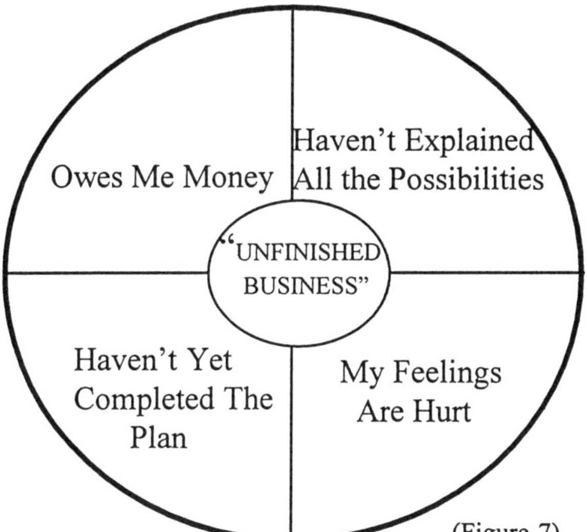

(Figure 7)

Given that we not only speak a great many languages on Earth, each with their own set of cultural perspectives, values and prejudices, within the English language alone, the interpretations which can be made of a single sentence are indeed astronomical. Given the examples of the interpretations of "money" and "unfinished business," we could make endless lists of other interpretations of concepts like "power," "freedom," "liberty," "peace" and likely even "love." I think the trick is to begin with a willingness, a mindfulness, that perhaps each of us is right AND accept that each other's views are also right. We need to begin individually, and collectively to use the whole brain--to find the common ground where all perspectives can be honored.

There is one more important difference about each of the processing modes that I need to present before pre-senting information about the development of skills. (See Figure 8). The person dominated by cerebral left thinking believes that knowledge gives one

HOW THE SPECIALIZED BRAIN LEARNS

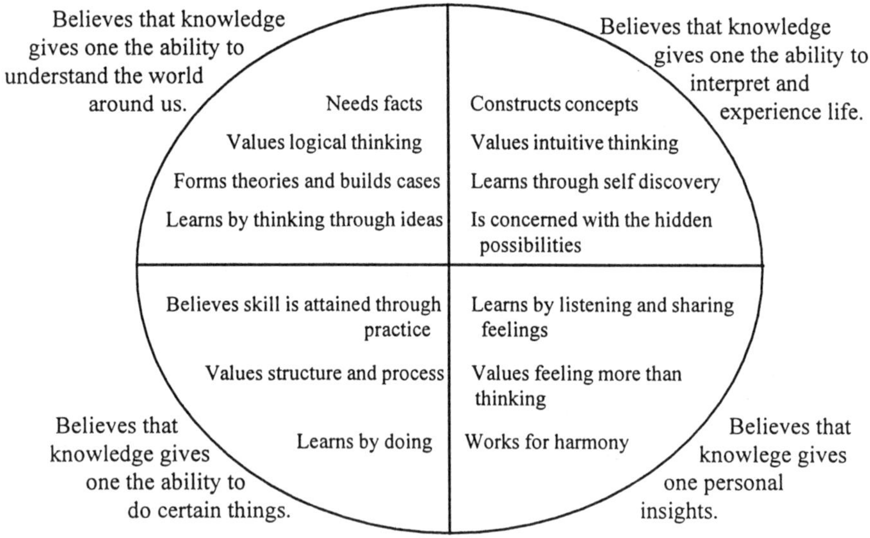

(Figure 8)

the ability to understand the world around him or her. That individual is likely to learn best through ideas, but there is a need for them to be grounded in fact. This person, as mentioned, values logical and rational thinking. The left limbic dominated individual, on the other hand, believes that knowledge gives a person the ability to do certain things. Thus, this person learns best by testing out ideas and theories. This individual values structure and process as a way of organizing what is experienced. There is also the belief that skills are attained through practice.

The person who uses the right limbic system as the preferred processing mode believes that knowledge gives personal insights. From this primary belief, this type or individual learns by listening and sharing ideas and belief systems. This in turn works to create harmony to integrate experiences within the self. Also a right processing mode, the person with a right cerebral preference believes that knowledge gives the individual the ability to interpret and experience life events. (Sound like me? MMMMMH). The individual dominated by this mode of thinking learns through self discovery. This person is concerned with the construction of concepts and deeply values intuitive processing. It is likely that this type of individual is concerned with hidden possibilities.

Development of Skills

The skills which characterize the four processing modes are also different. But before I talk about these, let me talk about how all these preferences develop in let me talk about how all these preferences develop in the first place. You remember in a previous chapter I talked about the child who imitated the body postures of his father. It seems we develop our preferences, our language and even our skills based on some pretty simple notions about the feedback we get from the environment. One of our basic drives is to love and be loved. So when my mother said something like "Oh, you are so creative" as I presented a little picture I had drawn to her, for posting on the refrigerator door, the message that I "got," was that if I made more pictures or did more creative things then I would get more recognition; in short, I would get more love. I suppose I could just as easily have given her a successfully completed math problem; in which case I might be sitting here writing a book of mathematics, rather than one that creatively attempts to find a common ground between the fields of psychology, physiology, neurology, physics and astrology.

Very early in life we learn as individuals what works for us and what doesn't work. Often, we tend to take the path of least resistance. Doing more and more of those things which are easy for us and for which we receive some kind of recognition, rather than pursuing those things which are difficult or for which we receive little if any recognition from our parents, our friends or our teachers. Interestingly, as we grow, and particularly when we enter school, there is the opportunity to receive multiple kinds of feedback. In my case, the cognitive skills of my parents were quite different. My mother reinforced my creative aspects and my activities which had to do with other people. My dad was my counselor for the math and physics, but because he wasn't as available as my mother, both in terms of feedback and time, I found it much more desirable to do the creative and group activities.

Unfortunately, I did not learn from my dad, until later in life, the ability to engage in reflection at the end of the day. This was despite the fact that he modeled this characteristic for me. When I was a young child, my dad built a forty gallon acquarium right in the wall of the dining room. It was filled with the most wonderous exotic multi-colored fish -- angel fish, black mollies that tracked our fingers when we tapped on the glass, and neon tetras. We also had prolific guppies with their own little special "nursery" that we put the momma fish into late in her pregnancy. Then there was that special partitioned off place where we put the male beta--the fish with the long flowing fantail who would aggressively fight another male to the death. (We only had one male and one female in their own little special place). While I remember laying quietly next to my father, seemingly lost somewhere among the floating fish, I never really got what he was doing. It seemed pretty boring to lay there for at least an hour every day just watching the fish. Yet in his way, that was his time of reflection. He just never guided me to watch with wonder, the gliding gentle motions of the fish. He didn't verbalize that in watching them, through just being quiet, we could change the meaning of the day's events. We could allow the harshness of conversations to melt in the unhurried floating of the fish.

I just had the sudden insight, that I really did learn to be reflective at the end of the day. Because I do it all the time now. I just didn't know how important that gift from my father was until just this moment.

Through his quiet way, he showed me, that one doesn't have to do anything, doesn't have to instruct another in the fine art of fish appreciation. That gift has always been with me, but it hadn't entered my awareness until I was willing to call it forth. So it seems now, that in this moment of time, instead of regretting lessons that I thought I could have learned earlier, perhaps I didn't need those gifts until just a few years ago.

My mom was generally a limbic processor, a person concerned with both people and things. She was highly organized, a maker of lists, a person who believed that everything had its place. Every drawer and every closet were carefully organized, books were placed on the shelves in descending order according to size. Plastic and paper bags were always kept, folded a precise way and stored in their separate designated places. I remember during my elementary school years several occasions when mother would go on a cleaning spree. I loved it because her cleaning meant that my twin brother and I would meet my dad for lunch downtown. It was one of the few times we ate "out."

Meanwhile, my mother was home cleaning and scrubbing every vertical and horizontal surface in the house -- the walls, the windows, the oven, the basement steps. She cleaned every inch of the house, and often my own bedroom, throwing out some of my most treasured rocks, broken crayons, and trinkets I obtained for my imaginary store. In a funny sort of way, I learned that there needed to be "secret" places for me that my mother would not find. Over a good many years, those "secret" places for storing my treasures, spilled over into the "secret" intimate things that I did not share with her. Hence, although I cannot trace this understanding backward in time, other than to the event I just described, there was a gradual breakdown in communication. I learned to share the creative parts, as the only one in the family representing this quadrant. I was taken to be frivolous, ungrounded, and fanciful. But I dutifully participated in all the activities for which my mother was the leader -- Blue Birds and Camp Fire Girls (we didn't have Girl Scouts in my home town), Job's Daughters, and church activities.

So while my own skills developed along lines of reinforcement and feedback, they also developed according to certain types of negative feedback. Following my high school years my mother developed a drinking problem. I suspect that since she was a "super" mom, being as equally involved with the activities of my brother as my own, when we left home at the same time for college, there was no way she could see to fill the void. Instead of applying her skills and working with other younger children in the community, many of whom she knew, she withdrew into herself. In my small town there were no mental health facilities, no support groups. A person who developed deviant behavior was, in short time, shunned by the community. Her friends visited less and less, the bridge games became less frequent because she always had too much to drink. So she sought meaning in the skills she knew she had. She became even more compulsive in the cleaning and organizing of the household. Although there were few visitors, and my brother and I rarely came home from college, she went on several major redecorating ventures -- changing the draperies, re-wallpapering, and buying new furniture. My dad who was generally a left brain processor, with a dominance in the left limbic system, viewed her activities as something to "do."

One particular occasion, early in my college years, illustrates how negative feedback can be as influencing as positive feedback. Growing up organized, I was beginning to take great pride in my new college apartment. But over Christmas vacation, I saw my mother becoming "enslaved" by her organization, she was becoming obsessed with cleanliness. I offered to cook dinner one night -- pizza I think. I do remember it was something that we rarely ever had when I was growing up. I knew that it was very important that I clean up properly. So I took extra care not only to take care of the dishes, but to actually wipe all the counter tops and even sweep the floor. I then sat down to chat with my dad over the noise of the television. My mother came into the kitchen, and standing with her hands on her hips, surveyed the area. With that she began to pull out the kitchen polish, to move all the counter top items and polish the counter tops. She polished, not "cleaned" every appliance, carefully fitting them back into her imaginary grid in which objects needed to be within a prescribed inch of each other. I watched, feeling hurt, anger and bewilderment. And somehow, in that moment of time, I learned that neatness was O.K., being compulsive was not.

Our beautiful and perfect home has now become a prison for my mother. She doesn't like my brother's children to be there because it makes too much of a mess for her to clean up -- even when my sister-in-law and I are careful to clean and organize the best we can. A house with nearly 2,500 square feet is simply too much for her to care for, yet all the cleaning people she hires do not satisfy her. She desperately wants to move with my dad to a smaller place but can't get over the barrier of what to do with all the "stuff." And at age 78, it is too much effort to organize all the garage sales.

My dad on the other hand, with a strong left limbic system, stays in the "safekeeping" mode. He yearns for status quo, unchanging, stable. At age 83, he would be perfectly happy to stay in the large house. Although he rarely pursues his hobby of rock cutting any more, he cannot bear to part with the boxes and baskets of rocks that fill the basement. These are things, from his perspective, that need to be saved. But I could see my mother's influence on my last visit home. All the containers of rocks now have labels! They are now sorted by color, type and size.

Having used my family and my background as only one illustration of how skills develop, I want to make some brief comments about how these skills get organized into the professions, vocations and jobs that we pursue. As I have stated under general characteristics of the left cerebral mode, there is concern with technical, financial and problem solving tasks. This makes for fertile ground for auto mechanics, computer programmers, bankers, and politicians (not diplomats as they also have a very active right limbic system). Those with a left limbic mode are concerned with process, the "how" of things, the organization, planning and sequencing of events, regardless of the topic. Persons with strong preferences in this area are the PTA and conference organizers, the janitors, the hospital and organization administrators, and conservative consumers.

The right limbic dominated person develops skills in teaching, non-technical writing, music appreciation and is skilled in expressing ideas as they relate to values and principles. They are the team players, the social workers, and the Presidents of advocacy groups. Real estate agents have preferences in both limbic styles of processing. Those with a right cerebral mode have skills in conceptualizing, those who make the long range strategic plans. They are the artists, the advertizing agents, whose creative aspects reflect cultural and social change. They are the visionaries, the mystics, those who choose to be on the "cutting edge." Quoting Anatol Brillard's final words as a drama critic, these are the ones who choose "the wonder, the terror, the *exultation* of being on the edge of being" (Ackterberg, 1991).

Hemispheric Differences

While we have spent time looking at the brain as if it had four quadrants, let's begin lumping them together by focusing on the hemispheric differences and similarities. The negative aspects of the right hemisphere are that alone, it is like a sail with no rudder, its tendency to see patterns leads at times into the mental disease of paranoia -- seeing things where none exist, because of a pre-occupation with visual patterns. According to experiments performed several years ago by Stuart Dimond, a psychologist at the University College in Cardiff, Wales, the right hemisphere, without the correcting influence of the left hemisphere, tends to view the world as more unpleasant and hostile than the left hemisphere would view the world by itself. Yet to discount the vision and the wisdom of the right hemisphere is tantamount to considering abortion for a mother known to have syphillis, thus depriving the world of Beethoven!

Persons dominated by their right hemisphere frequently are "natural" lefties, but not always. They have been shown by experiments and clinical studies to deny problems, deny hostility and avoid inter-personal conflict. The problem with this denial is that it manifests itself in the body in the form of "psychosomatic" complaints. In other words, people may develop disease in their body when there is really none present, due to over-imagining or over-imaging. This does not however, and I offer this as a word of caution, mean that symptoms are any less "real" to them. Pain is real to the person who believes they are in pain. And pain, like some of the other symptoms we experience, triggers physiological adaptive responses. But the adaptive responses may be excessive, thereby creating the necessity for surgery and other extreme measures. Again, I am not suggesting, as in the case of peptic ulcers or arthritis, that surgery is not warranted; I am suggesting that the *causal* factor may be psychosomatic, not physiological. The physiological responses are just adaptive measures the body employs while seeking balance.

As we examine the left hemisphere more closely, we recognize that it controls reasoning, abstract thinking and speech. By itself, the left hemisphere can function in the world much better than the right -- information worth noting for caregivers of those with traumatic head injury. That is, I should suggest that those with a left hemisphere would function better in Western culture, the inverse would be true for those functioning in an Eastern culture. The point I want to make is that without the oneness with the universe and creativity might be totally lost. Without the right hemisphere our ability to engage in the absurd would be tampered, and we would be in danger of losing our sense of humor.

It has been suggested that the two hemispheres of our brain perceive themselves in direct competition with each other for survival, at least if I am speaking metaphorically. It is sort of like having an IBM computer on the left and a MAC computer on the right. One hemisphere seems to do the thinking and one seems to do the graphics. If I could be one who could participate in goal setting for us as individual, for us as a human species (despite the grandiosity of this position), I would suggest that our mission is to get the two hemispheres, or two brains or two computers to talk to each other. We need to interface the gap in a user–friendly way! Given my comments about brain dominance and its influence on cultural development, isn't this precisely where we find ourselves as a humanity? There seems to be little interface between the Western and Eastern cultures in our global community.

My sense is that it is time to stop the war as it were, to pit the left hemisphere against the right hemisphere, the Western Culture against the Eastern culture. It is time to focus on the connection and the wholeness. Our knowledge of how the brain functions has undergone much revision in the last twenty years. We now know that the analogy of the IBM and the MAC computer is not really accurate because certain kinds of thinking do come from the right hemisphere. One might suggest that the left hemisphere does "vertical" thinking, looking for all the events that chain together, like putting pearls on a string. The right hemisphere engages in what we may call "horizontal" thinking, more like putting together a jigsaw puzzle and not having an awareness that the picture is not complete until the last piece is in place. Differences between the hemispheres, simply stated, can be understood by suggesting that the left brain takes events apart, while the right puts them back together; each leading to a different kind of understanding. The left hemisphere is reductionistic, the right is holistic.

This can be illustrated in a story taken from a book called *Maps of the Mind* by Hampden-Turner, written in 1982:

> Long ago in the days of debtor's prisons, a merchant found himself sinking even deeper into debt to a money lender. Finally, the money lender revealed what he really had been after, the merchant's daughter. The debt would be forgiven, if . . . . Realizing that the father and daughter were aghast at the offer, the wily financier invited both to take a walk with him along a gravel path. Here he proposed that "Providence shall decide." "I shall take two pebbles from this path," he said, stooping quickly as he spoke and gathering two stones, "And drop them," he did so . . . "the white one and the dark one into this black bag. You will escape prison if your daughter agrees, without looking, to pick one stone from this bag. If it is the white one, she goes free and your debt is forgiven. If it is the dark one, she is mine." Reluctantly the merchant agreed, but his daughter's heart beat wildly. She was sure, well almost, that two dark stones had been put into

> the bag. It was a trial she could not win, and to unmask the money lender's subterfuge would be equivalent to not choosing, and so sending her father to prison (p.108).

According to Edward de Bono, the 1970 author of *Lateral Thinking,* and the originator of the terms "vertical" and "lateral" thinking, the choice which this young woman faced was an exercise in vertical thinking, a logical either/or with disaster at each end. In this particular case, the faulty premise underlying the "choice" was contrived by a villain, yet we do not need villains to have inadequate beliefs. Errors of belief occur repeatedly in attempts to solve problems with vertical thinking alone. Try for yourself to choose in the daughter's place. Was she really caught in a double bind? Let's continue with our story to find out.

> She put her hand in the bag, withdrew a pebble, cried "Oops!" and dropped it "accidentally" amid the hundreds in the gravel at their feet. "I'm so sorry," she exclaimed, "Clumsy of me. But you can tell the color of the pebble I chose, by the color of the one remaining in the bag (p. 108)

Thus, our young heroine engaged in lateral thinking. This method of problem solving, using the right hemisphere, which assists the left, provided an alternative when the left hemisphere beliefs proved faulty. Yet to fully understand the brain we need yet an additional perspective. One which begins to go beyond that which we can see.

The Evolving Brain

I suppose the title of this section may be a little unnerving for those who believe that I am here going to tackle the Nature versus Creation argument. No, at least not here. I want to only offer another perspective on brain functioning, again by using a metaphorical model. One only has to look at the events in the last fifty years or so to recognize, whether or not, we are indeed evolving. In high school, I typed papers on an old standard upright, non-electrical typewriter, with metal rings around the keys and a carriage on the left hand side that had to be "thrown" to get to a new line. Today I sit here with my computer, laser printer and a color monitor. At my office is a computer complete with CD ROM, capable of multimedia presentations, animat-d colored slides and sounds, should I use them. I have just returned from a conference at which we looked at the "ergonomic" design of computers and to my delight I found one with a split keyboard, each half of which could be elevated on an angle to more approximate the natural position of the body when we are standing at rest with our palms facing the middle of the body, rather than turned over as they are now to work on a flat surface.

While my son grew up being introduced at an early age to a computer, we now "speak" daily with "electronic mail", via the computer. Our children will move from Nintendo as the game of choice to virtual reality. Our methods of cooking have changed from conventional ovens to convection ovens; we have changed or are becoming aware of the need to alter our diets from being meat eaters to becoming vegetarians. And while a simple thing like toothpaste was invented as early as 2000 B.C., we now have teeth whiteners, breath fresheners, and plaque removal all combined into one glorious swish in the mouth!

The point is, like a spiral, as we invent new material possessions, we make new adaptive responses. Adaptive responses that not only affect our physiology, but our personality and our cognitive abilities. So slow we think change happens that we don't even see it. But I would respond with a resounding "No, this is not true." We live in an enclosed terrarium, surrounded by roughly three miles of air space. Too long we have been deluded into thinking that the bombs we dropped on Hiroshima have no effect on us. That slow, hardly noticeable change does affect us. In a laboratory where I did some research for my doctoral degree, I was able to see the real evidence of change in the brains carefully preserved in formaldehyde. The corpus callosum, the band of nerve tracts connecting the right and left hemispheres of the brain, is thicker now in human brains than it was fifty years ago. Could it be that the radiation from the bombs has caused an adaptive response, which has, in turn, caused not only physiological but organic change? On a deeper level, were these, though negatively perceived human acts, interfered with and realigned as part of a grander plan? A plan which has created an evolutionary thrust so powerful as to move us more and more into whole brain thinking despite ourselves?

I think evidence of evolution is precisely the phenomena we see in our schools. More and more children are identified as hyperactive and as having Attention Deficit Disorder (ADD). As a practicing therapist, I see this as real evidence that as a human species we are developing the latent right brain. ADD children and hyperactive children learn through interaction with things and toys; they learn through experience, not facts and figures. So they can't sit still in our classrooms where creativity and feelings are stifled. The continued labeling of those who are different doesn't change the educational system, despite the federal laws which support inclusive public school education.

We are caught in the midst of our own evolution! And lest this civilization perish, like the mythical (or real?) civilizations of Atlantis and Lemuria, I can only point out these insights that they may serve to further our awakening. We need a "re–viewing" of where we have been, that we might more clearly see where we are going. My perspective is that we stand on the brink of a new era wherein our technology could be that which connects us -- which serves as the corpus callosum between the global hemispheres, assisting us to make decisions as a planetary community. Or our technology could lead us into separation, a denial of all that makes us human. The choices are ours.

Paul MacLean, then of the National Institutes of Mental Health, in 1969 developed the concept of the "Triune brain." (See Figure 9). His research suggested that the human brain is composed of three layers superimposed on each other which carries its history and function that developed in the various evolutionary stages during the ascent of mankind. The oldest and most primitive part of the brain is called the reptilian brain, according to MacLean. It has also been called the "R–complex." The functions of the R–complex in humans is similar to the brains in most reptiles living today. This part of our brain is concerned with primitive behaviors like establishing territory, growling, foraging for food, hoarding, greeting one another and forming social groups.

Think for a moment how these primitive behaviors appear in our daily lives. Look around your neighborhood and see those homes which have fences, or distinct boundaries, marking off in a way, territory that belongs to a particular family. Look around your home and notice your own "hoarding" behavior: that pile of used clothing, broken radios and miscellaneous items no longer needed, that seem to be waiting for the garage sale that never comes.

TRIUNE BRAIN

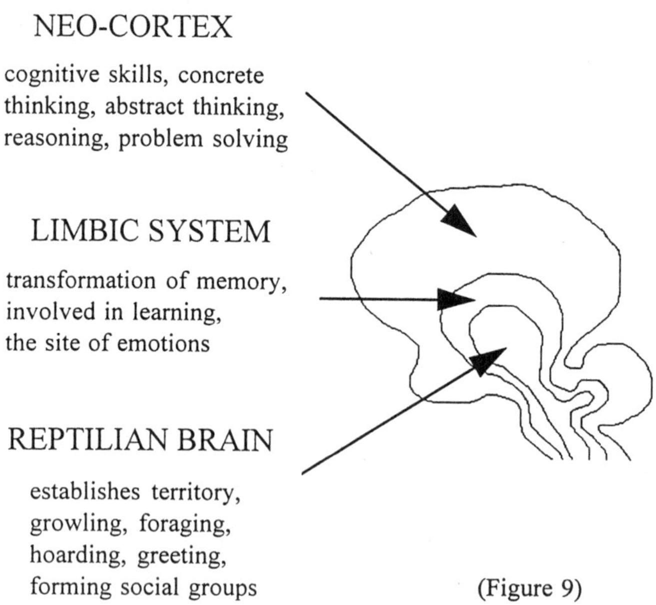

(Figure 9)

Think about your "greeting" behaviors and recall a time when you were walking down a street and you nodded or said, "Good Morning" only to be ignored. You likely concluded that something was really wrong with the *other* person, because in some sort of way, he or she violated some unwritten rule that suggests it is "polite" to speak when spoken to, even if we are talking about strangers. Recall too, those persons who seem mere acquaintances, the ones you "chat" with about the weather, the spouse, the pets. If one day one of these acquaintances appeared before you and began going into intimate details about his or her relationship, it would appear quite out of place for you. Once again, you would have a sense that some social order had been violated. You see, in our culture, we have a certain non–written, non–spoken understanding of the kind of dialogue we have, depending on whether or not the one we are speaking to is a stranger, an acquaintance, a friend or a lover. Within these invisible boundaries, we have rules about space, or how far we stand from each other during our conversations. It is perfectly acceptable to hug or hold hands with a friend or lover, but not something we would ordinarily do with a stranger. Likewise, it would seem strange with our loved ones if we shook hands with them in the morning and only said: "Hello, how are you today?" Whether or not we are aware, mindful as it were, of these behaviors as related to our reptilian ancestry, we cannot deny their presence.

Moving up the evolutionary ladder, as it were metaphorically, we would find the middle layer of our brain which is called the limbic system or the paleo–ammalian brain. In our four quadrant model of the brain, this system is regarded as both the "safekeeping" system, and that which is responsible for regulating our emotional behavior. The input from the limbic system is critical to learning as it is felt that information which has an "emotional tag" is learned faster and retained longer. Recall for a moment when you were learning how to ride a bike. It is likely you did not learn to ride it by staying on (or with mom or dad hanging on), but you learned to ride by learning how not to fall off! Remember all that learning? All those scrapes and bumps? The crashes into the bushes? The curbs that seemed to jump up from nowhere? Limbic processing recorded those emotional reactions. It does not provide a logical, rational answer for the "feeling." This accounts for the students who "feel" their answer is *right,* despite the professor or the teacher's opinion to the contrary.

We are just now revisiting, as it were, this part of the brain. As a society we are learning to redefine intimacy in the absence of sexuality. We are, in our countless talk shows recognizing that feelings are just as important as the events, the facts. As if we were riding a pendulum gone out of control, swinging to reclaim the feeling part of us, it seems all of life's events become amplified. The unattended part of us comes forth, with a rage and a violence yet unheard of in our social history. The over-reliance on our left hemispheres, our need for productivity and material goods smacks us in the face with our escape into drugs, into the psychedelic spaces of the dream world -- wherein our views of reality are not quite as harsh. While these events could be interpreted as a society, both locally and globaly gone out of control, my benevolent side would only view these events as man's need to come into balance --

recognition that the pendulum of change swings from the impoverishment of the 1920's and 1930's to an age of industrialization and materialism. Then slowly, but perhaps with more speed, more urgency, the pendulum swings back to a new spiral of recognition -- an evolving perspective of our yet unspoken yearning for wholeness.

So impassioned am I with our own evolution, I see in my own writing that there is that pull to move toward my own right cerebral processing mode -- to the mode of dreams and creativity. You no doubt see the shifts between the logical linear content related to the functioning of the brain and the creative and social or feeling interpretations I make on a larger scale. So I offer only a mindfulness of the detour, not an apology, as I move again into a description of the Triune brain functions.

The third or most advanced and most recently evolved layer of the brain is the neomammalian brain or the neocortex as described by Paul MacLean. This part of the brain comprises by far the most weight of the three pound human brain mass. It is the site of most of our conscious thought; indeed it serves as the functional descriptor for functioning of the left and right cerebral hemispheres.

Let us take another of those quantum leaps and go on another journey. A journey back into our bodies, a journey through time.

Contacting the Evolutionary Brain

Lie down in a comfortable position . . . and begin

deep breathing . . . breathing in all the goodness . . . pleasure . . . and loving that you can . . . breathing out the resistance . . . negativity . . . and tension . . . breathing deeply . . . feeling safe and secure.

We are going backward . . . on a journey through time . . . deep into the structures of the possible human that you are . . . allow yourself to picture a balloon . . . and enter into that structure now . . . deep in the recesses of your brain . . . you have entered the reptilian brain . . . allow yourself to begin feeling what it must have been like to be a fish . . . knowing that the more deliberately you are involved in this process . . . the more mindful you are with your awareness . . . the more connections you will have with that part of you.

Begin to imagine that you are moving like a fish on your belly . . . gliding on the floor . . . start with your arms out in front of you . . . and push your right arm forward . . . pushing from the shoulder . . . and hike up your right hip . . . keeping the legs straight . . . then push forward with your left arm . . . pushing from the shoulder with the elbow straight . . . and hike up your left hip . . . making sure to move forward (or imagine moving forward) only one half of your body at a time . . . then try going backward . . . again imaging moving only one half of the body at a time . . . moving the arm and leg in the same direction . . . notice that movement is generally in your spine . . . then look around as a fish . . . and sense the instability of your environment . . . your own cautious movements.

Sense your gradual evolution . . . although you are still on your belly . . . allow imaginary movements of your legs . . . notice as you pull your body forward with your left arm . . . that your right leg wants to automatically bend . . . no longer are you tied to movement with just half of the body . . . the body is evolving . . . allowing you to move faster and faster . . . remember what it was like to be a reptile . . . and let those memories come into your awareness . . . sense too that movement seems patterned . . . as does thinking . . . and that from this reptilian body, your habits . . . your continual methods of striving come forth . . . your routines . . . and little rituals come from this structure deep inside of you . . . and from the reptilian part of you, your sense of protection of your territory comes . . . the creation of stability . . . continue to imagine crawling along . . . and thank this reptilian part of you for the habit patterns it provides . . . for the sense of stability in your own being.

Feel yourself evolving now into an amphibian . . . begin now to imagine pulling yourself along with your arms . . . bending first one then the other . . . notice that your head now comes up . . . and the rest of your body seems to follow along . . . notice how your senses have changed . . . check the sounds and smells . . . continue to imagine moving until you are directed to once again move up the evolutionary ladder.

By breathing in and breathing out . . . allow yourself to gradually evolve . . . imagine coming first to a position on all fours . . . rocking first back and forth in this position . . . not unlike a new-born baby . . . then with courage and curiosity . . . begin moving forward . . . sense that you have arrived at the limbic system . . . that part of your brain which resembles a three petal flower . . . sense the greater freedom in movement . . . in your spine . . . your head . . . your neck . . . imagine actively exploring the world with your hands . . . and imagine that you could gather food and bring it to your mouth.

Notice the change in your emotional state . . . open your eyes just slightly . . . and sense the change that vision provides you as you begin crawling around . . . sense the gift of hearing . . . and you move forward and backward . . . in circles to the left . . . and circles to the right . . . as you continue to move notice you are developing friends . . . seeking mates . . . forming groups with a social order . . . feel this deep connection with all in that species . . . knowing that from this awareness . . . your sense of nurturing and family emerges . . . from this part of your brain you sense how others feel . . . you have compassion . . . the ability to reflect on where you have been . . . and from this seat of emotions deep in your brain, you begin to form memories . . . memories that are tagged with emotional events . . . those that are positive . . . and those that you have determined are negative . . . and as you move in this primitive state . . . notice the source of dominance and aggression . . . anger and the fighting that originate from this primitive structure in the brain . . . as you imagine crawling thank this part of your limbic system for the ability to process emotions.

Now begin the process of evolving one more time . . . allow yourself to imagine rising up to your feet . . . sense the muscles becoming more massive . . . see yourself becoming a great ape . . . moving about the room . . . lumbering somewhat awkwardly . . . awaken to other perceptions . . . those beyond sight and sound . . . those senses which alert you to the presence of others . . . in front and in back of you . . . and as you move up the evolutionary scale . . . allow yourself to lose the protective furry covering . . . standing now . . . vulnerable and immensely inventive . . . begin imagining moving around the room . . . with your eyes open.

Sense the growing structure of the neocortex . . . or the neomammilian brain . . . the new mammal . . . see the ambiguous relationship you had with the earlier brain . . . hold in your awareness that somehow between crawling and walking . . . you took a quantum leap . . . a giant step . . . with the breath of the Divine you became human . . . with your own Pandora's box . . . capable of idiosyncrasies . . . silly little habits and behaviors and patterns . . . that are not a part of you now . . . but are of time . . . and begin moving faster now . . . fusing past into present . . . dissolving the boundaries . . . sense that in you there is an incredible computer in the left half of the brain . . . and in the right half, you have a movie projector that makes visions . . . visions which will allow you to make yet another transcendence . . . moving faster now . . . faster as you begin to bridge the present with the future . . . remember with a sense of knowing . . . that you have yet another quantum leap to make . . . this time a giant step for mankind . . . conscious for the first time in all recorded history of your own evolution . . . you are moving toward oneness . . . one with all creatures . . . with Mother Earth . . . uniting the world within to the world without . . . moving away from need . . . and want . . . and separation . . . away from the reptilian and amphibian structures . . . you are evolving at this very second . . . with your own body . . . with movement . . . with sound . . . with gestures . . . fling yourself into the dream . . . into the expanded human that is you . . . and do it NOW.

Then lie down or imagine yourself lying down . . . sinking into the wonder of all that you are . . . reflect and bring into conscious mindfulness the process that you have been through . . . and with full presence . . . and without judgment . . . let the images rise and allow yourself to acknowledge them . . . what you remember about being a fish . . . what you remember about being an amphibian and a reptile . . . what you remember about becoming a mammal and an early human . . . what you remember about becoming an extended human.

In discussion of this process, it is appropriate that I share some thoughts from Jean Houston, author of *The Possible Human* (1982) and with whom I did this process again in her Mystery School workshops in 1991. She suggests that as you allowed yourself to get in touch with the structures of the brain which represent stages you have passed through, you evoke awareness of your own evolution. This enables you to recognize that you have grown and in this process, parts of you have died or become extinct. This reflects that you have either physically or psychologically outgrown old stages and are thrust forward by the evolutionary desire that is within.

The intent of the exercise was to bring forth your awareness of development of all species, but also an awareness and a remembering of the stages you went through *en utero.* The development of the fetus follows that of all other species; that is what is meant by ontological development -- it follows the phylogenic development of prior species. As you experienced "evolving" from a fish to an amphibian, you psychologically evolved in a way to foster greater movement in a more open environment. As you experienced being an amphibian, the intent was to assist you in remembering the connection in moving from water to land. The genius of the reptile was to bring forth old survival mechanism. In transcending them or evolving past them, it was hoped there would be a reformation of the "stick-to-it-ive-ness," which for some has not evolved, rather remains at the level as "stuck-in-it-ive-ness."

Mythical remembrances of early mammals and the great ape was designed to bring into your awareness your abilities and desires to communicate, to socialize, to be gregarious and funny. Entering into the stage of early man was to remind you of your abilities to acquire skills and crafts, to take risks and explore one's reality more widely. Rising to the fully evolved human was an attempt to assist you in remembering your own interior space as much more complex than you may have recognized and to begin the deepening connection with others.

To imagine the extended human was an attempt to allow you the opportunity to have access to your role in becoming a co-partner in the evolutionary process and to stimulate awareness that you are beginning a new phase. You therefore stand now on the brink of being open to extraordinary experiences, using your intuitive processes and your mystical remembrances.

Chapter 4 **Personality Types**

People are different in fundamental ways. They want different things; have different motives, purposes, aims, values, needs, drives, impulses and urges. They *believe* differently; they think, conceptualize, perceive, understand and comprehend differently. The belief that people are fundamentally alike appears to be a twentieth century notion. Probably the idea is related to the growth of democracy in the Western world. If we are equal, then we must be alike.

In 1920, Carl Jung disagreed. He proposed that people are different in fundamental ways even though they all have the same multitude of instincts to drive them from within. While one instinct is no more important than another, Jung maintained there were preferences for how we "function"--and those preferences Jung called "psychological types." Because psychological types may give us clues about how we think and how we feel, these states are worth exploring, particularly since we have established in a previous chapter *how* thinking and feeling get reflected in the physical body.

Let's begin to look at these differences, not in terms of good or bad; rather for the purpose of examining those differences so that they might be understood. In attempting to understand the theory of Carl Jung, it seems appropriate to intuit some of the ancient social, religious, political and psychological factors that may have led to the development of his theories. In short, a brief look into the ancient civilization of the world of the Greeks seems warranted, for reasons which will become apparent in a later chapter. From Holcolm's Oracle we find the following:

> Tell us, Master, how it was in the beginning.
>
> In the beginning special gifts were given to different groups of people. The caregivers were endowed with compassion for the less fortunate. The engineers were given the ability to see what was not yet there. The carpenters were given patience to set straight lines and perfect angles. The technicians were provided with diligence so that they might conscientiously follow the blueprints and detailed directions of others. The experimental scientists were given the certain belief that the world could be manipulated according to their vision of it . . . . And finally there remained one last group and one last gift. These were the explorers. To them was given the gift of curiosity that they might forever observe the world as it is and seek to understand the many wonders of the world and the special gifts given to others.
>
> But what of the evaluators? You have not mentioned their special gift.
>
> Halcolm smiled. The evaluators, dear children, were spread throughout all the other groups, each endowed with the special gift of their own group, and each using that gift in a special way.
>
> But does that not make for much arguing among evaluators about who has the most special gift of all?

Halcolm smiled (Patton, 1986, p. 39).

This story may serve as a framework for beginning to understand psychological types. From early historical perspectives to present theories, each contributing theory has espoused evaluation and understanding of the human condition from a particular point of view. And each view has caused much arguing among the theorists. Our problem it seems, is that as our society and culture changes, we cling to theories of the past, so reluctant are we as a humanity to allow the emergence of new ideas in the midst of our change. More critically, we have not learned from the past and we have not gleaned from it the greater wisdom.

Grecian Decentralization of Personality

How different was the world of the Greeks! Close your eyes now and go with me on a mythical journey . . . a journey back in time . . . as far back as you can go . . . until there was just Gaia . . . the Earth who came out of the darkness so long ago, no one really knows . . . she lies quietly beneath Uranus, the Sky . . . so magnificent was the sky sprinkled with stars that young Earth looked up at him and fell so in love . . . and their union . . . the union between Father Sky and Mother Earth brought forth many living things . . .

Gaia was a bountiful mother who brought forth first the Titans . . . so large were these first gods that Gaia needed to create mountains to serve as thrones. . . . Yet Uranus was not proud . . . so ugly were his children with a single eye in the middle of their forehead, he called them Cyclops . . . while not handsome, they were exceedingly strong smiths . . . hurling lightening . . . thunder . . . and thunderbolts across the sky . . . so as to make even the stars fade. . . So unhappy was Gaia to have her children banned to the heavens for their looks . . . she bade the last male grandchild, Cronus, to subdue his father . . . and so it came to pass that Uranus fled to the farest reaches of the universe . . . giving up his power.

Mother Earth made Pontius . . . the boundless sea . . . her husband . . . and from this union grew a luxurious abundance . . . of trees and flowers . . . flora and fauna . . . such as the Universe had never seen . . . and from her bosom . . . Mother Earth called forth the dust of Man. Cronus, who became the lord of the Universe . . . after banishing Uranus . . . now began to fear that one of his own children . . . might rise up and slay him . . . so he consumed each newborn god by swallowing it . . . his wife Rhea mourned deeply for her children . . . so when she gave birth to the god Zeus . . . she hid him . . . wrapping him in swaddling clothes . . . and sending him away to a secret cave on the isle of Crete . . . then Rhea cleverly wrapped a stone in place of the baby Zeus, and it too was consumed by Cronus.

In the time that ensued . . . Zeus was tended by gentle nymphs . . . he was nursed by a goat with great horns from which flowed ambrosia and nectar . . . the food and drink of the gods . . . so great was the treasure of the horns . . . that Zeus gave them to the gentle nymphs who raised him . . . for it was known throughout the land . . . that he gave them horns of plenty which could never be emptied . . . . soon Zeus was to take his first wife who was known as Metis . . . goddess of prudence . . . who offered good council for Zeus not to overthrow his father Cronus . . . so cunning was Metis . . . she made for Cronus . . . a magic potion which would render him unconquerable . . . instead . . . it made him so sick he vomited up . . . the stone that was to have been Zeus . . . and his five other children . . . the gods Hades . . . Poseidon . . . Hestia . . . Demeter . . . and Hera . . . as Cronus saw his children rise before him . . . he too surrendered and fled.

Then Zeus . . . mighty in power and wisdom . . . shared his power with his brothers and sisters . . . calling upon the Cyclops to forge mighty weapons to do battle with the Titans . . . for Poseidon, the Cyclops made a trident . . . so forceful that when he shook it . . . the earth shook . . . and the water frothed up into waves as tall as the mountains . . . for Hades, the Cyclops made a cape of invisibiity . . . and for Zeus himself, the Cyclops fashioned lightning bolts . . . . In time a terrible battle ensued and Zeus, the victor . . . commanded that the Titans to be banned to Tartarus . . . with Atlas, the strongest of the Titans . . . sent to the end of the world . . . to carry forever the vault of the sky on his shoulders.

Angry with Zeus for banning her sons . . . Mother Earth brought forth two terrible monsters . . . Typhon and Echidna whom she sent against Zeus . . . imagine Typhon's horrible hundred heads touching the stars . . . red hot stones pouring from his gaping mouths . . . hissing like a hundred snakes . . . and roaring like a hundred lions . . . he waged terror and ravaged the land. . . . on and on until hardly a creature was left . . . until the courageous Zeus threw well aimed thunder bolts at Typhon as he tore up Mount Aetna . . . pinning him far underground . . . where the monster lies to this day . .

. belching fire, lava and smoke.

Mother Earth sighed in resignation . . . allowing her own healing . . . rebirthing the planet to a state far better than before the battles . . . she was pleased that the Cyclops . . . being both masons as well as smiths . . . built a towering palace on top of Mount Olympus . . . a palace so great in height . . . it touched the sky . . . and it is said that Iris . . . dressed in a gown of iridescent drops ran a rainbow path between Olympus and earth.

It is said that Zeus then took another wife . . . Hera . . . and on that day Mother Earth gave the bride a little tree that bore golden apples of immortality . . . she planted the tree in the garden of the Hesperides . . . and ordered three nymphs to watch over it . . . but not all was well in Olympus. . . Zeus loved Olympus . . . but would often sneak down to earth . . . take on various disguises . . . and marry mortal girls . . . in one of those moments of passion Zeus thought he had seen jealous Hera coming . . . and to protect his newest bride Io from her wrath . . . he turned Io into a cow . . . Hera, pretending nothing was wrong demanded to have the cow for a gift. . . she then tied poor Io to a tree . . . and sent her servant Argus to watch over her . . . he was of course the best choice . . . as he had 100 eyes placed all over his body . . . and it is said that he could see in any direction . . . . In time Zeus became so distraught . . . he sent his son Hermes to rescue Io . . . disguised as a shepherd with a special pipe . . . Argus who was so bored . . . welcomed the company . . . but soon fell into everlasting sleep . . . the loss of Argus infuriated Hera . . . who sent a vicious gadfly to torment poor Io . . . in exasperation she fled to Egypt . . . when the Egyptians saw her they fell to their knees and worshipped her. . . and so it was that Zeus then turned Io back into human form . . . with a promise to Hera that he would not look at Io again . . . and so it seems Io had not suffered in vain.

Hephaestus, the god of smiths and fire . . . son of Zeus and Hera . . . often stepped into the arguments between his parents . . . so often did he side with his mother . . . that Zeus grabbed him by his legs and threw him out of Olympus . . . nursed to health by a gentle sea goddess . . . Hephaestus built robots of gold and silver to assist him in his workshop . . . robots so gentle it is said that they had tongues of silver . . . to apease his guilt, Zeus gave to Hephaestus . . . Aphrodite . . . the beautiful goddess of love who was said to be without mother or father . . . a being of light who burst forth from the dawn . . . between them they bore a son Eros . . . a mischievious being . . . who delighted in shooting arrows into the hearts of unwary victims . . . upon which it is said, he laughed mockingly.

Now it happened that Metis was to have another child with Zeus . . . and she sat inside his head . . . hammering out a helmet . . . and weaving a splendid robe for the coming child . . . but Zeus suffered from the pounding in his head . . . and all the gods came to offer assistance . . . Hephaestus grasped the tools and split open his father's skull . . . and out sprang . . . Athena . . . fully grown . . . wearing the robe and the helmet . . . her grey eyes flashing . . . she was destined to lead the armies with Nike the spirit of Victory . . . constantly at her side.

Athena was fond of a certain city in Greece . . . and so was her uncle Poseidon . . . both claimed the city . . . and after a long quarrel . . . they decided that whoever gave the finest gift should have it . . . taking his trident . . . Poseidon struck a cliff . . . and water gushed forth . . . alas it was sea water . . . and not very useful . . . Athena on the other hand . . . planted an olive tree in a nearby crevice . . . and since it was judged to give food . . . oil . . . and wood . . . it was decreed the greater gift . . . so it was that Athena ruled wisely and well over the city of Athens.

Apollo and Artemis . . . the male and female twins . . . children of Zeus . . . grew rapidly as all gods did . . . . one day Zeus sent Apollo to win for himself the oracle of Delphi . . . which was guarded by a Python dragon . . . while the dragon unleashed his fury . . . spitting fire and venom . . . the thousand shafts of silver arrows shot by Apollo . . . were too much . . . and the oracle of Delphi was Apollo's . . . his twin sister Artemis . . . was a cold and pitiless goddess . . . so vain she asked Zeus . . . her father . . . to grant her a wish to forever remain young . . . and that she never be asked to marry . . . Zeus granted her wish and Artemis was off . . . to hunt in the hills . . . with her nymphs and hounds . . . bathing in the cool moonlight . . . a young hunter Actaeon found her breathtaking . . . but the vengeful Artemis. . . wanting never to be seen by a mortal . . . turned him into a stag . . . who was brought down to an untimely death by his own hounds.

The great myths tell us that Orion . . . was the son of Poseidon . . . a modest but great hunter . . . to whom the King of Chios promised the hand of his daughter if he . . . Orion would kill all the great beasts . . . so Orion hunted as he had never before . . . but the King . . . not wanting to loose his daughter . . . drugged

Orion . . . and put out both his eyes . . . blind and helpless . . . Orion staggered over the seas in search of the sun . . . to restore his eyesight . . . upon doing so he found the goddess Artemis . . . the only man she ever tolerated . . . and together they rejoiced in each other's company . . . Apollo, in a fit of jealous rage . . . sent a scorpion to attack Orion . . . although Artemis was angry . . . she could not stay that way . . . and in reunion . . . they hung Orion's image in the skies . . . so the great hunter would not be forgotten.

Hermes . . . merriest of all Olympians . . . was god of shepherds and travelers . . . but he was terribly mischievious . . . sneaking out of his cave . . . he stole . . . then disguised fifty of Apollo's best cows . . . the enraged Apollo stormed into the cave . . . demanding the return of his cows . . . and driving poor Hermes into the count–enance of their father Zeus.

Hermes, realizing he had to tell the truth . . . then led Apollo to his cows . . . delighted with the reunion . . . Zeus made Hermes the herald of the gods . . . he gave to him a golden hat with wings . . . and winged sandles . . . and a cap under which he could hide his magic tricks . . . while he was a popular god . . . to the Olympians . . . as well as other mortals . . . there was the time when he had killed Argus . . . the hundred–eyed servant . . . and Hera had tried to punish him by giving all gods a pebble . . . intending to stone poor Hermes to death . . . but so glib was Hermes in his defense . . . the gods applauded him . . . and in so doing . . . he was showered with stones . . . not hurting him . . . but leading to the belief that stones piled along the wayside . . . are signs of Hermes' presence . . . a guardian for all travelers.

Hades . . . the eldest brother of Zeus . . . was a gloomy and forlorn god . . . preferring to guide the souls of the dead to the river Styx . . . he lived with his ice-cold queen Persephone . . . unhappy because she had been kidnapped by him . . . snatched from the loving care of her mother Demeter, goddess of the harvest . . . who ran desperately searching for her daughter . . . so grieved that all nature wept . . . flowers wilted . . . trees lost their leaves . . . the fields grew barren and cold . . . bent with grief Demeter turned into an old grey woman . . . when she discovered that the evil Hades had captured Persephone . . . her grief turned to anger and she informed Zeus . . . to bade Hermes release her daughter . . . or the earth would perish . . . so it was that Persephone was released from the deaththrows . . . but upon leaving she had eaten a pomegranate . . . believed to be the food of the dead . . . for a while the reunion of mother and daughter blossomed . . . but Persephone grew sad . . . for she had eated the deadly fruit . . . Zeus decided that the two should not be separated forever . . . but for every seed Persephone had tasted . . . she had to return for one month . . . to the underworld . . . . Every year thereafter . . . when Persephone was with her mother . . . the earth burst into bloom and flourished . . . it was warm and bore fruit . . . but in the winter when she had to leave . . . the earth turned barren . . . Demeter being a kind goddess . . . taught mortals to sew seed during the barren months . . . and to reap of the harvest just before the long winter . . . so it was that summer and winter . . . spring and fall came to the planet Earth (D'Aulaire, 1962).

Ah, yes, the Greeks walked with Truth (Apollo)

and Beauty (Aphrodite) on either side. They traveled with Hermes, danced and drank with Dionysus, sailed the seas under the guardianship of Poseidon. Even Zeus, the embodiment of might and power, was a first among equal, in no sense were the other gods his satellites. Soul, for the Greeks, was an unbreakable relationship between humans, gods and nature which encompassed even death. *Psyche* stretched from the eminent to the transcendent. The concept of psyche gave the Greeks their infinite love and delight in nature and an extraordinary courage in exploring it. Into every nook and cranny of the world, the spirit of the gods had already ventured. Thus, men crossed the seas in the path of Odyssus (Hampden-Turner, 1982).

The Greeks have been criticized for being idolatrous, but perhaps it has been forgotten that if there are many gods or many potential personalities within human capacity, then multiple images broaden even liberate our compulsions by offering the possibility of fuller personalities.

So great was the Age of Pericles, Charles Hampden-Turner, author of *Maps of the Mind* (1982) suggested it witnessed the height of the Athenian Empire, the establishment of democracy, the centralization of the Delian League in Athens, the poetry of Pindar, the sculpture of Myron, the building of the Parthenon, *Antigone* by Sophocles, the medicine of Hippocrates, and the first production of *Oedipus Rex.* Athenians worshiped gods whose polycentric values pulled outward like a centrifuge. But to the Greeks, it was a natural theology with the universe being made up of gods as well as man, so that the gods personified force fields of *this* world. Drama was a concerted effort to elevate the consciousness of a whole community. The function of the play was not entertainment; the human play, heightened by pretending, was to learn rules of behaving so as to avoid the consequences of real life tragedies. The Greeks believed in a rhythmic universe of contrasting joys and pains. They deplored excess just as Zeus had hurled thunderbolts, thus banning the Titan to Tartarus.

In short, the finest human ideal, honed to god-like perfection, swung to and fro, in dynamic opposition. Virtue required each person to steer between intellect and impulse, human folly was less a consequence of badness in people than it was a misjudgment in combining values. The tragic hero triumphs, over-learns the winning combinations but employs them in new circumstances with disastrous results. Thus, Cronus moved by fear of having Mother Earth punish him for banning her children, instead swallows his own offspring, only to be tricked by Metis into vomiting them up and thus surrendering in the end.

Greek drama and democracy, viewed as wholes, were celebrations of harmony, not dichotomy. Their ideal was both the attainment of heroic extremes and the realization that harmony requires one extreme to yield to the opposite. What was heroic about Oedipus was his painful change from ignorance to knowledge, freedom to determinism, vigilance to blindness, sovereignty to exile. Could it be that unity requires a separation and a coming together as Apollo and Artemis discovered? When Pericles delivered his famous funeral oration in 430 B.C., he knew the soul of Athens would never die . . . "mighty indeed are the marks and monuments we have left" (Andrews, 1967).

The Entrance of Carl Jung

Much of the information on Carl Jung (1875–1971) had been gleaned from the text *Maps of the Mind* by Charles Hampden-Turner (1982), as well as from the writings of Jung himself *(Modern Man in Search of a Soul,* 1933 and *Psychological Types,* 1971). Some have described Jung as a mere disciple of Freud. In truth, Jung pioneered word association tests and earned an international reputation before he met Freud in 1907. He published his major dissent from Freud's position just five years after their first meeting.

However, Jung borrowed from Freud the concepts of "consciousness" and "unconsciousness," a mind mediated by a defined "ego," and a source of psychic energy called the "libido." Beyond these similarities, the differences are profound. Freud's model tended to be mechanistic, analytic and reductive to basic causes. Jung's model was organic, expansive and unfolding to purposive ends. Jung never subscribed to the supposition that science and religion were incompatible.

Jung ascribed to the psyche, four functions which he called "thinking," "feeling," "sensation" and "intuition." Jung maintained most persons have a preferred function and at least one auxiliary. From Jung's position, Western culture was dominated in its thinking function. Technological Man had gained the world but lost his soul. Jung proposed rounding of the psyche following the inner way of T'ai Chi -- from thinking to intuition to sensing to feeling -- to the very depth of the unconscious where lies the knowledge of good and evil.

Jung's concept of the unconscious was much

more elaborate than Freud's. There was a personal unconsciousness of dimmed memories and repressed materials and there was a collective unconsciousness at a deeper level. Jung's unconsciousness had a primordial structure and coherence, like a burial chamber of priceless antiques, hints of an archetypal structure proposed by Saint Augustine. For Jung, unconscious processes were primordial, psychic processes transformed into images via symbols and metaphors.

Jung proposed that when the ego uses a dominant function to engage the environment, it will develop a "persona," at its outer edge. This persona or "public relations facade," is a compromise between the ego as it aspires to be, the social functions demanded of it, and the limitations of the life situation. Unless a balance of these elements is attained, a persona rigidifies into a stereotyped mask. Ideally, the persona is a supple protective coating that facilitates daily encounters.

As the ego has a persona in front, it also has a "shadow." Jung proposed the shadow to be the split-off part of the ego which has been repressed or rejected. To confront one's shadow is to encounter one's unrealized potential -- the functions never developed. The shadow, therefore personifies both the evil and isolation and the hope of reconciliation.

Jung proposed that beyond the shadow in the journey inwards to the unconscious lies the "soul image." In men it is called the "anima," or female spirit; in women the "animus," or male spirit. The soul image is the contrasexual archetype of the ego. Jung proposed that in romatic love, we fall in love with our soul image which blinds us to the real nature of the other -- that we are in love with the "idea of life," with our inner striving for completeness and balance.

Like Freud, Jung proposed the psyche's structure is animated by the energy of the "libido," a life force which in high intensity, energizes will, affect and performance; in low intensity, it energizes attitudes, interests and possibilities. Jung maintained energy shifts toward one value, but consciously or unconsciously it flows back: tension–relaxation, openness–closure, evaluation–decision. He proposed there were natural instincts which were balanced by spiritual instincts and that spiritual instincts have some archetypal model guided by the wisdom of the ages. Thus Mind, for Jung, was united with the body.

A Deeper Look at the Wisdom of Jung

> If I do not want what you want, please try not to tell me that my want is wrong. Or if I believe other than you, at least pause before you correct my view. Or if my emotion is less than yours, or more, given the same circumstances, try not to ask me to feel more strongly or weakly. Or yet if I act, or fail to act, in the manner of design for action, let me be. I do not, for the moment at least, ask you to understand me. That will come only when you are willing to give up changing me into a copy of you" (Keirsey & Bates, 1984, p. 1).

During his clinical years, Jung worked with schizophrenics and noted some dramatic personality reversals. On the one hand, were persons who dealt with the concrete or engaged in people–oriented activities, and there were those who dealt with the abstract or thing–oriented activities. Thus in formulating his four–fold model he initially divided cognitive activities into four quadrants. (See Figure 10).

JUNG'S COGNITIVE ORIENTATION

Concrete People	Abstract People
Concrete Things	Abstract Things

(Figure 10)

Perception, in Jung's opinion, included the ways of becoming aware of things, people, events or ideas. It included information gathering, the seeking of sensation or inspiration and selection of the stimulus to be attended to. According to Isabel Myers who translated Jung's work into the well known Myers Briggs Type Indicator (Myers & Myers, 1980; and Myers & McCaulley, 1985) the meaning of perception as Jung used it, was not always clear to other writers who analyzed Jung's position. Myers proposed Jung used the word "percep–tion" to mean "becoming aware." In his model then, perceiving functions were placed in diametrically opposed quadrants (See Figure 11). He divided these perceptive activities into two categories that he labeled as "sensing" and "intuition." Sensing refered to perceptions observable by way of the senses, sensing establishes what exists.

JUNG'S PERCEIVING FUNCTIONS

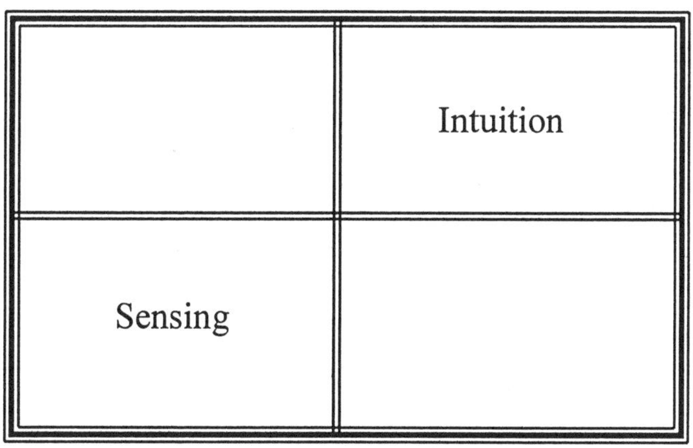

(Figure 11)

Because the senses can bring to awareness only what is occurring in the present moment, persons oriented toward sensing [perception] tend to focus on the immediate experience and often develop characteristics associated with this awareness such as enjoying the present moment, realism, acute powers of observation, memory for detail and practicality" (Myers & McCaulley, 1985, p. 12).

Intuition, according to Jung, refered to the perception of possibilities, meanings and relationships by way of insight. He characterized intuition as "perception by way of the unconscious" (Myers and McCaulley, 1985, p. 12). Intuition permits perception beyond what is visible to the senses, including future events. Thus, persons oriented toward intuitive perception may be so intent on pursuing possibilities that they may overlook actualities. They may develop characteristics that could be defined as imaginative, theoretical, abstract, future-oriented, or creative.

Jung proposed that in addition to perceiving (S and N functions), a person used a "judging function" (See Figure 12).

JUNG'S JUDGING FUNCTIONS

Thinking	
	Feeling

(Figure 12)

He used the term "feeling" (F) and "thinking" (T) to refer to relational functions that are directed "toward bringing life events into harmony with the laws of reason" (Myers & Mc Caulley, 1985, p. 12). Judging functions in Jung's model were diametrically opposed to perceiving functions. Jung maintained that feeling was the function by which one comes to decisions by weighing relative values and merits of the issues. "Feeling relies on an understanding of personal values and group values; thus, it is more subjective than thinking" (Myers & McCaulley, 1985, p. 12). In other words, people who use feeling to make decisions have a concern for human values as opposed to the technical aspects of problems. They have a need for affiliation, a capacity for warmth, a desire for harmony and a time orientation that includes preservation of the values of the past.

Thinking on the other hand, is a way of using judgment by making logical connections. Thinking, from Jung's perspective, relied on principles of cause and effect and therefore tended to be impersonal. Persons who are primarily oriented toward thinking may develop characteristics associated with "analytical ability, objectivity, concern with principles of justice and fairness, criticality and an orientation to time that is concerned with connections from the past through the present toward the future" (Myers & McCaulley, 1985, p. 12).

In the perceiving mode, sensing (S) functions deal with present time, while intuition (N) functions are future oriented. This infers that decisions made by sensing (S) functions are pragmatic while decisions made by intuition (N) are concerned with possibilities (See Figure 13).

JUNG'S EXPANDED MODEL

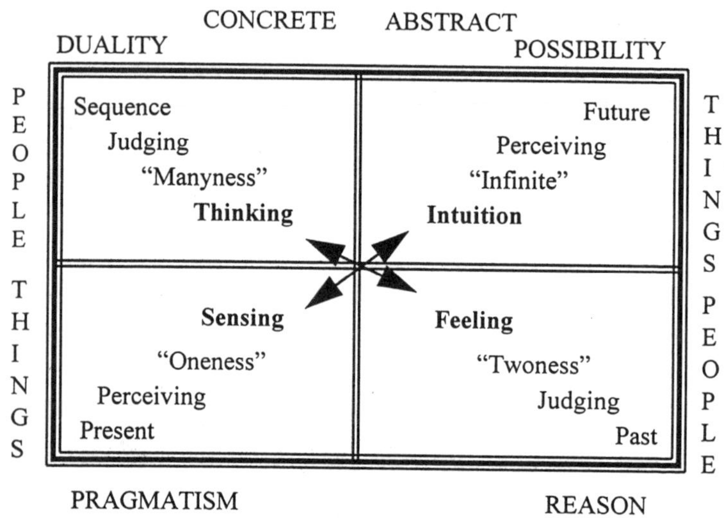

(Figure 13)

In the judging mode, feeling (F) functions deal with the past while thinking (T) deals with sequence or the relation of past, present and future events. Judgments made using feeling (F) functions deal with dualistic choices of like or dislike, good or bad. Information is regarded as positive or negative, good or harmful for survival. Persons who use feeling (F) as a judging mode prefer to see their world in black and white -- coincidently typical of American culture. One is Democratic or Republican, Catholic or Protestant, rich or poor. One wins or looses in the cooperative enterprise.

The thinking (T) function operates very differently. As noted in the expanded model, it is a rational, reasoned process in the exercise of judgment. Unlike sensing

(S) which is concerned with "oneness," feeling (F) is concerned with "twoness," intuition (N) with "infinite" possibilities and thinking (T) is concerned with the "many." In thinking, the choices are not limitless as with intuition, but are not bounded by singleness as with sensing. In summary, the four functions direct conscious mental activity toward different goals.

> *Thinking* seeks rational order and plans according to impersonal logic,
>
> *Sensation* seeks the fullest possible experience of what is immediate and real,
>
> *Intuition* seeks the broadest view of what is possible and insightful,
>
> *Feeling* seeks rational order according to harmony among subjective values.

The key to the dynamics of the theory lies in the assumption that the four functions pull in different directions. To compare personality to a ship at sea, we take it for granted a ship needs a captain with undisputed authority to set the course and bring the ship to the desired port. The ship would never reach its destination if each helmsman in turn, aimed in a different direction. In type theory, one of the four functions is the preferred or dominant function. It determines what is the desired direction and keeps the ship on course.

Now I am sure that you have a sense that all this feels vaguely familiar. Of course, one only has to look briefly at the information on the four cognitive processing modes to determine a great deal of overlap. And you thought all along that "personality" was something else, that it was not related to thinking. Perhaps you are more familiar with the true genius of Jung as he described the orientation to the inner world. As you may know he used the words "extraversion" (E) and "introversion" (I) [I prefer to use Jung's original spellings]. To many lay people the term extravert means *sociable* and introvert means *shy.* The Jungian descriptions are, however, broader. In the extraverted attitude, energy is directed outward toward objects and people in the environment. There is a desire to act on the environment, to affirm its importance and to increase its effect. Characteristics associated with an extraverted attitude may include an awareness and reliance on the environment for stimulation and guidance, an action-orientation (which may sometimes include an impulsive way of meeting life), frankness, an ease of communication and sociability. The extravert directs energy outward and simultaneously is energized by the environment (See Figure 14).

In the introverted (I) attitude, energy is drawn from the environment, and is consolidated in one's position. The main interests lie in the inner world of concepts and ideas. Persons with an introverted attitude may develop characteristics of liking concepts and ideas, having a reliance on enduring concepts more than transitory external events, having a thoughtful, contemplative detachment, and enjoying solitude and privacy. As an orientation to life, the real criterion is the determination of whether the focus and interests are on things and people external to the self (extravert) or internal to the self (introvert). One deals with acquiring and scavaging and the other deals with conserving and self-discipline.

INTROVERTS / EXTRAVERTS

Extraverts	Introverts
Introverts	Extraverts

(Figure 14)

Type theory assumes children are born with a "predisposition" to prefer some functions over others. In Jung's model, the environment becomes extremely important because environmental factors can foster development of each person's natural preferences, or the environment can discourage development by reinforcing activities that are less satisfying and less motivating, making skill development more difficult. Assuming for the moment, that the environment is reinforcing, children are motivated to exercise their dominant function, becoming more skillful, adept and differentiated in its use, not unlike using a process as described in cognitive development. With the reinforcement of constant practice, the preferred function becomes more controlled and trustworthy. A sense of competence thus comes from exercising a function well.

While this development of a preferred function is occurring, there is a "relative" neglect of the opposite pole of the same preference. For example, a person who develops sensing in a highly differentiated way is likely to become an astute observer of the immediate environment. As development occurs, the person may develop some of the characteristics assumed to follow from this acute awareness: realism, practicality and common sense. Further, while attention is being given to the specifics of the environment, that person will spend less time and energy using intuition (the bi-polar opposite). In other words, sensing persons spend less time focusing on the future. Since they focus on practical applications, they may have less interest in theoretical issues, and a focus on reality gives them less time for focusing on the imagination. While this example has looked at sensing, the opposite would be true for the intuitive person. Likewise thinking and feeling polar opposites have less time available to develop the bi-polar opposite characteristics.

The work of Carl Jung stands out as critically important, because his frame of reference was broad enough to encompass both the conflict and the fulfillent models of human development. His work had a clinical and a theoretical base; bcause it was also developmental. Jung's model was predictive enough to be used as the theoretical basis for the Myers Briggs typology, as a guide for career counseling; reductive enough to serve as a guide for psychotherapy and dream analysis.

Application of Jungian Typology

In the completion of my doctoral degree which examined Ned Herrmann's model in depth, I also studied Jungian Typology, seeing an immediate overlap. In a workshop with Pat Battle & Associates of Columbia, Maryland, I had an opportunity to have first hand experience with typology. Using the *Myers Briggs Type Indicator,* each participant having completed the instrument, then assigned him or herself to a particular category which described one of their strong preferences. We were asked to come up with a list of things that we liked about being an introvert or an extravert (See Figure 15). I placed myself in the introvert group

WHAT I LIKE ABOUT BEING AN	
INTROVERT	EXTRAVERT
I like being alone I prefer to talk with people one at a time I like to sit and reflect I like in-depth conversations I like to ponder things in my head	I like being open I meet people easily and have been described as outspoken I am full of energy I am confortable in a group I have few worries I like having fun I like to move things along I am generally self confident

(Figure 15)

because my world is dominated by concepts and ideas.

Quite frankly, although I was only a contributor to the list, I like being alone. Being alone is not a sense of loneliness for me. I prefer to talk with people one at a time, to delve, as it were, into their world of ideas. Obviously, this means I much prefer the in-depth conversations and have little patience for people who just want to "chit-chat." I like to ponder things in my head and sit for long periods of time in reflection, in contemplation. Interestingly enough, we are not as bi-polar as it would seem. There were characteristics about the extraverted type which were also true for me. I have few worries, I like to move things along, I am full of energy and I am self-confident. I mention these things, not so much that you have a chance to figure out who I really am (introverts don't like that very much), but so that you can see that rarely do people fit just into one category or another.

In the workshop I was describing, we were then asked to identify some things we did not like about our own preferred type (See Figure 16). The interesting thing about this exercise was having a directed experience with opposite types. I was surprised, for example to see that extraverts generated an even longer list than introverts. I made a faulty assumption that as a group, extraverts spent little time in reflection. I had discounted that in their "openness" they rarely "hide" things. Due to their verbal nature, the group could have likely generated even more characteristics had the introverts not stopped them (because we felt inadequate or were tired of their expounding?) What did come to me as a surprise was their awareness that they did not like to get overcommitted. It seems they have an all-inclusive

WHAT I DON'T LIKE ABOUT BEING AN	
INTROVERT	EXTRAVERT
I'm sometimes afraid to go to new places I'm sometimes jealous of people who make friends easily I sometimes have difficulty getting motivated	I don't like being alone I don't like being accused of not listening I don't like being called insensitive I don't like that I get overcommitted I don't like that I sometimes jump to conclusions

(Figure 16)

need to be included and seem to volunteer for lots of activities, As take charge people, they also assume leadership of many activities in which they engage. What was particularly interesting was to discover that extraverts as a group, really don't like being alone. They don't know how to use their time for extended periods even though they have a great many interests.

It seemed from the outset then, that each of us, if we chose, could assist the other who held an opposing view of life. In the exchange that happened in the group, I also understood that none of the characteristics on this list identified by the extraverts fit me! At first, I was again reminded of my constant sense of differentness I felt growing up. Then I realized, it was not that time period which needed my self-reflection. It was my "illness." Again, always backward in time I reflected. Perhaps because I was able to find strength and courage within, I, in a manner of speaking, transcended the feelings of being afraid to go to new places or get motivated to do something. More importantly, at that moment in time, I was again reminded, that although I would regard myself as warm and friendly, capable of great sympathy as well as passion, I am not sure that I have *ever* felt jealous. In fact, I have a hard time even understanding the concept. It implies some kind of yearning for something that someone else has; my yearning has always been to find the deeper part of me and "jealousy" simply doesn't fit in my world view. Yet I could not discount that jealousy is a fundamental experience for many people.

It was then I began to wonder about the possibility, as I went through my illness, as I "healed" my physical body, perhaps I transcended many of the emotional ways of processing information, perhaps I moved, as it were, to a different understanding. Could it be that awareness of who we really are moves us into a state of love -- a state that is so powerful as to change our world views? These questions would remain unanswered for a good long while, long after completion of the workshop and even my doctoral dissertation. It seems, in retrospect, that my life is like a constant garden. The questions are like seeds that are planted in my awareness, but they do not sprout until all the conditions are right, until the ground has shifted to make a more firm foundation. Then when the ideas blossom, it is hard to rembember when the seeds were first planted -- so long do they lie dormant.

Back to the workshop on personality types. It

must have been like a time of spring planting, because many many seeds were planted. I remember that the workshop got more interesting when Pat asked us to to identify what it was that we did not like about the opposite type (See Figure 17). In this case, it seemed as if ammunition was again given to the extraverts. But

WHAT I DON'T LIKE ABOUT	
INTROVERTS	EXTRAVERTS
They are losers They are not team players I can't "read" them They take too long to start things They are hard to talk with	They are noisy They engage in too much chit chat They take up too much of my time They talk foreever on the phone They are sometimes irresponsible They make too many assumptions They don't have much depth

(Figure 17)

it pointed out another difference, at least to members of that group, that perhaps, there was something else going on. Later in the afternoon, we would explore which of us in the introverted group had strong "judgment functions."

For me, lost in a world of ideas and concepts, deep in a state of contemplation, I began to have a sense of how profoundly we needed each other. I hadn't thought I was "hard to talk with." If that were true, then perhaps for me to have an extended relation–

ship with an extrovert, I needed not only to be patient as they wove, as it were, their way toward me, in the exchange of dialog but I needed to invite them into my space -- grabbing their attention in multiple ways. I would need to reach, search and find one of their many interests to sustain an "us–ness." Contained in their "manyness" was a "twoness!"

Yet perhaps the most enlightening part of the morning session was when we then generated a list of what we really needed from the opposite type. (See Figure 18). It was in that moment that I came to a far different understanding not only of opposite types, but of the need for them. Neither can exist successfully without the opposing life approach. The introvert needs the extravert to engender enthusiasm, the extravert needs the introvert to listen to them.

WHAT IS NEEDED FROM	
INTROVERTS WHO NEED EXTROVERTS	EXTRAVERTS WHO NEED INTROVERTS
They engender enthusiasm	They really listen to me
They are generous	They have a calming effect
They come up with new ideas	They don't need as many "strokes"
They are willing to take risks	I value their ability to think clearly

(Figure 18)

The introvert needs the generosity of the extravert and the extravert needs the calming influence of the introvert. So the real value in looking at typology, at least for me, at the time, was to begin to discover that as we define ourselves, we become who we best are *in relationship.* Whatever the nature of relationship, whether that be with a stranger, a friend, a business associate or a lover, we have the unlimited opportunity to discover something about ourselves. In that discovery, we can re-identify ourselves. So another seed was planted. I reasoned that I had a whole brain -- and that if much of what is called typology comes from the perceptions I make of the world through my interpretation of life events, what if the duality that I perceived to be out there was really "in here!" Was that what Jung was trying to tell us all along? Was the introverted side of me the "persona," the extraverted side "my shadow?" Were the "yin" and "yang" elements (which composed a whole), just the deeper reflection of my soul? Into the coffer these musings would go -- to brew, simmer, take root and grow until the time had come for the harvest.

As I began to work more and more with the interrelationships between Herrmann's model and Jung's model, I saw more and more similarities. I began to see the wisdom in each of the different approaches. (See Figure 19 for the full table of Jungian Typologies).

It was as if I had come in contact with a living, breathing Yin and Yang. No longer could I accept just that introverts needed extraverts, there was more depth than that. I was to discover that opposites were not rigid labels assigned to one of my illustrations, but that the characteristics were like a careful tapestry woven

JUNGIAN PERSONALITY TYPES					
		Sensing Types		Intuitive Types	
		With Thinking	With Feeling	With Feeling	With Thinking
INTROVERTS	Judging Types	**ISTJ** I Depth of concentration S Reliance on facts T Logic and analysis J Organization	**ISFJ** I Depth of concentration S Reliance of facts F Warmth and sympathy J Organization	**INFJ** I Depth of concentration N Grasp of possibilities F Warmth and sympathy J Organization	**INTJ** I Depth of concentration N Grasp of possibilities T Logic and analysis J Organization
INTROVERTS	Perceiving Types	**ISTP** I Depth of concentration S Reliance on facts T Logic and analysis P Adaptability	**ISFP** I Depth of concentration S Reliance on facts F Warmth and sympathy P Adaptability	**INFP** I Depth of concentration N Grasp of possibilities F Warmth and sympathy P Adaptability	**INTP** I Depth of concentration N Grasp of possibilities T Logic and analysis P Adaptability
EXTRAVERTS	Perceiving Types	**ESTP** E Breadth of interests S Reliance on facts T Logic and analysis P Adaptability	**ESFP** E Breadth of interests S Reliance on facts F Warmth and Sympathy P Adaptability	**ENFP** E Breadth of interests N Grasp of possibilities F Warmth and sympathy P Adaptability	**ENTP** E Breadth of interests N Grasp of possibilities T Logic and analysis P Adaptability
EXTRAVERTS	Judging Types	**ESTJ** E Breadth of interests S Reliance on facts T Logic and analysis J Organizatopm	**ESFJ** E Breadth of interests S Reliance on facts F Warmth and sympathy J Organization	**ENFJ** E Breadth of interests N Grasp of possibilities F Warmth and sympathy J Organization	**ENTJ** E Breadth of interests N Grasp of possibilities T Logic and analysis J Organization

(Figure 19)

together with the skills of a master weaver, as if so carefully orchestrated as to elude us. I discovered that full expression of any particular characteristic existed to the extent that it was allowed to be demonstrated. AAAAAH HAAAA! But allowed by whom? Was I beginning to find the mysteries of being human? The illusions?

Could it be that in our collective consciousness as a humanity, that those "shadow" parts of ourselves remain hidden because we have not called them forth ourselves? Could it be that we hold onto an illusion, that we cannot be all that we can be because we believe it is someone else's fault? That the stifling and repression we feel is due to a lack of our own mindfulness? Our own unwillingness to unravel the mysteries of who we are?

I started first to look at the most bi-polar expressions of personality concentrating on the polarities of the introvert and the extrovert. I applied them to my own life and some of my relationships. But it wasn't until I carefully examined the wholeness of each type that I began to have some insight. First I extended my examination to the opposite types of an INFP and ESTJ. How could such polar opposites comfortably exist? Ironically, these were the type characteristics of myself and of my former husband! I discovered, interestingly, that the "perception" (P) aspect in the INFP is characterized by "adapability". While the "extraverted" (E) aspect of an ESTJ is characterized by a breadth of interests. This then, became the meeting point for my relationship with my former husband.

The thing that kept our ten year marriage together was my ability to adapt to his breadth of interests. His preference for using judgment to make sense of the world using logic and analysis (T) in our discussion was compatible with my introverted perception of the world which allowed me a depth of concentration (I). However, our "way of being" in the world was decidedly different. I make sense of the world by perceiving, by becoming aware of things, people, events and ideas. As an introvert, I prefered the world of ideas and concepts. He preferred a world of people and things, and more importantly made sense of the world by judging, by bringing life's events into harmony with the laws of reason. Herein lay the fundamental differences.

As we unsuccessfully "coped" with my illness, he sought reason, logical reasons. I tended to seek inspiration, to play with ideas; to live my outer life with feeling, my inner life with intuition. In that moment, long after our divorce, when I was able to recognize that perhaps he had been a guide for me, a teacher, was the moment I recognized his orientation was to stay in present time while mine was to rage off into the future. And it was this piece of wisdom that led me to working with my body, moment by moment as described in an earlier chapter. In other words, on some level I picked up the wisdom he offered. My willingness, although not consciously acknowledged to move from a future to a present world view, caused a perceptual shift. I caused a shift in my own consciousness.

So I invite you, if it seems appropriate, to spend considerable time pondering the type table, to find your own characteristics and those of your friends and loved ones. I think it more helpful, not to focus on type per se, but to look at the wholeness that can come when we are willing to appreciate the mutual usefulness of the opposite type (See Figure 20 at the end of the chapter).

So I again offer that we need not only to seek the words, but the wisdom of those who have gone before us. Perhaps because Jung chose to honor the the original definition of psychology, he remains for me a champion. Perhaps because he retrieved concepts of the soul. But then, perhaps Jung has lived on past his dying, because . . . because he was inimitably Jung.

> The modern man . . . is not eager to know in what ways he can imitate Christ, but in what way he can live his own individual life, however meager and uninteresting it may be . . . Tired of this warfare of opinions, the modern man wishes to find out for himself how things are. And though this desire opens bar and bolt to the most dangerous possibilities, we cannot help seeing it as a courageous enterprise and giving it some measure of sympathy. It is no reckless adventure, but an effort inspired by deep spiritual distress to bring meaning once more into life on the basis of fresh and unprejudiced experience. Caution has its place, no doubt, but we cannot refuse our support to a serious venture which calls the whole of the personality into the field of action. If we oppose it, we are trying to suppress what is best in man--his daring and his aspiration. And should we succeed, we should only have stood in the way of that invaluable experience which might have given a meaning to life. What would have happened if Paul had allowed himself to be talked out of his journey to Damascus? (Jung, 1933).

MUTUAL USEFULNESS OF THE OPPOSITE TYPE

Thinking Types	Intuitive Types
To teach To persuade To conciliate To arouse enthusiasm To connect with others To forcast how others feel To appreciate the thinker himself	To analyze To organize To weigh the evidence To find the flaws in advance To hold consistently to a policy To reform what needs reforming To stand firm against opposition
Thinking Types need Feeling Types	Intuitive Types need Sensing Types
Sensing Types need Intuitive Types	Feeling Types need Thinking Types
To explain what other intuitive means To deal with having too many choices To supply ingenuity to problems To gain a sense of vision To seek the "impossible" To see the possibilities	To remember things that seemed irrelevant To notice what ought to be attended to To bring up pertinent facts To read over a contract To keep track of detail To have patience
Sensing Types	Feeling Types

(Figure 20)

Chapter 5 Beyond the Brain into Consciousness

In the preceeding two chapters, I presented information about the brain and personality so we might begin to appreciate the really wonderful gifts that we have -- that we might begin to look at ourselves through a different lens. My intent was that we begin to appreciate the wholeness of who we are. As long as we look for the differences, they will be there, because we usually find what we are looking for. So I delve again into understanding the body with the intent that I want to be responsible for my experiences, to be as fully present as possible, to be mindful, not just some rag doll who gets tossed to and fro because of my inability to take a closer look at myself, or because I perceive someone else has more control over me.

Because my experiences initially started with one of the senses of the body, I think that a closer look at them serves as an appropriate starting place. I think we need to really appreciate the senses that have been *gifted* to us -- the senses of sight, hearing, tasting, smelling and touching. In attempting to understand the senses, I discovered that they are all directed outward. They are not reflectors of what is going on inside us (at least until we call that awareness forth). We can remember what our senses do, but we can't get them right this minute to actually do what they are designed to do. Try it . . . go ahead. Smell the bucket of fish after it has sat in the sunshine for several hours. Smell it now. No? O.K. Then get cold. Get really cold, so cold that your fingers ache and get numb. Are you doing it yet? Probably not. The best you can do is tap into the *memory* of what the fish smelled like, or the time you were really cold.

Now that I have made the suggestion that our senses may not be all that we thought they were, let's go one step further. Why do you think you are cold? You think you are cold because a long time ago, some-ne, likely one of your parents or a teacher, suggested that you must wear a coat because if you don't you will "feel cold." So you got the idea that cold was related to temperature and warmth was related to wearing cloth-ng. Repeatedly, from infancy onward, this scenario was acted out over and over and over, until your brain developed a particular pattern. You developed not only a belief that when it *is* cold, you will *be* cold, but your body developed a physiological response. Sound famil-ar? This is not unlike the child who emulates his father, and in so doing, takes on his body postures. This is not unlike development of the personality, in that we seek those things which feel good to us, for which we get reinforcement or experience a sense of well-being.

We could go on through each of the senses in this way, but I hardly think it necessary. The point is, we learned *meaning* about each of our senses through our life experiences and those interpretations we made in earlier moments of time. As adults, no one questions us about what it "means" to be "cold," or smell something "awful," or touch something "soft." So our senses are a product of our social conditioning. They can't be torn from the fabric of our experience anymore than feelings can be separated from our thinking patterns.

Can it be that this is the "collective conscious–ess" that Jung refers to? Just as learning to drive a car starts in incremental steps until we have habituated them into a larger motor plan? Could it be that the meaning we assign to each moment of experience, be–gins to exist in a larger whole so that we don't have to again interpret each of life's events, one by one as they happen? Can it be that as we habituate interpretation of our senses, our feelings and our thoughts that they not only go into a larger whole for each individual, but they begin to collect in a larger whole outside of self, as a whole for each species? Is this sort of like the "hun–dredth monkey" phenomenon, wherein a monkey on a distant island suddenly uses tools in a new way because all of the monkeys in the neighboring island, one by one began using tools in a particular way so as to form a group "idea" or interpretation of tool use? And that eventually, through a means I will try to describe later, this new learning gets into the "stuff" of the imagination of all members of the species?

Bear with me as I deviate to deal with the ques–tions that come fast and furious. *Can it be that in each moment of time as we misinterpret the deeper meaning of our life experiences, over eons and eons of time, we instead created a world of illusion?* A world of illusion in which we feel we are separated from each other, choosing instead to compete with each other and finding fault? A world of illusion in which our experiences have been torn apart, separating mind from body, thought from feeling, sense from experience? Have we instead made of our own inattentiveness a world of limitation, need, want and isolation? Has it really been of *human* making that we have created a world put asunder to suffer all that is external as appearing to *be* the human experience as the existentialists have proported? Can it be that the ancient separation of soul from body leads us now into the illusions that care of the body is assigned to a physician, care of the mind is assigned to a psychiatrist and care of the soul is assigned to the church? If all this is true, then the world as we know it, the reality which we experience day by day, is not of our personal making! Much of what we experience is inherited, physically, socially, culturally! This presuposes that we can get out of the morass. We can, each of us individually begin to affect our own beliefs, which in turn can affect the mass consciousness. Such is the hope I have for humanity -- that the miracles will come out of our ordinariness.

If it is true that our senses give us the opportunity to experience our external world, and that the meaning and the emotion that we assign to them comes only from our life's experiences, then we begin right now, where we are. Since we can't relive our lives, or redo the history of the human species, then we have to use the only means available to us. We again circle backward to take advantage of imagery. Imagery is not bound by vision, but by all the senses. We need an experience that uses imagery and the metaphoric thinking of the right hemisphere coupled with the language labeling of the left hemisphere to jolt us, as it were, into a different awareness of who we really are. Let's imagine for a moment what Jean Houston calls a multitracking exercise. Consider, for example, these phrases:

"touching the sound of winter,"

"smelling the tingle of the wind through the pines,"
"listening to the softness of puppy breath."

In this last example, "listening" is usually associated with hearing, "softness" with touch, and "puppy breath" with "smell" plus I suppose all those warm fuzzy emotional thoughts you have when you conjur up an image of puppy.

Stay with this for a moment. Can you sense that as you read through these simple phrases that you had some sort of feeling of expansiveness? "Touching the sound of winter," calls forth in me a feeling of peace, a vision of whiteness, a comfort in being touched; a "soul" awareness of the wonder of the stillness. Can it be that when these single images are combined--that out of this process there emerges a whole, greater than the sum of the parts? Is this what we mean by "consciousness," a state of awareness that *transcends* the moment, that calls forth a deeper response? One that requires us in the moment to make a quantum leap -- to evolve, as it were?

The evolution that we learned about in school and that you experienced previously in an earlier chapter, was the evolution of the physical form. You learned in school, for example, that the single-celled creatures of the oceans were the predecessors of more complex forms of life. A fish is more complex and therefore, more evolved than a sponge; a horse more complex, and therefore, more evolved than a snake; a monkey more complex, and therefore, more evolved than a horse, and so on up the evolutionary ladder to the human being. In terms of evolution of the form, the human has been regarded as the most evolved of all species. We have learned, in other words, that evolution means the progressive development of organizational complexity.

This definition of evolution is an expression of the idea that the organism that is best able to control both its environment and all of the other organisms in its environment is the most evolved. "Survival of the fittest" means that the most evolved organism in a given environment is that organism that is at the top of the food chain. According to this definition, the organism that is the most able to ensure its own survival, most able to serve its self-preservation needs is the most evolved. But what of the evolution of emotion, the evolution of thought? Are we, as a human species, not far more advanced than those forms of us who appeared thousands of years ago, carrying clubs and seeking rudimentary forms of shelter?

I contend that this definition of evolution is inadequate. It is rooted in Darwinism. A kind of thinking that seeks not to understand *relationships* between species, or relationships among species, but pits one against the other in some kind of arbitrarily designed heirarchy. This is not to suggest Darwin's thinking at the time is less noble than it was. He too, was a product of *his* environment. His thinking came at a time when the invisible was being torn apart from the visible, the Creator from his creation, knower from the known. Mind and consciousness were encased in a body, incapable of understanding itself.

My understanding of evolution will come out bit by bit as we go further. But for the most part, I cannot separate evolution from consciousness any more than I can separate mind from body. When two humans en-age one another, they are, in terms of organizational complexity, equally evolved. If both have the same intelligence, yet one is small minded, mean and selfish, while the other is magnanimous and altruistic, I say that the one who is altruistic is the more evolved. If one human intentionally sacrifices his or her life to save another, I say that the human who sacrificed his or her life was one of the most evolved among us.

Remember the buckling of a bridge in San Fran-isco where many worked for hours to save those who were trapped as result of the earthquake? Time and time again rescuers took great risks with their own lives to free those still trapped in the rubble. Even earlier there was the incident of a plane that left Washington D.C. and on take-off and ended up in the Potomac River. There was one man who stayed in the water, time and time again rescuing another, until at last he gave his own life. Going back even further, we are told that Jesus foresaw the plot against his life, even to the details of how his friends would act and react, yet he did not run from what he saw.

Much of humankind has been shaped by the power and love of those who gave their lives for others. Our humanity is shaped by those who remembered the connections, in spite of themselves. Yet ask any hero, any fireman who pulls small children from the lapping jaws of fire, or any rescuer who pilots the helicopter over a mass of trees looking for the fallen skiier, if he or she thinks of themselves as a "hero." No, likely, in the moments of crisis, the wisdom comes forth. People perceive themselves as ordinary stating, "Oh, it's what anyone else would have done." There is then, deep in our psyche, our soul, deep in the history of humanity, a deeper awareness which lies dormant, waiting to be called forth. Unfortunately, we only evoke that deeper wisdom in times of crisis, not during our ordinary waking moments.

Even so, our deeper understanding tells us that a truly evolved being is one who values others more than him/herself and that he or she who values love more than the physical world and what is in it, is the most evolved. With this in mind, we must now bring our understanding of evolution into alignment with this deeper insight. It is important that we do this because our current understanding of evolution reflects a phase that we are now leaving. By examining this understanding, we can perceive how we have evolved to now, and what we are in the process of leaving behind. By reflecting upon a new and expanded understanding of evolution, one that validates our deepest truths, our thoughts, our emotions and our senses; we can see what we are evolving into. We can "seed" or plant a way of being in the world that is different in terms of what we experience, what we value and how we act.

Our current understanding of evolution results from the fact that we have evolved until now, by exploring physical reality with our five senses. We have been, until now, five-sensory human beings. The path of evolution has allowed us to see the basic principles of the Universe in concrete ways. We have seen through the five senses that every action has a cause and every cause has an effect. We see, for example, that a stick is a tool, and we see the effects of how we choose to use it. As we examine the deeper meaning through mindfulness, we notice that the club that kills can drive a stake into the ground to hold shelter. The spear that takes life can be used as a lever to ease life's burdens. The knife that cuts flesh can be used to cut cloth. The hands that build bombs can be used to build schools. The brains that coordinate the activities of violence can coordinate the activities of cooperation.

We are beginning to see, or we are remembering, that when the activities of life are infused with reverence, they come alive with meaning and purpose. We see that when reverence is lacking from life's activities, the result is cruelty, violence and loneliness. The physical arena is a magnificent learning environment. It is a school within which, through experimentation, we come to understand what causes us to expand and what causes us to contract, what causes us to grow and what causes us to shrivel. We are discovering what nourshes our soul and what depletes it, what works and what does not.

When the physical environment is seen only from the five-sensory point of view, physical survival appears to be the fundamental criterion of evolution because no other kind of evolution is detect- able. It is from this point of view that "survival of the fittest" appears to be synonymous with evolution.

When perception of the physical world is limited to the externalization of our five sensory modality, the basis of life in the physical arena becomes fear. The need for physical dominance produces a type of competition that affects every aspect of our lives. It affects relationships between lovers and between superpowers, between siblings and between races, between classes and between sexes. It disrupts the natural tendency toward harmony between nations and between friends. The narrow-mindedness of separation and competition that sent warships to the Persian Gulf, sent soldiers to Vietman and crusaders to Palestine. The disconnected feelings resulting in judgment that separated the family of Romeo from the family of Juliet is the same judgment and prejudice that separates the family of the black husband from the family of the white wife. The negative life experiences that set Lee Harvey Oswald against John Kennedy is the same that set Cain against Abel. Brother and sisters quarrel for the same reason that corporations quarrel -- they seek power over one another.

The power to control the environment and those within it, is power over what can be felt, smelled, tasted, heard or seen. This type of power is external power. The problem is that external power can be acquired or lost, as in the stock market or an election. It can be bought or stolen, transferred or inherited. It is thought of something that can be gotten from someone else, or somewhere else. One person's gain of external power is perceived as another person's loss. The result of seeing power as external is violence and destruction. All of our institutions -- social, economic and political -- reflect our understanding of power as external.

To lighten up a bit, we have, nearly since the beginning of time, been using the wrong mathematical formulas. We have assumed that in order to have power, we had to take it from somewhere else. We believed that as we "added" power (to ourselves, our community, our society or our govermnent), we became mindless that we had, in fact, "subtracted" it from elsewhere else. In this scenerio, we have neglected the wisdom of the ordinary folks. Ask any mother of eight children how she manages to love all of them. The wise mother will tell us that she "multiplies" her abilities to be loving, she does not "divide" them!

Our deeper understanding then leads us to another kind of power, a power that loves life in every form that it appears, a power that does not judge what it encounters, a power that perceives meaningfulness and purpose in the smallest details upon the Earth. This is authentic power. When we align our thoughts, our emotions and actions with the highest part of ourselves, we are filled with enthusiasm, purpose and meaning. Life becomes alive with the sights, sounds, smells and touches of all things that surround us. When life is full, we have no thoughts of bitterness. When we transcend our survival needs to recognize that we all share in the resources of this planet, then we will have no memory of fear. We can become joyously and intimately engaged in our world.

Authentic power has its roots in the deepest source of our being. Authentic power cannot be bought, inherited or hoarded. An authentically empowered person is incapable of making anyone or anything a victim. An authentically empowered person is one who is so strong, so empowered, that the idea of using force against another is not part of his or her consciousness.

As we evolve from five–sensory humans into multi–sensory humans, our five senses, taken together, form a single sensory system that is designed not only to perceive the physical reality, but other realities as well. The perceptions of a multi–sensory human extend beyond the physical reality to the larger dynamic of systems. The multi–sensory human is able to perceive, and to appreciate, the role that our physical reality plays in a larger picture of evolution and the dynamics by which our physical reality is created and sustained.

Multi-Sensory Experience

Find a place where you can sit quietly . . . begin first to notice your breathing . . . breathing naturally as you get centered in your own experience of who you are . . . then begin breathing first with the air coming into the right nostril . . . and then the left . . . track the air as it fills your lungs . . . and reaches your brain . . . and flows down to your fingertips . . . then breathe in through the top of your head . . . track that air and see where it flows . . . then breathe through the soles of your feet . . . and follow the air up through your body.

Allow yourself to follow the breath as it leaves the body . . . and fills the space around you . . . feel the breath caressing the space between your toes . . . and get a sense of the color of your breath around your arms and around your legs . . . breathe more deeply and as you exhale . . . follow your breath as it touches the tree in your backyard . . . and allow that breath . . . like droplets of water to nestle on a tiny leaf . . . look at the world through the green eyes of the leaf . . . and smell in the gentleness of the butterfly as it drinks in the single droplet of water.

Breathe in again and as you breathe out in short breaths . . . follow the rhythm . . . into the beat of a distant drum . . . coming faster and faster . . . the rhythm beginning to affect your left foot as it begins to tap out a slow rhythm . . . a rhythm that takes on form and swirls around and around . . . spiraling to a ski slope in the Alps and encircling the neck of a giraffe . . . let the spiraling stop as you feel the edges of a single spot on the neck of the giraffe.

Smell the busy flurry of a hive of bees . . . as you allow your feet to be immersed in a bowl of jello . . . squish the golden light between your toes . . . and hang upside down on the monkey bars . . . flap you arms like a chicken and imagine pedaling your legs on a giant bicycle . . . tumbling head over heels into a space surrounded by the soft sounds of green pines . . . lick the pinkness of peppermint ice cream . . . as you smell the softness of puppy breath . . . basking in the warmth of the sun . . . holding the moon in your right hand.

Imagine being in the space between the kernals of popping corn . . . as if in your expansion . . . you hold each kernal suspended in space . . . like the electrons floating in an atom . . . while you hear the humming of "row, row, your boat" coming from your left finger . . . while the big toe on your right foot tickles the ear of an elephant . . . spinning and spinning through time . . . sensing Santa Claus and his sleigh running over the tip of your nose . . . as you become a wave licking the soft shore. . . turning into first a cube then a ball . . . to be held in the palm of a tiny child.

Trace triangles on the left side of your brain . . . and play tic tac toe on the tummy of a black bear . . . seeing the taste of honey drip through the trees in a pine forest . . . that makes the crickets giggle . . . and the baking bread in your oven sigh . . . now draw circles around the arteries in the palm of your left hand . . . that fly through the air with the grace of a Canadian goose . . . to land softly on the whisker of a tiny kitten . . . growling at the silence of winter.

Connect from your heart . . . a golden thread to the sun . . . on which Christopher Columbus sails . . .

bumping into the back side of your head . . . sending out notes that surround a golden harp . . . that melts into a sunflower . . . from which you sniff the nectar of life . . . becoming a newborn fawn snuggled in the sleeve of your coat . . . watching a volcano erupt . . . with the thundering hoofs of a mountain ridge . . . overlooking an African plain . . . floating high above Jupiter . . . who remembers Abraham Lincoln . . . splashing in a fountain . . . shoeless in the middle of Washington D.C. . . . which has just turned the Washington Monument upside down . . . and from which you spin the Earth like a top.

Yawn now . . . letting the Easter bunny run down your tongue . . . in search of the holy grail . . . marching through endless time . . . listening to the purr of the ancient Sphinx . . . as it nestles in a mound of snow . . . falling on the beak of an eagle . . . as he rises to greet the sun . . . as the East moves toward the West . . . calling forth remembrance of one heart . . . one mind . . . scattered throughout space . . . like droplets of endless time . . . transformed into stars . . . that twinkle in the middle of your left eye.

Awaken now . . . to a new awareness . . . an awareness of a being capable of endless images . . . images connected together so as to allow a pouring forth of all that is creative within you . . . making a larger whole . . . than the sum of your imagined parts . . . . Awaken now with new intent . . . to recognize that it is you who is the thinker of the thought . . . the doubter of the doubt . . . the dreamer of the dream . . . you as maker of meaning are now armed to go forth . . . not with weapons . . . nor wealth . . . not with new knowledge . . . nor old remembrances . . . you as maker of meaning goes forth . . . in your own ordinary way . .

. to welcome the miracle of being a multi-sensory human . . . capable of dreaming the impossible dream . . . and inventing your own miracles.

The Omnipotent Mind

I trust from the process above that you not only have a sense of expansiveness regarding the abundance of information which comes to you through the senses, but you literally have a different sense of who you are. Have you for example, ever really held the moon in your left hand? Or felt the edges of a spot on a giraffe's neck? Or listened to the purr of the ancient Sphinx? Probably not. So you may have discovered that not only can we expand our awareness of who we really are through our senses, but that when our senses are intermixed with events in the objective world, we can make new meaning when we re-order the relationships between time and events. In that process, we find new connections. Yet it is more than that. In finding new connections, we alter the sense of who we are in the Universe.

Now I ask if you had any problem imagining Jupiter remembering Abraham Lincoln? No? Then from what place in you did this wisdom come? Can you not acknowledge that everything that exists on this earth is but the product of the imagination of someone else? Wasn't there a scientist somewhere who said that that ball of something out there in space is called Jupiter? Like the lemmings rushing to the sea just because they have done so for countless years, we all looked up (metaphorically) and said, "yes, yes, that *is* Jupiter." But wasn't it just as easy to make Jupiter into a personification of something else--a being who remembered? And didn't you just want to giggle at the thought of Abraham Lincoln being shoeless in a fountain in Washington D.C.? Yet isn't that exactly what he would have done if he could have caught a glimpse of his "shadow," the opposing force to his sternness and wisdom? I can certainly imagine that a man who chose to unite the country, would have, deep within his soul, a sense of playfulness.

It seems to me, that we have arbitrarily assigned states of being to objects in our physical universe. In separating ourselves from our experiences, we have in some arbitrary way decided that some things are "dead" and some are "alive." And from that, we have tended to draw only on the wisdom from those things that we thought were "alive." We have looked, for the most part, to other people for an explanation of our experiences. As an eternal cosmic gardener, I plant this seed in your awareness, that it might begin to take root, so that later we can explore in greater detail the possibility of consciousness existing in every aspect of our physical world, in the rocks and the trees, in the planets themselves.

Let's pause in reflection a moment to re-enter the world of the Greeks. So powerful are their teachings, they are found alive and well today, hidden in our deep remembrances, hidden in the very language we speak. Could it be for example, that just as Rhea hid the baby Zeus in swaddling clothes in fear of Cronus, that was the seed planted in consciousness which evoked the Mother of Moses to do the same thing? Can it be that in our celebration of Thanksgiving, we celebrate abundance from the fullness of the horn of plenty, yearning to partake of the nectar of the gods which nourished Zeus in his upbringing? Is the language we use to describe the burdens of the world that we carry on our backs any different from Atlas being banned to carry the weight of the world on his shoulders?

Can it be that the story of Mother Earth giving a little tree with golden apples as a wedding present to Zeus and Hera, be the seed which would, at a later time, be impetus for the story of creation and the garden of Eden? Are our children of today, who are convinced that their mothers have eyes in the backs of their heads tapping into the archetype of Argus, who had eyes all over his body? Are the words of the politicians merely the silver-tongued phrases which came from the mouths of the robots created by the god Hephraetus? Can it be that the birth of Christ, which came out of a union, not between woman and man, but between woman and God, merely be another instance of how beings come to this planet?

It is stated in the Greek myths that both Athena and Aphrodite did not have biological parents; Aphrodite arose from the sea and Athena burst in full adult form from the head of Zeus. Is it an accident or a prototype that Athena would be a goddess of war; Aphrodite, a goddess of all that was beautiful? Is this the persona and shadow Jung talked about in regard to the feminine principle? Could it be that the ancient Greeks had a deeper and more real relationship with their entire Universe, as evidenced by Mother Earth banishing Uranus to the end of the Universe, Apollo and Artemis hanging the image of Orion in the sky? Can it be that our ancestors were far wiser than we?

The endless questions come pouring forth. The intent is to move us deeper and deeper into consciousness. To slow down the movies of our lives. But let's do it in incremental steps getting practical for the moment. We have discovered that thoughts are triggered by our experiences, our beliefs and our attitudes (however ancient or buried they might be). Thoughts can also be triggered by our willingness to become conscious of our own thinking process. This is tricky business because the brain is always on. It does what it likes to do best, it thinks thoughts. If, for example, I say to you "do not think about the red pen." *Do not think about the red pen.* You may find yourself saying O.K., I won't "think about the red pen." Yet in that instant, I trust, you recognize that you are thinking about the red pen in the *very act of telling yourself you will not think about it!* This is pretty much the way we lead our lives. In choosing not to think about something, we haven't the foggiest notion how not to think about it! It hasn't occurred to us to think about something else. The principle is pretty simple. You cannot sit and stand at the same instant in time.

Deepak Chopra, author of *Quantum Healing,* 1990, wrote that we think about 60,000 thoughts a day. This means that we have an enormous potential for focusing our thoughts on anything we want (calling Uranus back from the far ends of the Universe, or creating an eternal spring of the year out of our yearning for connection). Yet for most of us, the thoughts that we think are about 95% the same thoughts we had yesterday and the day before. *In fact, we keep recreating our problems in every instant in time that we give our attention to them.* Look at the model in Figure 21. Let's say that I am going through the difficult time of divorce. I have a fight with my husband. As soon as I get to work, I tell a co–worker (focusing my awareness on the events from the night before) about the incident. At lunch, I meet a friend and tell the same story, again using focused awareness about a slightly different incident, fused with the memory of how I told the story earlier in the morning. In the middle of the afternoon, I have a call from my mother and again I relate the events of the last twenty–four hours, now adding more and emotion to my story.

THE MIND BODY MATRIX

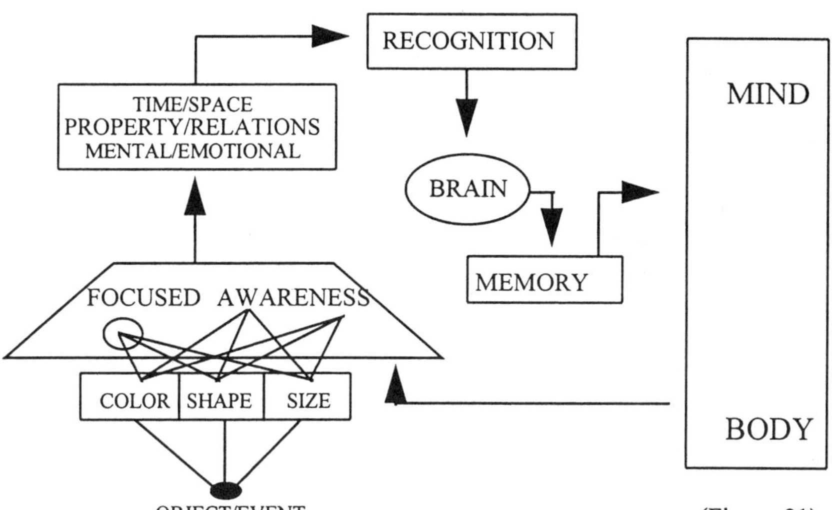

(Figure 21)

On my way home I stop for a drink with a friend

of my husband, and in asking for his advice, I retell my story for the fourth time that day. In each of these four instances, I am re–creating the problems all over again. Not only do I re–tell my problems, but in the process of giving them my full attention, in each instance the problems not only multiply, they become a little more and more distorted because I have taken events out of context. Then I began to add my own interpretations -- interpretations made in moments of anger and frustration. Personally, I know I am a very clever person and know something about the personalities and cognitive preferences of my friends, so I was even able to adapt my stories to fit their sympathies. In short, I discovered that I was giving my problems momentum. I added fuel to the fire. The more emotion I evoked, the more images I called forth, the larger the number of receptors that fire off in the limbic system. I was literally *creating* a larger and larger memory bank!

What we haven't recognized until recently is how the "stuff" of our lives gets into our bodies. According to the findings of Candice Pert, a researcher at the National Institutes of Health, neuropeptides are the chemicals which serve as communication links between brain cells. Her research, replicated at a number of other prestigious laboratories, suggests that neuropeptides have been found in receptor sites in every cell in the body. *This implies that memory is at the cell level, not just in the brain!*

It is at the cellular level that emotion and associated thoughts are stored. It is as if our body is listening to itself. If I talk about my boss as being a "pain in the neck," the cells in my neck get the message to do pain. It is as if my word is law in my own universe! If I have a "gut feeling that everything is falling apart," the cells in my gut, in my stomach, hear that it is time to fall apart. I am suggesting that the language we use directs the thoughts and emotions to the cellular level of the body. I am suggesting too, that this body is a fully functioning whole. The body is conscious, aware of every feeling, every thought, every emotion. This means that intelligence is *in the body*. It is in every organ, artery, vein and nerve. In a general state of health the liver *knows* how to eliminate waste products, the heart *knows* how to regulate circardian rhythms, the intestines *know* how to absorb nutrients and eliminate waste products. Each of these bodily systems, while having their own intelligence, also respond to the immune system.

Deepak Chopra suggests that the immune system serves as a mirror between thought and feeling. Our immune cells are evesdropping not only on our internal dialogue but on our external dialogue. He suggests that the immune system listens to the conversations we are having with ourselves at every second of every day. If we are having "contaminated" conversations -- you know the kind where we blame the other person, where we whine and give up all power and awareness -- that contaminated information gets into the body at the cell level. Well, just imagine lots and lots of these kinds of occurrences over a long period of time. Each contaminated cell can only do what it is biologically directed to do -- it divides in half; and those divide in half; and so on and so on and so on. We then start having little colonies of unhappy cells, which make unhappy tissue, or muscle. This then is the *origin* of all disease processes.

In a sense, all along I have been talking about the

mind. It is not in the brain, nor in the intelligence of the organ. It does not live only at the cell level. It is the product of all the interactions. Traditionally, when we "think" about the mind, we are really thinking about the brain as our source of thinking. Thinking, however, comes from the mind, the mind of which is neither exclusively tied to internal or external structures. The mind is infinite and is nonlocal, suggests Deepak Chopra. It is a part of a larger field of information.

Rupert Sheldrake, a research scientist with the Noetic Institute in California, suggests that the mind is part of a "morphogenetic" field into which thoughts are projected and received. His work, along with those scientists exploring the frontiers of quantum physics, suggest that the mind is infinite. It is capable of many, many correlations at the same time. We can play golf, digest food, kill germs, plan an investment strategy and ponder the color or our new coat all at the same time. By suggesting that the mind is nonlocal, it means we can call forth from memory the last golf game, what we ate for lunch, the last time were were sick and the color of shoes we wore at our son's wedding last March, in just the blink of an eye! Not only can the mind go *backward* in a time/space continuum, it goes f*orward.* We can project what we will say to our buddies about the bet we have won over the football game, we can imagine cool lemonade waiting for us at the clubhouse following a tennis match, we can anticipate the sense of being clean and fresh after a shower, and so forth. The point is, we do these kinds of activities all the time and this is all ordinary stuff here.

The mind, being limitless and timeless, is also "spaceless." However else would you be able to hold the moon in the palm of your hand? The mind, being larger than self, allows us to have intimate experiences with all aspects of places, events and people which would otherwise be denied us. The mind, according to Deepak Chopra, in his audio tape series *Magical Mind, Magical Body,* 1991, monitors the stars and the planets in a single instant. Our biological rhythms are the expression of the entire cosmos. The cycles of day and night, influenced by the sun, affect our sleep patterns. The cycle of the moon affects the female 28 day menstral cycle. Deepack suggests that to separate ourselves from the rest of the cosmos is an artifact of our sensory awareness. It is a misperception of who we really are. It is a denial of our multi-dimensional heritage.

We are moving deeper and deeper into the realm of consciousness, of meaning that we assign to things and events in the world, and in our daily lives. I would like to create another model so that we have something concrete to deal with, and again, a metaphorical or mythical model. For the sake of discussion, let's say that consciousness comes from the heart -- not necessarily the biological heart, but from the center of the being (again having no reference to the physical body). Let's assume too, that there are four components to consciousness which we could arbitrarily call the mind, the will, love and vision. (See Figure 22).

Our mind, composed both of the thoughts we think and those which we intuit "that just come to us", as a component of consciousness, has for the most part, like our senses, been traditionally projected outward. We have used our "minds," as it were to gather information about who will acknowledge us. Our educational system has, in fact, been built on this premise. Our

BIOENERGETICS OF THE HEART

(Figure 22)

educational system is not designed to teach us to learn more about ourselves, to use our minds for reflection and self discovery. In our educational systems, teachers give us grades, and those grades serve as an external sign of what we know. Just as our senses can't give us information about what is going on inside us, neither has our conscious mind been trained to reflect and engage in self discovery.

Ponder our educational system in depth for a moment. Have you ever noticed that there were times when you were sure that you knew something, but the teacher told you that you were wrong? Or perhaps you recall a math class when you knew the right answer but since you could not do the computation, the problem was considered only half right? This means then, that grades are not a reflection of what it is that we know, rather, grades are a verification that we know what the teacher knows or wants us to know! It seems that the more education we get, the more confused we get, because we are continually asked to keep validating different things.

Consciousness of the heart gets "hooked" into the mind through the *illusion* that we must learn and do things like everyone else. We get "hooked" into believing that all education and all learning comes from outside us. We devalue and learn not to trust our own internal resources. Thus, when our jobs fail, when we are not adequately prepared according to other people's standards, we are booted out and suffer *abandonment* or separation. Without the ability to know our own beliefs and transcend them, we are not able to determine our own unique reasons for being here and we continue to live life outside of ourselves. We, in our defense, continue to make judgments about others and the world around us, rooted in the inability or unwilingness to determine for ourselves, our own course of action. Following this course of action not only leads us into separation, but we fall prey to fear.

Will is a second component of consciousness. We have tied our "will" to ancient concepts of ego, which we have also directed outward. We have assumed that our will is related to how much *control* we have. Our will has been tied to external concepts of power discussed earlier. We speak of "will power" to loose weight, to stop smoking, to give us courage to change jobs, or redefine our relationships. This business of will is very confusing when it comes to making choices. It seems we only get two choices. Either "we get it" (all the money, power, security and love we want) or we get hurt; we feel *betrayed.* As if in putting our faith in the "system," (again focusing control outside ourselves). IT fails and we "get ripped off." Sometimes when we do "get it" (all the money and power we want), we get addicted to it, and when we get addicted to it, we increase the chances of loosing it and starting all over. Or if we don't loose everything, we at least get hurt.

Consciousness of the heart gets "hooked" into will through our belief that we have control of our lives, other people and what goes on in the world around us. Thus when we fail to see beyond our limited impressions of ourselves, when we are not open to guidance from the mirrors provided by those whom we would label as different from us, we loose all sense of control. When we continue to dispute that there is a Divine Plan, we again separate soul from experience, mind from body, thought from feeling. This then leads us into the experience of betrayal -- the *sickness unto death.* Because we are so clever about how we have organized our illusions, we likely suffer guilt and thus further convince ourselves that we were not entitled to the abundance of the universe.

Love, as a third component of consciousness, was intended as a way of displaying our feelings. Instead, our emotions have become more a reflection of our *beliefs* not only about ourselves, and others, but the world around us. Not being able to express feelings in the moment, they have become distorted over time. Consciousness of the heart gets "hooked" into emotion, generally concerning our beliefs about male and female. We have assumed that our lives will work better "if only" we can find the right partner, the right lover, the right soul mate. We have not yet reached a stage of wholeness and, like the yin/yang symbol, been able to see all that is considered feminine and all that is considered masculine is encoded within us, regardless of our gender (like Athena and Aphrodite). Without the sense of wholeness, we are forever doomed to face *rejection,* assuming is it related to the universe not giving us our other half.

Historically, vision refers not to sight, but insight, wisdom. As a final component of consciousness, like our mind, our will, and our emotions, we have directed our vision outward. We have used our creative expres–ion as an attention–seeking devise that allows us to compare our importance with others. We have kept vision tied only to the sense of sight. We want to look how others look, we wear shoes on our feet that match in color and style. If a three year old wants to wear one pink shoe and one orange shoe, we discourage that kind of expression. We express ourselves not only through visual style, but language style, and even in the shape of our bodies! In short, we express ourselves in ways that are approved by others. If the cultural model is to be thin or muscular, as it is in this country, then females try to be thin and males try to be muscular. If the female model is to be large and robust, as it may be in some Middle Eastern countries, then it is desirous for the female to be large.

Consciousness of the heart gets "hooked" into our vision, our creative expression when we hold onto the *fantasy* that we must look like everyone else, we must act like them. If the model is to be thick and robust for women as it is in the Middle East, then alas, we are only worth more camels! When our visions of ourselves do not match those of the collective, we find that we exper–

ience *disappointment.* However, disappointment comes from the faulty judgments we make about ourselves, and about the very models we have emulated. Thus, we loose all capacity for vision, for looking at and expressing ourselves.

So how can we possibly make sense out of this business of being human when we have been raised through eons and eons of time to believe that our consciousness is directed outward? I can only suggest that we begin the process of seeking answers to the questions which have been nagging us since the beginning of time. I urge you to ask the deeper questions, to move beyond the surface impressions, to explore you for the magnificence that you are. In this way maybe you would fall in love with yourself. What a delicious idea! A person who is more loving, as far as I know, attracts all the love he or she can handle. A loving person who no longer projects will outward, but who seeks to find the meaning of each experience, comes to an understanding through vision, through wisdom, that control does not exist outside self. By taking these components of consciousness and directing them inward, making new relationships between them, we become even more conscious.

I have spoken before about how our life changes when all our activities become infused with reverence. When we recognize that our mind is timeless, spaceless, and we devote our activities toward what I call Divine exploration, then we are forever blessed with sufficient *learning* in this lifetime. As we direct our will inward, reflecting on what we have learned then we gain *authentic* power. A power that, like the mind, transcends time and space. We move into a knowing that we are part of a grander plan, and that our willful exploration only deepens the mystery. As we use mind and will in this manner, we begin to recognize that as beings we are indeed timeless, and ageless. While the form may change, there will remain, preserved in eternity, that soul seed. When we are willing to use our vision, not for physical sight, but for gathering the wisdom of the heart, then we are moving into *expression* of the "I am" self. As we move into full awareness of our capacity for love, we come to recognize that this is what *preserves* the mind and body, the spirit and the soul (See Figure 23).

THE "I AM" SELF

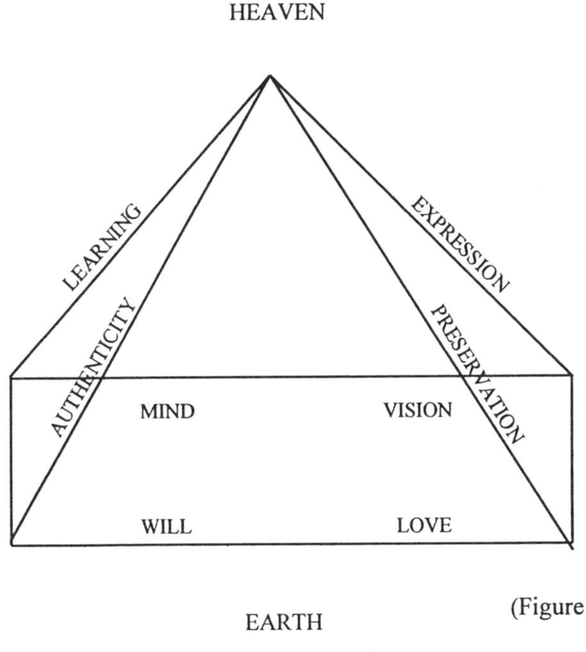

(Figure 23)

> We are not sure [the scientists tell us] but we have accumulated evidence which indicates that the key to understanding the universe is you.
>
> This is not only different from the way that we have looked at the world for three hundred years, it is opposite. The distinction betweenthe "in here" and the "out there" upon which science was founded is becoming blurred. This is a puzzling state of affairs. Scientists, using the "in here--out there" distinction may not exist. What is "out there" apparently depends, in a rigorous mathematical sense as well as a philosophical one, on what we decide "in here."
>
> The new physics tells us that an observer cannot observe without altering what he sees. Observer and the observed are interrelated in a real and fundamental sense. The exact nature of this interrelationship is not clear, but there is a growing body of evidence that the distinction between the "in here" and the "out there" is illusion.
>
> Access to the physical world is through experience. The common denominator of all experiences is the "I" that does the experiencing. In short, what we experience is not external reality, but our interaction with it (Zukav, 1979).

To find the answers we want, we ask questions not of others, but of ourselves. If we want really big answers, it is my experience we need to ask really big questions (See Figure 24).

CONSCIOUSNESS OF A HEAL-THY BODY

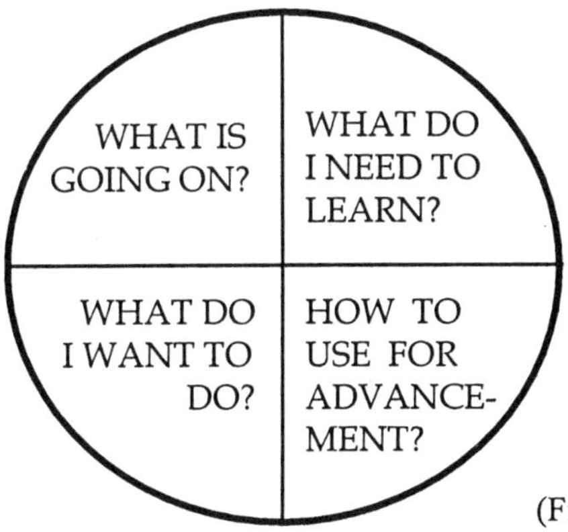

(Figure 24)

Chapter 6 The Vibrating Universe

We now venture even further into the unknown, stretching from the objective reality into an ever expanding subjective reality. We move out of the realm of the left hemisphere into the right; we move from thinking and sensing to feeling and intuiting. We venture into a new way of looking at the human body. In this venture we begin to cross thresholds of time and space, thinking like our most eminent physicists. We cross cultural boundaries, looking from Western to Eastern philosophies, tapping into the knowledge of the ancient mystics.

On some level, all of us would agree that we are energy beings, that is, we have often felt the "energy" that drives us. We can feel a depletion of energy when we are tired. Likewise, when we feel a surge of power, we say we are "inspired" or "energized." While we are familiar with using the term "energy" this way, we have not yet allowed a deeper meaning. Our physicists give us a very helpful metaphoric picture.

Imagine a straight line, like a guitar string. Now pluck that string. If you did that, it would vibrate. Now imagine taking the two ends of the string and putting them together so that they make an imaginary orbit. It wouldn't matter if it was your finger that "plucked" the orbital cord, or an electron or even a planet! All known material in the physical universe is fundamentally composed of vibration. Further, an electron in one place can get "in tune" with an electron in a far distant place, whether the electron is in the body, in a plant, or even in a planet. Just as we could pluck a single string on a guitar to create vibration or sound, all other strings next to it would begin to vibrate in sympathy with it.

Let's back up a moment and make this a little easier to understand. I assure you I do this, not so much for your understanding, but for my own. Let's talk about vibration in terms of sound. We know that we are constantly surrounded by sound. We have two openings in our head through which we hear sound. In fact, the making of sound is the way we communicate with each other. On a more subtle level, even the motion of our bodies makes sound. To exaggerate this point, rapid movement of your hand next to your ear, creates a "whirling" kind of sound. Sound, then, or vibration, is any acoustical disturbance that is composed of many frequencies. Since our bodies both create and receive sound through hearing, speaking and moving, it may be well for us to look at the nature of sound as a key to understanding a deeper reality of the body.

Let's go back to that guitar string. Let's say that we could put that string on a frame and stretch it tight (See Figure 25). If we were to pluck the string in the middle at a half-way point, we would notice that the string vibrates between the two points of attachment. If we could look at this in slow motion, we would notice two symmetrical arcs. According to Itzhak Bentov, author of *Stalking the Wild Pendulum,* 1988, this is called a "standing wave."

If we were to pluck that same string at one quarter of its length, we would notice a remarkable difference. With a slow motion camera, we would see that there would be two standing waves, one between the middle distance and the end of the frame closest to where we touched the string, as we noted before. But now, there would be a second wave, from the middle point to the farthest connection to the frame. It would vibrate in the same pattern as the first half; in other words it would create a symmetrical pattern. If we moved our finger even closer to one side of the frame, we would create even more waves, but each time the wave form would double. The creation of waves would follow a mathematical formula using integral numbers (numbers that are not fractional); so we would create two waves, then four, then eight and so on, each time we moved our finger up the string. The sound would of course be higher in frequency and the little string would vibrate faster and faster.

NATURE OF SOUND WAVES

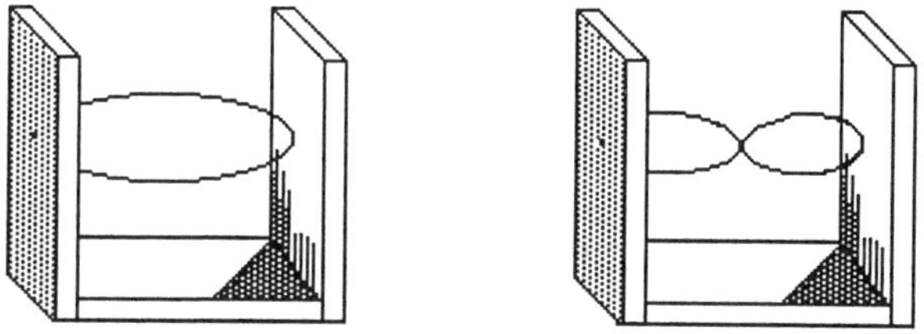

(Figure 25)

Now, let's apply what we know about sound to a stationary object. Let's take a thin sheet of metal and clamp one edge in a stationary position (See Figure 26). Keeping the metal sheet horizontal, let's place fine grains of sand on the metal sheet. Then let's take a violin bow string and draw it across the free edge of the metal sheet until it creates sound. As we continue to draw the bow string on the metal, we would notice that the grains of sand start to move, and they begin to collect in certain places and form a symmetrical pattern.

VIBRATIONAL EFFECTS OF SOUND

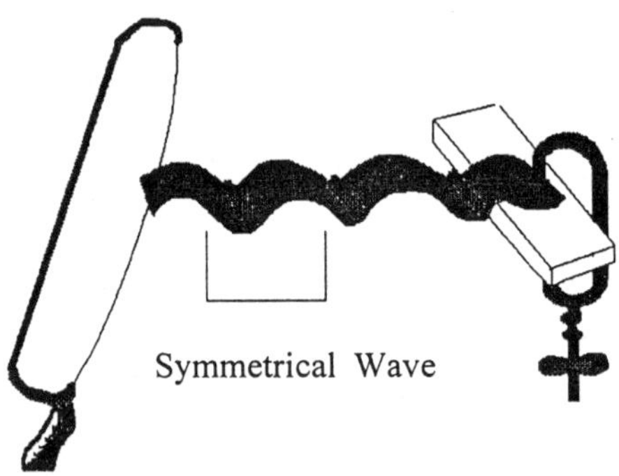

(Figure 26)

It seems the bow string creates standing waves on the metal which are active areas that vibrate up and down, moving the sand. Yet like the areas on the string in the frame which did not move, there are areas on the metal sheet which are quiet areas where there is no vibration. This is where the grains of sand migrate. In other words, we might refer to these as low energy places, or places where matter accumulates.

Just as sound affects a piece of metal, a two–

dimensional surface, it affects three-dimensional objects as well, like our bodies. But since it is easier not to use our bodies for the moment to illustrate this point, let's assume we have a transparent box that we fill with water. Into this fluid, we would place solid particles that have the same specific gravity as water. In other words, the solid pieces would not sink to the bottom, but would randomly float in the liquid. If we vibrate the six walls of the cube with sound, we would notice movement of the particles. Only this time, they move to create *order* out of the randomly dispersed particles. (See Figure 27).

ORGANIZING EFFECTS OF SOUND

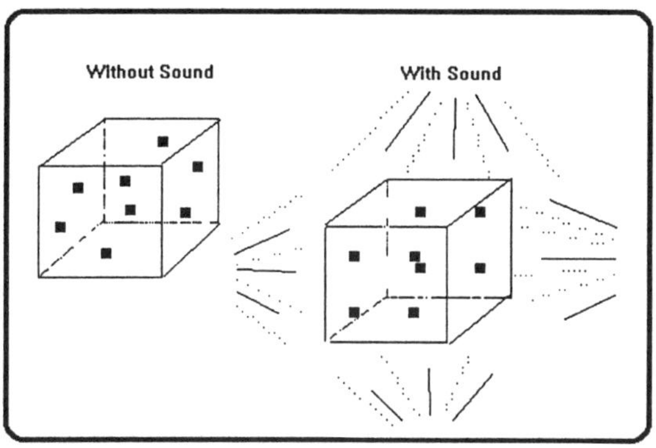

(Figure 27)

Interestingly, if we could introduce different sounds, low and high tones, we would notice that these floating particles would begin to arrange themselves differently. They would begin to take *shape.* The lower the vibration, the greater the density, the higher the vibration, the farther apart the particles are.

Let's now change the nature of our experiment. Let's get a shallow glass bowl and fill it with water. (A glass bowl makes it easier to see what we are doing). Now drop a pebble into the bowl of water. You would notice that the pebble is the source of mini ripples or waves, spreading evenly across the water. Let's now make this a bit more complicated and simultaneously drop three pebbles into the water. (Oh, and by the way, this is not a story about a villain so it doesn't matter if you use white or black pebbles!) If you could look at this in slow motion you would see that there are ripples which spread out from each pebble you dropped. But with the three pebbles, as the ripples spread out, they begin to cross and interact with each other (See Figure 28). This creates a complex pattern which Bentov would call an "interference" pattern.

INTERFERENCE WAVE PATTERNS

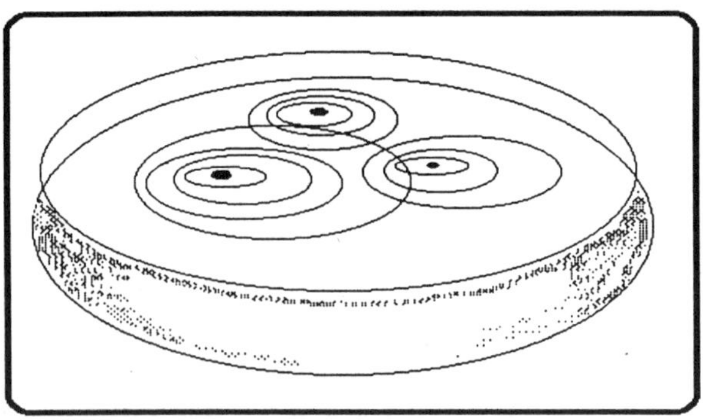

(Figure 28)

We seem to be on a roll here. So let's continue with our experiments with sound, then we will try to apply them to our understanding of the body and the nature of the physical universe. In a different experiment, let's say that I could create two wave patterns of identical frequency and amplitude and superimpose them on each other. I would, of course, have to have either a sound generating machine (or sounds from a computer) which I could in some method measure, say with an oscilloscope. I guess you will just have to trust me on this. Anyway, if the sounds were exactly the same, the vibrational patterns would be the same. The peaks would match the peaks and the valleys would match the valleys (See Figure 29).

CONSTRUCTIVE INTERFERENCE

(Figure 29)

But when I measure the effect of combining these frequencies or sounds, the wave form is twice the height of either of the original frequencies. It seems that they reinforce each other. Bentov, as my resource, suggests that this is called "constructive interference." Other writers have called this "resonance." So not only are these wave patterns in harmony, they create an effect that is greater than the parts.

Now what happens when we use frequencies or sounds that are not identical in wave form? What if they were exactly opposite? We would find, in this case, that the peaks match the valleys and the valleys match the peaks and they cancel each other out! In effect, they create a "flat line." This is known in physics, as well as electricity as "destructive interference" (See Figure 30).

DESTRUCTIVE INTERFERENCE

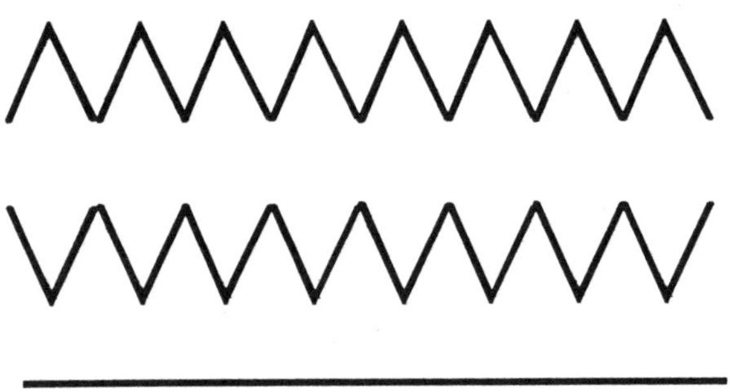

(Figure 30)

Now let's look at what happens when we change the frequency of two sounds. Sound can be measured in beat frequency or cycles per second. Let's see what happens when one sound, say 50 cycles per second, is superimposed on another, say 60 cycles per second. Now it gets very interesting (See Figure 31). Where the wave height or amplitude oppose each other, we see the destructive interference -- the cancellation effect. Where the amplitudes match or reinforce each other, we see the increase in the peaks and valleys -- the constructive interference.

MODULATING EFFECTS OF SOUND

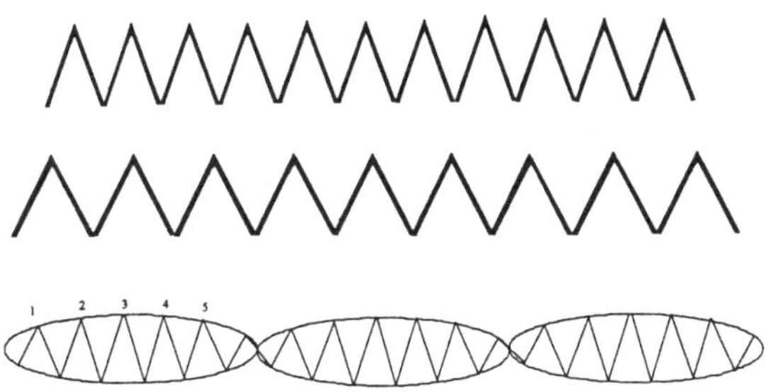

(Figure 31)

When these are put together, this makes an entirely new wave pattern, said to be "in phase." Of greater interest is that the very nature of the pattern is different, it is slower than the first two. The resultant difference between 60 cycles per second and 50 cycles per second is 10 cycles per second. So the entire pattern has been slowed down. Bentov refers to this as a "modulation" of the basic sounds.

So far, we have been examining the physics of sound and the vibrational effects of sound. These vibrational effects are also related to movement, just as the flapping of your wrist in the air created vibration that we call sound. But let's take an even deeper look at the nature of vibration itself. Remember our bowl of water with the three pebbles. Suppose you could quick freeze the bowl of water just after dropping in the pebbles, so as to freeze the ripples on the surface of the water. If you were to lift the thin layer of ice that formed on the surface, leaving the remaining water and the pebbles on the bottom of the pan, you would notice an interesting phenomena. If you were to hold the ice to a light source and look through it, you would see three pebbles suspended in the air (although they are of course, still in the bottom of the bowl). In holographic fashion, somehow the surface of the ice has stored the information about the whereabouts and the shape of the pebbles. Sound or vibration, then, is *a way of storing information or knowledge!* (See Figure 32).

I think the implications for this basic understanding of sound are profound. If we begin to look at the physics of vibration and energy, it gives us a different way of looking at the physical universe and our place in it. Can it be that here is a reasonable explanation why we feel such peacefulness sitting quietly on the beach looking at the sunset? Or walking on the crisp grass after a warm summer rain? Is it possible that at the sub-atomic level our body, begins to resonate with the sub-atomic structures around us -- the plants and the rocks, the fish and the animals? Or is the physical universe in some way "modulating" our cellular structure? I think so. In those moments that we become reverent, when we become mindful, we slow down the stresses of life so that we become "in tune" with our surroundings, we get in touch with the harmony of universe.

VIBRATION STORES INFORMATION

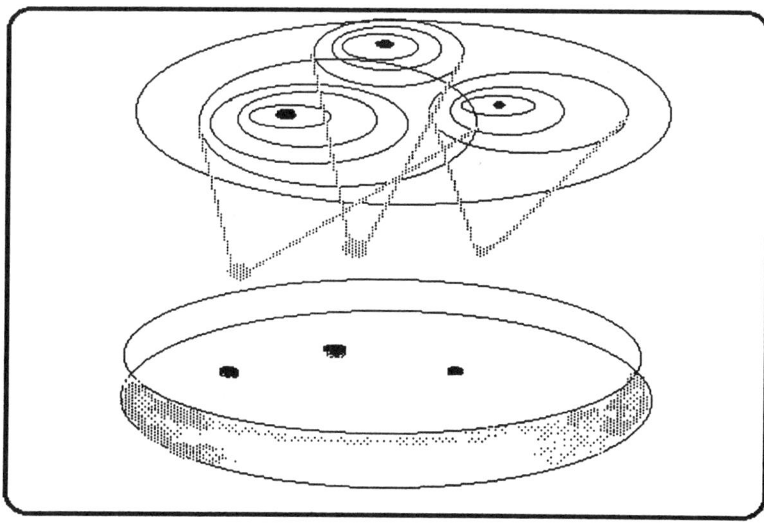

(Figure 32)

Our most intimate moments suggest that lovers truly connect in a very profound way, not just emotionally but biochemically and electromagnetically. Perhaps that feeling of intimacy comes because we have surrendered all need, at that moment, to be different; we have moved into a oneness. At the biochemical level, we have come into phase with each other. Slowing the universe down, we begin to breathe as one.

Yet even in our waking moments, can it be that

when two people of opposing viewpoints interact with each other that they, from a point of view of a physicist, have a modulating effect on each other? Probably, if they are willing to stay in relationship. If not, the wonders of physics suggest that opposing types may set up destructive interference patterns, thereby canceling the strong effects of polarization. So either way, by relating to each other, each person benefits. I think the same is true for two people who are very much alike. They literally reinforce each other, they double the effect of the energy. They set up constructive interference patterns that are contagious to everyone around them.

All of this is, of course, true when we are working with ourselves. When we are willing to confront the "shadow" which Jung referred to, we literally cancel its effects. This is likely what happens when people suggest they have had a "transcending" experience. Vibrationaly, they have released negative patterns of thinking and feeling as those patterns came in contact with positive patterns of loving and forgiveness. When we use the higher cerebral processes of thinking and intuiting, perhaps we also modulate the effects of emotion and even our sense of needing to have things stay the same. The cerebral hemispheres, as more sophisticated structures with more complex neural circuitry which have more recently evolved, have a higher vibration pattern than the limbic system.

It gets really fascinating when physicists tell us even more, shifting now from vibrational understanding to understanding the very nature of our sub-atomic structure. Physicists suggest that electrons don't really follow an exact orbital path (and neither does a planet for that matter). Electrons are more like probability patterns that make up the electron shell. Electrons can be everywhere and no where at the same time! They represent probabilities of interconnectedness. This suggests that it no longer makes sense to fix a fragment (a single electron, a molecule, a cell, an organ, or a body) because it will deteriorate with the fixing. It deteriorates because we have tampered with its nature; it was only a probability pattern in the first place! Not only that, but what it was connected to will change. This then, means that we must begin to focus on the whole and not the part.

Let me say this another way. Imagine you could go on a journey into the middle of an atom. Let's say the atom is about the size of planet earth. Scattered throughout are several white grapes, at various distances. In the middle, is one small, barely discernable cherry pit! These grapes represent the electrons in an atom. The cherry pit represents the nucleus. This analogy is intended to shift our perceptual thinking. While our physicists remind us that at the sub–atomic level, the human body is composed of electrons and protons whirling around a central core or a nucleus, their deeper analysis suggests that the body is composed of 99.99% space with very little relegated to the state of matter. In fact, if you could take all the "matter" of the physical universe (all those electrons and protons and nuclei) and squash them into a single solid form, you would have an object about the size of one grain of rice; regular rice, not long grain! This causes us to ponder what is in all that space? Is it a no–*thing*–ness? Is it a form of non–material intelligence? Would we want to call this God?

No longer is it appropriate to focus on the form,

we need a bigger lens to look at the "space." We need a world view which looks at the body, in terms of the internal space and the external space. We need to come to a deeper understanding of the body, and in so doing, we must come to a different way of describing it. Physicists are suggesting that by looking at the body in terms of an interactive field of intelligence or energy, we gain a better understanding not only of its function, but how the body breaks down in the first place.

We live in an interactive universe. Understanding the whole cannot come from understanding a single unit because each unit is part of the whole. If we focus on the whole, we could come to understand a single unit. The emerging model suggests we live in a holographic universe, and within that universe, each seemingly separate unit is, in fact, a holographic projection of the whole.

Energy of the Subtle Bodies

The energy in the physical body vibrates at a low enough rate that it can be seen, hence leading to the belief that it is real rather than an artifact of our perceptual constructs. Just like our experiment with the bow string on the metal, matter accumulates around low energy or low vibrational points. If we are willing to move into an understanding of the body as a hologram, we begin to get a much better picture of who we really are. Let's, for the moment, picture an egg-like structure surrounding the physical body. (See Figure 33).

The yolk could, metaphorically, be related to the physical body, because the energy vibrates at a low enough level that it can be seen. The "stuff" surround–ng the physical body is a what Rubert Sheldrake, a bio–ogist with the Noetic Institute of Sciences, refers to as a field of energy. He contends this field of energy is called a "morphogenic field," which is created by the body and that this field, in turn, creates the body --

THE HUMAN ENERGY FIELD

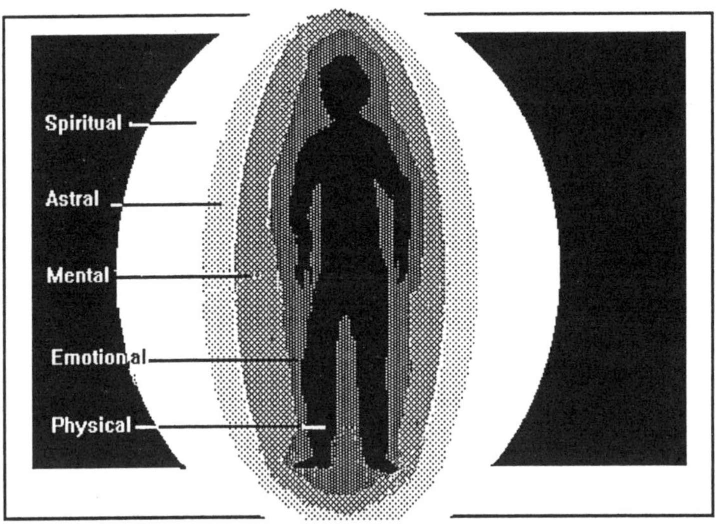

Etheric Template is not shown (Figure 33)

sort of like a mini self–contained universe. In other words, thoughts and emotions, as vibrations, create different resonance patterns around the body through the process of sympathetic vibration. The body sets up wave patterns around it called constructive wave patterns as described previously. Clairvoyants have been known to call this field of energy the "aura." The field of energy, as an interchangeable field, interacts with other energy fields (other people, plants, and even planets in the solar system) and again, through the process of resonance, sends vibrational patterns back to the more dense physical body.

Positive affirmations or pleasant thoughts are regarded as having a higher vibration than negative thoughts and emotions. So as long as positive thoughts and emotions are being projected into the resonant field, and being fed back to it, the body maintains a state of health. But when we get into states of competition, judgement, fear and anxiety, these lower vibrations are also projected into the field. Since we live on a planet which has a gravitational pull that affects even the tiniest atom or electron, gravity affects the vibrational field around the body, causing all that has been projected to spin and come back into the body through acupuncture or meridian points. There are other structures in the body which also respond to changes in vibrational level, most of which are located at the cellular level.

It may be easier to think of the aura or the energy fields as levels of consciousness. The lower the consciousness, the lower the vibration; hence the more dense the structure. The lower three energy fields which can be seen and felt (which I will describe in a minute) constitute the lower end of the vibrational field. The upper levels of the energy field where the energy vibrates at a much faster rate, cannot be seen by the naked eye. They can however, be "intuited" or "seen" by clarivoyants.

What I am proposing in this model is that we indeed have a self contained universe with components of both "heaven" and "earth" represented in the physical form. If we think of fields in terms of vibration, then it is within the natural human capacity to achieve complete awareness. In fact, it is our natural birthright. The upper realms of consciousness are not reserved for the mystics and the monks! They are ordinary expressions of mindfullness (See Figure 34).

As we examine the details of this holographic body, we would notice that beyond the obvious physical body, there is an energy field called the *etheric body* (not shown in Figure 33). According to Barbara Brennen, a former NASA research scientist and author of *Hands of Light,* 1987, the etheric template is the site at which energy is converted into matter. It corresponds directly with acupuncture meridian links which affect both the circulatory and nervous systems in the physical body, thereby contributing energetically to cellular patterns of physiology. Other writers have referred to this layer as the *health band,* as it is associated with automatic or autonomic functioning of the nervous system. The etheric body acts to both send and receive the frequency exchange between the physical body and the energy of the other subtle bodies. It is this energy field which is manipulated through a process called "therapeutic touch." While there are pain receptors throughout the body, there are also pain receptor sites in the etheric template which may be perceived as processing channels. It is suspected that pain *originates* from the etheric template as energy blockages from the emotional and mental fields work their way through this field into the physical body.

EXPRESSION OF CONSCIOUSNESS IN THE ENERGY FIELDS

PLANES OF REALITY

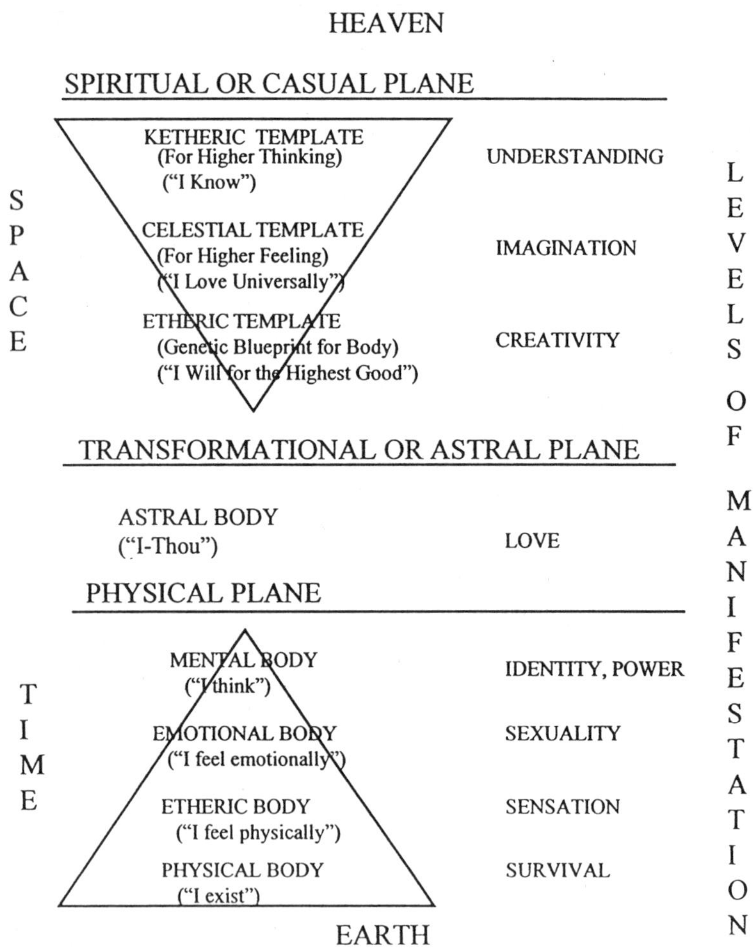

(Figure 34)

For the lay person, this energy field is one with which we can all have a direct experience. It is the field which can be seen by an untrained eye. Let's do a brief experiment to see the etheric template. Sit in a dimly lit room, one that has a white background. Then put your hands in front of your face at a distance of about two feet with the palms facing you. Relax your eyes or soften your gaze and focus on your hands. As you move your fingers apart, notice that there is a faint grayish or pale blue aura, or a transparent field around your fingers. (See Figure 35). What you are actually seeing is not an artifact of vision, but is the etheric body.

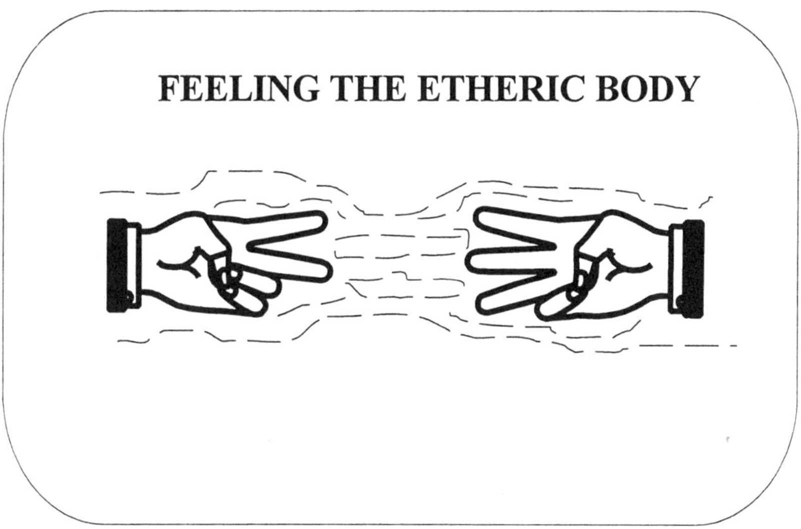

(Figure 35)

If you were to move your hands over your arms and legs without touching them, keeping a distance of about one inch from the extremity, you may be able to feel temperature changes. Heat is generally an indication that energy is moving faster in a particular area than another. You may also be able to feel the energy blockages. They just feel more "dense." To do this successfully, it is also suggested that you trust your intuitive feelings, as this is more of a subjective experience than an objective one. For some, it helps to close your eyes and focus your attention on what your hands are feeling. This etheric body that you are experiencing extends about an inch from your physical body, and it follows the general contour of each body part.

The second layer of the human energy field, can be found by placing your palms so that they are facing each other. Gently move them together and apart, covering a distance from two to four inches. As you focus your attention on the space between your hands, you may have a vague sense of a slight elastic pull between your hands. If you are unable to feel this field in this manner, try holding open the palm of the right hand. Then draw imaginary circles with the left index finger on the palm of the right hand (See Figure 36). Do not touch the palm and be sure to be at least two inches from the right palm. Try making circles clockwise, then counter clockwise. In these two exercises you have been working with the second layer of your energy field which has been called the *emotional* body. You may be able to feel this energy field on other body parts, but it is especially noted in the palms, the soles of the feet, and around the face and head. Some writers suggest that *this energy field may be the primary originating site of disease and illness in the physical body as it houses all unresolved emotional issues.* Still other writers speculate that this energy field is an interactive field attached to energy grids which support the physical planet. (A comment will be made about this in a later chapter). This energy field carries a great deal of power if one were to be conscious of it. Those whom we would regard as "charismatic" would have a powerful and energized emotional body.

(Figure 36)

The second layer is concerned with emotional feelings and reactions to events in life. So although the layman has full awareness that emotions are as "real" as the physical body, he or she may have the outdated notion that feelings originate in the brain. The emotional body "houses" feelings which are projected outward from the physical body. Emotions result from the pairing of sensations (like heat, cold, or touch) with thoughts as the body moves through time and space in an interactive way. The interpretations become emotions only when attached to thoughts (which are a higher vibrational level). For example, fear may arise from a thought of incompetency, or a perception of being inadequate which is associated with being really cold. This might result in a "flight" response, or a running from the situation. On the other hand, when aggression or the need to strike out to defend oneself is paired with anger, it might result in a "fight" response. These emotions (which are really distorted views of the self) are stored until triggered again by like events. The retriggering of the earlier memory then becomes paired with yet another sensation and creates in its place another self view. As events which occur in single moments of now . . . now . . . now . . . are accumulated in time, they form patterns (in space) which we may more commonly call "personality patterns" or "habitual ways of being."

Because the universe is interactive, as are our relationships, the emotional field serves as the point from which we receive thoughts as feelings projected to us by others. In other words, your employee need not tell you directly that you are a "pain in the neck," if it is even a thought, it will get into your body! While you may not pick up the thought "telepathically," you will likely pick it up through other senses. You will "feel" that your employee doesn't like you. The choice about what you do with this information is of course, up to you. The phenomena also works the other way, regardless of whether the information is positive or negative. You may be the one who is projecting the thoughts or emotions. I need to point out here that it truly does make a difference if you are the one sending or receiving the thoughts and emotions. About 80% of what we think about someone else stays in *our* auric field, only about 20% gets into theirs. So if you thought you could "do someone in," by thinking negative thoughts, guess what? You are the one who will suffer the most because of the judgments and criticism! Because the projections stay in your energy field, you will have to deal with them sooner or later. There is a pretty powerful suggestion here and it is to stop finding fault with each other! It may save our lives.

As an aside, understanding the power of the emotional body from a vibrational sense may give us a beginning understanding as to why prayer may be so important in aiding healing. Positive thoughts projected into the field of a person who is ill, enter the emotional field, and pass through the etheric template which transposes the energy. Usually the energy of the ailing person is "boosted," as it is interpreted by the body as a higher vibration. It therefore impacts on cell division, creating possibilities for "healthy" cells to emerge.

Within the emotional field are energetic tendencies or *miasms* which predisposes an individual toward manifesting a particular illness. Miasms are believed to be the emotional memories which may be inherited genetically or acquired during an individual's lifetime. If unpleasant memories are not resolved, they may be root causes of chronic diseases. According to Richard Gerber, a Detroit physician, and author of *Vibrational Medicine,* 1988, miasms may be acquired as result of an infectious agent, however, the infection is not the miasm. The disease causing organism may be eradicated by antibiotic therapy, but the subtle energetic trace, the memory of the infection, may persist at an unseen level, perhaps in the emotional field. Miasms which reside in the emotional field may weaken the natural bodily defenses, creating a tendency toward manifesting different types of illnesses at a later date.

An understanding of miasms may offer a different way for us to understand the recurrence of diseases such as cancer or ulcers, repeated heart attacks, and for conversion of HIV positive responses into AIDS. Even if the diseased tissue is removed, or chemotherapy applied, unless there is, at the same time, a removal of the emotional event(s) which caused the trauma, it is likely to reoccur or be manifest in a more chronic form. Added to this, is the possibility that the body "remembers" the trauma of the surgery, the invasion of the body or the state of being tied to artificial support systems. I intentionally use this phrase "the body remembers" because I trust that we have firmly established that memory is at the cellular level. Evidence for this was suggested in the work by Candice Pert in an earlier chapter. I also made the suggestion that sound or vibration is a way of storing information or knowledge.

Our picture of health gets more complex as we delve into our interconnectedness. As infants we are birthed through the energy field of the mother, and are cuddled by numerous relatives, thereby subjecting the infant to all the uncleared emotional traumas of each person that he or she encounters! While this "sharing" of emotional fields has been presented as being related to childhood, it is really a lifelong process. We share with each other all the unresolved issues since the beginning of time!

In one sense, it doesn't matter if you believe in reincarnation or not. If you did, then I would suggest that all of the experiences of life imprint on the soul as well as the physical body. *The point of death is to release the soul from the body, so that it might be cleansed or returned to a state of coherent vibration.* Once a soul is cleansed, it can then, if it so chooses, enter another life cycle for more learning and discovery. The soul however, carries the imprint of all previous learning. This may account for our absolute "knowing" when there are no logical answers. Instances of "knowing" may be moments of tapping into the information stored at the soul level. If you are not comfortable with this interpretation, then let's stick to biology. Since memory of life's events is stored at the cell level, which in turn affects the DNA and RNA which is passed down from generation to generation, then we still have all the memories of humanity imprinted in our biology. If one chooses only to stay with a vibrational interpretation, then we "get" a little bit of everybody else into our bodies through interaction of our energy fields. In this case, I can speculate that we may be able to tap into deep cellular knowledge of each other.

In terms of illness, we are moving more and more into an interpretation of the body as a hologram, not just in itself, but as part of a larger whole. If one holds a belief that the body is an integrated whole, then each part is a necessary and contributing part. The removal of a single part is a disruption of the whole. We are dependent on our very environment and determined by it.

We return now to the third layer of the human energy field which is the *mental field.* In a balanced state, it extends from four to six inches beyond the body and as such, begins to lose the fine differentiation. It would appear as if entire limbs were encased in this field, so if looking at the hands, the field would appear more like a mitten than a glove. The fourth layer may also be referred to as the *para-conscious band.* It is a field wherein we pick up events previously called "unconscious" or "pre-conscious." For example, you may have had the experience of picking up the phone to call a friend just as they called you. Up until now you may have preferred to call this a "coincidence." But our physicists remind us *there are no coincidences in the physical universe. There are no accidents! There are only interactive fields of probability, which, when they meet, turn probability into positive or negative possibilities through constructive or destructive interference patterns or through a process called phase locking.*

The interactive field of our mental life, is associated with the linear processing of the left hemisphere. Science can now demonstrate that when we think positive, affirmative thoughts, we cleanse the more dense energy fields and reconstitute the physical body. If, however, we make judgments or criticisms about ourselves or others, these negative "thought forms" remain in the energy field as blockages and eventually, if left unresolved, work their way into the physical body as disease processes. Dr. Gerber suggests that the subtler the energy, the more powerful it is, therefore healing at the mental level is stronger and produces longer lasting results that healing the physical body alone. Post surgical patients can be self-instructed to visualize a healed organ or a body part in place of the diseased part. The neural circuitry of the body doesn't "care" if it is working with a real or an *imagined* part as we experienced in Chapter 2. The body does however, "care" about the integrity of the whole. *The body is a self-organizing, self-maintaining, self-renewing and self-transcending whole!*

Correspondingly, research from Harvard Medical School by Jerome Frank suggests that the diverse modes of medical treatment owe their success or failure to the patient's state of mind, not to the treatment itself. As a leading researcher on the "placebo effect," Dr. Frank confirmed more than twenty years ago that *what the patient thinks* about either the treatment or the prescriptions taken, has the greatest effect on the health outcome of the patient.

Again, I feel a need to digress here and write for a moment about the placebo effect. Most of us already know what this means in a general way. But we have confined our understanding to the realm of pharmaceuticals. In other words, our understanding is that if we are told that a particular medication will be good for us, we generally believe that this is true. Believing that it is true, as I have just mentioned, perhaps has more effect on the body than the medication itself. From my own experience, I had to determine the placebo effect of the diagnosis itself! My experience was that I did not have a brain tumor. But now, I can finally, make the bold statement that a *diagnosis alone may work just like a placebo.* Given the lengthy descriptions about how the energy works in the mental and emotional bodies, a medical diagnosis may just be a negative thought form. What we choose to do about it lies in the mystery of our willingness to accept an alternative point of view.

Generally, the choice is made to give up all authority which resides inside, trusting instead the opinion of a stranger, who is not only outside our experience, but is one whom we view is smarter or wiser than our own field of information. In other words, we discount and devalue our own wisdom. My sense is that in giving up our authority, our own personal truth, we at that moment in time begin to participate in the creation of the disease. This in turn sets up stress -- not the kind we would ordinarily talk about, as stressors in the environment. The stress is set up in our own energy field because there is incongruent information. The wisdom of the body which holds the ideas of wholeness may be suddenly challenged by the mental beliefs and whatever emotional charge any particular words evoke in us according to the severity of the diagnosis. Incongruent information sets up a destructive force field of interference patterns. Either the belief "wins" the war and the body dies, or we honor the wisdom of the body and alter our belief systems. It's is as simple as we choose to make it.

As we begin to accept some of these ideas, we come closer to understanding the mind–body connection. This allows us to "re–cognize" or re–think that our bodies are more fluid, more dynamic, more changing, and more creative than we have ever imagined. The physical body reflects our dreams, our feelings, our senses and our thoughts. . . indeed, our very souls. Because the energy field of the practitioner directly interacts with the energy field of the patient, the model of health care for the twenty-first century suggests that to be truly effective, the practitioner must first heal themselves before interacting with others.

These notions have major impact on our health care system. In the Western culture, we currently have a system of payment for disease management. It is suspected that this system will evolve into preventive health education. Traditional roles of health practitioners from nurses to therapists to physicians will drastically change. Not only that, but health will become a personal issue, not a social one! *If drastic changes are made in the financial management of illness, each of us will have to take responsibility for ourselves, and that means responsibility for our health -- responsibility for our feelings, our thoughts, and our bodies.* If health care survives a financial crunch, we will move beyond a model which implies that the body needs fixing to an arena where love, compassion, understanding and forgiveness are the tools of caring for health.

To directly experience the fourth layer of the energy field, one would have to go to sleep! For beyond the mental field is the *astral body,* the energy field which contains the vibrations associated with both lucid dreams (day dreams) and those dreams (or nightmares) we would associate with sleeping. In whatever form dreams take, (day dreams or night dreams), the content is usually symbolic or archetypal. Some writers have suggested that dreams come to us as starry messages, containing information that may seem too difficult for processing if that information came directly to us.

Whatever their content, if we look at dreams energetically, the information is processed in the right hemisphere of the brain. In other words, dreams are interpreted and recorded as information coming into consciousness via the astral level from higher vibrational realms. This in turn stimulates the logical analytic thinking of the left hemisphere which allows us then to have thoughts about the dreams. Often as dreams trigger receptor sites in the right hemisphere, the right limbic system is stimulated, and as if bypassing the left brain, emotions come directly into our awareness. We might call these sudden archetypal images "nightmares." Whatever you might want to call them, this is the material we have previously called information of the "unconscious."

Objective information related to the senses and the subjective information of dreams is necessary to maintain hemispheric balance. It is almost as if the left hemisphere is the most active during the day as many of our activities are heavily weighted in language. Then at night, the right hemisphere is most active, through the dream state. This "taking a dominant turn" as it were, or the interplay between the right and left hemispheres of the brain is necessary for the expression of the physical personality and for activation of the pineal gland in the brain. The pineal gland is linked to energy vortices throughout the physical body which regulate the flow of energy throughout the energy fields. In experiencing the astral body, you may have noted in the guided visual imagery exercises, which is sort of like lucid dreaming, that you felt expanded or had a sense of floating. Your limbs may have felt decidedly lighter or heavier, depending on your point of focus. If you experienced your limbs as lighter, you literally took for a moment a dimensional shift, you moved your awareness beyond the boundaries of the physical body.

It is important that I take a moment to talk about the importance of dreams. Fred Wolf, author of *The Dreaming Universe,* 1994, suggests that dreams are critical in the formation of our self–identity. In the dream state, many of us have had the experience of being able to manipulate life events in a different way than we would in the waking state. Our imaginary conversations are often conducted in such a way as to assist us in feeling empowered, or perhaps benevolent. We even experience our bodies as no longer being tied to the forces of gravity. We float in endless space, transcending perhaps the physical laws of the universe. Many of us have conversations with beings who do not have discernible features, whether they are archetypal images, angels, guides, or friends we know in our earthly life depends on the experiences of each individual.

What is important is that we have, through our dreams, experiences that transcend time. We can move backward in time and recreate our life stories differently. We even move forward in time, to other places and other events. Perhaps these experiences are real, as Fred Wolf asserts in another of his books, *Parallel Universes,* written in 1988. He suggests that in dreams we are projected into another time and space, and those events that we experience we bring back into the moment of now. Thus, it would seem, he offers a reasonable explanation for experiences such as deja vu. Through the dream state, we also have our first experience, although most of us have not thought of it as this way, of looking at ourselves from outside ourselves. We have the experience of watching ourselves. If any of you have ever had this experience, as I have, then ultimately we have to ask, where are we in this process? We can be the *dreamer* and the *one who is dreaming* (or watching) and the *subject* of the dream, all at the same time! So perhaps our dreams serve as an additional reference point for us to begin accepting the notion of living in a holographic body that is multidimensional, capable of many realities at the same time.

My friend and noted dream analysist, Marlene Myher would say our "dream" or behind sleep work of the Higher Mind descends into receptors of the right brain and is processed by beliefs and concepts formed and accepted by the left brain. This implies that often dreams are "worked over" by restrictions of the left brain beliefs. It is her opinion we must take our dream work more seriously when we understand that the brain itself is only the computor processing mechanism, not the formulator of original thought. Dreams embody a language of their own and must be learned and read by someone trained in the field, as they can be useful in clearing the four subtle energy bodies (which will be detailed in the following chapter).

Let me delve again into the world of physics, because I think there is some wonderful information here that applies not only to dreams but to consciousness itself, and ultimately to the physical body. Remember our pan into which we dropped the pebbles? Let's think for a moment not of pebbles but just events, being dropped into a quantum energy field. (See Figure 37).

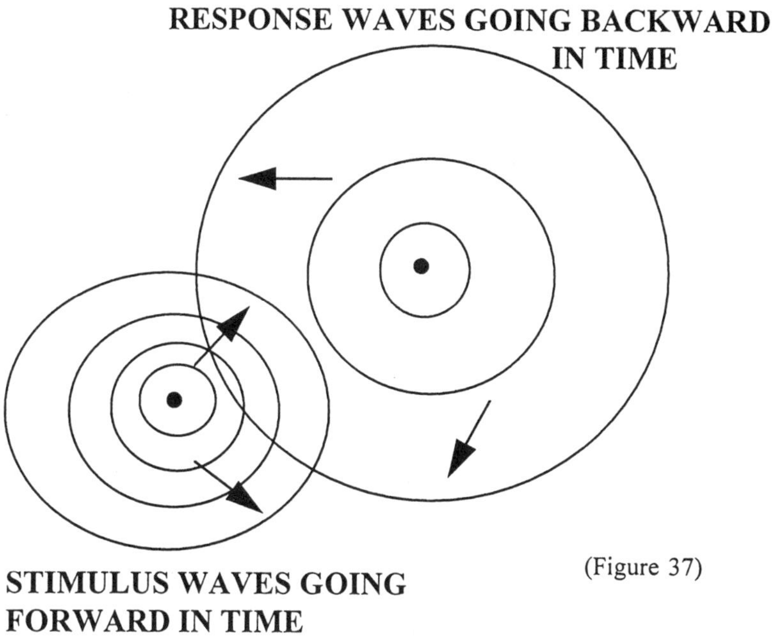

(Figure 37)

According to Wolfe, in his book *The Dreaming Universe:*

> Waves reinforce themselves in the space between the events and during the time between the events. Then they cancel each other out in the space outside these events and before the initial or offering effect and after the final or echoing event. The degree of cancellation depends on how similar the offer and echo waves are to each other. The greater the match, the greater the reinforcement between the events and the greater the cancellation outside of the events. . . The most

> significant thing of all, besides its bizarreness, is that two events are required before there is actually one event (p. 163).

In other words, the greater the number of events that there are, the more meaningful the initial event becomes. But to the body, it doesn't matter whether the "echo" or corresponding event occurs in space and time outside us, or if it occurs in the space and time of the dream world. So dreams, through the way in which they are constructed, can make life's events even more meaningful, or can cancel out the probability of that event making its way to our conscious awake state. Thus, dreams in themselves may be one of the natural ways in which the body heals itself.

Since I have just described a general principle of physics, then it applies to all of the energetic fields which I am in the process of describing. In other words, a single thought could send out a wave pattern. Corresponding thoughts could either reinforce it, cancel it out, or modulate it. The same is true when thoughts are paired with emotions. If we have a great deal of emotion attached to a thought, then the field effect is greater. It can only be modified by higher frequency patterns or if we had a series of responding life events, closely contained in time which were sufficient to provide echo waves to cause a cancellation effect.

For now, let's continue the exploration of the human energy field. The foregoing comments were offered as we are about to explore perhaps the most influential aspects of the human energy field -- the *spiritual or causal* body. But to continue to discuss the energy fields in terms of layers is a little misleading as the energy is so subtle that it cannot usually be seen or felt. It can be "intuited" or sensed by a skilled individual. However, for the sake of discussion, continual reference will be made to the energy fields as layers.

The fifth, sixth and seventh layers have generally been referred to as the *spiritual* layers. For the sake of discussion I will speak about each separately. Some writers have called the fifth layer the *karmic band.* Still others have referred to this field as the *etheric template* (not to be confused with the etheric body). Others yet call this field of energy the *Higher Self.* Whatever the name, it is through this field that we meet our challenges, overcome obstacles, and strive for higher consciousness. From an energetic perspective, life's challenges are opportunities, whether created in this lifetime or carried over from another. *Opportunities present themselves for mental activity, for a reformulation of our identity as human beings and for defining our personal truth as spiritual beings.* In other words, resolution of "karma" is the very foundation of evolution. It seems as though I can't stay in the safety of physics nor biology, as this is where we need to begin to bridge the gap into meta-physics.

In Hindu terms, *darma* has been used to describe one's life path or spiritual destiny, *karma* has been referred to as the challenges or the obstacles. If one believes in the notion of reincarnation and that planet earth is God's school, then each soul coming into a earth body selects those life lessons to learn which have the highest probability of evolving consciousness. It has been suggested by Barbara Brennan that the life pattern is encoded in the energy field in the seventh layer. This is the dynamic template which is constantly changing as the individual exerts free will choices in the process of living. As growth takes place, each individual has the opportunity to reach higher and higher levels of consciousness through the resolution of old patterns or karma. Interestingly, as each person progresses, so does the whole of humanity, so that each generation is usually able to sustain a slightly higher vibration. This then, is what is called evolution. It occurs within the species level and between levels, thus tadpoles evolve into frogs. They move in the transition stage from fish to amphibian, perhaps the only creatures left on the earth to remind us that evolution can take place within a single species' life span!

The sixth layer has been called the *celestial template.* It has also been called the *angelic body* or the emotional template (not to be confused with the emotional body or emotional field). It is in this realm that one experiences celestial love, a love that extends beyond human form, plant and animal life. It is important to point out that love, from a higher vibrational expression, is not the same as love from an attached emotional perspective. When a person has raised their consciousness to a higher vibrational level to truly recognize the connection with all of humanity and all creations on the planet, then that individual is likely able to experience and express unconditional loving. Still other writers suggest that the sixth layer may be related to soul evolution. It has also been said that mystics and "channels" enter other dimensional perceptions by accessing this energy field.

The seventh layer of the human energy field has been called the *cosmic band* which connects with universal consciousness. It has also been called by some the *ketheric template* or the template for the lower mental body. To work with the ketheric template, effort is directed at restructuring faulty belief systems. Paradoxically, this layer has traditionally been considered as the realm of the unconscious. Carl Jung suggested that once all the material of the unconscious has been brought to conscious attention and has been resolved, then one is closer to being at the entry of soul awareness.

From an energetic viewpoint, the notion of the "unconscious" is no more! It has been a product of social conditioning since the time of Freud. For hundreds of years we have been hypnotized into believing that only one with special training could enter the unknown territory of the "mind." What an interesting illusion! We live in a body, yet cannot access the information it contains? Previously, I stated Jung proposed that all unresolved material needed to be resolved in order for the soul to evolve. I propose that issues which have not served us need our attention for the purpose of "de-emotionalizing." We need to become detached from our experiences, we need a perspective that life's events are not personal. Life's events are simply choice states in which we decide what is worthy of our attention and resolution. Sometimes the mere awareness can release habitual patterns of behavior. In each moment of "now," we need to decide "what is it that I am willing to allow my spirit to be involved with." I can choose a slower path which focuses on the physical or I can choose to release the physical and look at the deeper meaning (or the higher perspective). It is a matter of perception. Does one choose to live life or evolve the soul? But then, if evolution is built into the system as an activity of the whole, maybe this is not the choice state which is available. Perhaps the choice is to determine for ourselves whether we want our lessons in wisdom or in woe. By this I mean, in applying principles of vibration, *what we give our attention to we create.* So if we focus on our problems, it is likely we are learning our lessons by woe. If we look for a deeper meaning, if we intuitively move into the solution and trust in it, then perhaps we are living our lives with wisdom.

As a field of consciousness, an interactive field of intelligence, it is the soul "layer" which yearns to evolve, yearns to dissolve the separation between the individual and God. The yearning of the soul to return to a state of love may cause the other energy fields to move faster. As fields move faster, they start a spin, forming a gyroscope -- moving thoughts and emotions through the etheric template. It seems as if the soul forces conscious attention of all unresolved mental and emotional issues in this life time (or in past–life times).

The moment a troublesome thought comes into awareness, a conscious person will attend to it looking as it were, into the linkages between thought and sensation. It truly doesn't matter if a definitive visual image or an experience comes forth, because some of the information has been stored for so many thousand years, it follows a convoluted path. If the information is negative, if it is in any way disempowering, it needs to be released. Let me say this a bit stronger. *Any negative event, whether it is an innocent comment from another, a perceived misdeed you have performed, or a thought of guilt must be released as it is not truth.* Each of us is whole and complete as we are, we are spiritual beings having a human experience. As we move more and more into the mysteries of the soul, we will come to recognize that we are part of a larger whole. We are but a seed in the heart of Earth; we are the dream of the Divine.

I would like to offer here a model I have developed which I find helpful in working with clearing my own consciousness and raising the vibrational level of my own body. I have borrowed some of the ideas I presented in Figure 34, so that we might begin to make a tie between the states of health and states of "disease." (See Figure 38). I have indicated ascending states of consciousness and the breakdown of consciousness which leads to the dymanic process of "dis–ease." Usually when the physical body breaks down it is because there have been energy blockages in the higher vibrations so that the body is not nourished. In other words, the energy is converted into matter, rather than used for rejuvenation and restoration of the whole system.

It is probably not so important that you remember the names of the subtle bodies, nor what they look like. It is more important to experience the fields, to expand awareness that each of us is more than a physical body.

Those who have suffered traumatic physical illness will often find that at some critical point, they transcend the pain in the physical body, that they have "moved out of the physical realm" and in so doing, have discovered not only the deep emotional realms, but an inner mental strength. For some, tremendous physical pain serves as an awakening to a sense of deep spiritual meaning for living.

DYNAMIC PROCESS OF "DIS-EASE"

CONSCIOUSNESS REFLECTED IN THE ENERGY SYSTEM

↑ EVOLUTION OF CONSCIOUSNESS

↓ BREAKDOWN OF CONSCIOUSNESS

REALMS OF PERCEPTION

KETHERIC TEMPLATE	I BELIEVE MY BELIEFS TO BE TRUE	JUDGEMENT AGAINST GOD	ISOLATION
CELESTIAL TEMPLATE	I LOVE WHAT I BELIEVE	JUDGEMENT AGAINST SELF	DENIAL ADDICTIONS
ETHERIC TEMPLATE	I WILL MY BELIEFS TO BE TRUE	JUDGEMENT AGAINST OTHERS	COMPETITION

REALM OF TRANSFORMATION

ASTRAL BODY	I DESIRE ACCORDING TO MY BELIEFS	REPRESSION INDIFFERENCE	SEPARATION

REALMS OF PHYSICAL REALITY

MENTAL BODY	I THINK ACCORDING TO MY BELIEFS YES/NO DUALITY	STAGNATION FRUSTRATION	DEPRESSION OBSESSIONS
EMOTIONAL BODY	I FEEL ACCORDING TO MY BELIEFS	ANGER, HATE	GUILT
ETHERIC BODY	I AM ACCORDING TO MY BELIEFS	HOPELESS, FEAR, ANXIETY	PAIN
PHYSICAL BODY	I EXIST ACCORDING TO MY BELIEFS	GRIEF, SHAME	**DISEASE**

→ BREAKDOWN OF THE BODY

(Figure 38)

Experiencing the Subtle Energy Bodies

Lie in a comfortable position . . . and begin breathing deeply . . . breathing in the love, pleasure and happiness . . . and breathing out the resistance, negativity and tension . . . scan the physical body . . . letting go of the tension in your feet . . . your legs . . . your knees . . . your hips . . . letting the tension flow out of your pelvis . . . and your stomach . . . out of your upper back . . . and your shoulders . . . breathe in deeply and as you exhale . . . relax your upper arms . . . and your lower arms . . . your hands and your neck . . . let the tension flow from around your mouth . . . your nose . . . your eyes . . . and the top of your head.

Allow yourself to come in contact with the temple of your physical body . . . with the seven bioenergetic fields . . . imagine now, as in a dream state . . . that you can see your body . . . and with your own love and intention . . . you can clear and experience the energy fields . . . see the etheric field . . . through which flow the streams of vitality . . . see the light bluish field floating around you like a shimmering web . . . with sparkling light points which form the energy matrix . . . upon which the physical matter of your tissues are shaped and anchored . . . see your self gently running your fingers over the outside of your body . . . not touching, but keeping your hands about one inch from the body . . . gently, like stroking long streams of angel hair . . . move the energy from the head . . . down around your head and shoulders . . . draping the energy around your hands and fingers . . . moving gently the energy toward the heart . . . then beginning at your toes

. . . gently stroke this field up your legs . . . your hips . . . your back and your stomach . . . to your heart.

Now allow yourself . . . your dream body . . . to re–enter and lie with your physical body . . . and thank this dream being for working . . . with your etheric template . . . then expand into this field with your awareness . . . allowing the starry messages to awaken you to your true self . . . a being of rainbows of light . . . clouds of swirling colors . . . containing symbols and pictures of all that you are . . . sense this wonder now.

Then move beyond . . . expanding your awareness into the emotional field . . . notice the fluid motion of this energy . . . as it swirls around you . . . extending about three inches from your body . . . bathing you in liquid light . . . breath this clear light into the physical body . . . feeling safe and secure . . . loved by yourself and your Creator . . . knowing that your feelings are as important as your body.

Check your breathing again . . . breathing in the light and love . . . expanding now into the mental field . . . a field of energy composed of an even finer substance . . . noting how thoughts move through the emotional fields . . . slowly tracking . . . slowing down the life pictures . . . breathe in the light into your mental body . . . letting go of the need to think . . . to plan . . . to intuit . . . following only the words on the page . . . clear any discomfort or fear . . . that may be tied from your thoughts . . . to your emotional body . . . allowing yourself to remain suspended and safe in a field of light.

Move beyond your mental body into your spiritual body . . . like the negative of a photograph . . . see all the possibilities that you are . . . expanding your awareness into a space . . . nearly two feet around your body . . . at this level, sound as vibration, creates matter . . . imagine transparent lines of energy floating in a field of cobalt blue around you . . . and get a picture of these patterns of your life . . . see if there are issues which resolve around a general theme . . . which you may wish to reinforce or release . . . imagine that with your loving intent . . . you can clear all unresolved issues . . . and do it now.

As you breathe . . . expand into your angelic essence . . . see yourself transformed in a field of shimmering light . . . like mother of pearl sequins . . . radiating from your body . . . like the glow of a candle . . . sense that you are part of the loving connection . . . with all beings . . . with all animals . . . and plants . . . with all parts of the universe . . . see the light and love in all that exists . . . sensing now a deeper connection . . . coming into your awareness . . . your own ability to hold unconditional love . . . for yourself and others.

Stretch now to the edges of your being . . . until you contact your soul . . . a field of energy floating around you . . . encasing your body like a golden egg . . . strong and resistant to penetration . . . containing all of who you are . . . and have ever been . . . move now into the knowing that heaven and earth is contained within . . . there is no authority outside of yourself and your own experiences . . . you are the awareness . . . the angelic service . . . the universal knowing . . . imagine now that you are surrounding this egg shape with tiny shimmering triangles . . . containing the light inside . . . reflecting the love to the outside . . . ask if you choose . . . that this image be retained for your highest good.

Thank yourself for this experience . . . for higher awareness . . . ever present thinking and feeling . . . and be greatful for the structure of your physical body . . . that you have a vehicle . . . with which you can move love . . . from place to place . . . breathe in slowly and gently . . . then make contact with your hands to the chair . . . and refocus your eyes or come into full awareness . . . in your own time.

Some of you may have been very comfortable contacting your subtle bodies, the energy or auric fields; having either a clear sense of each or a visual image. As you do this process repeatedly, you become more and more aware of your subtle bodies. The awareness of our subtle bodies comes in large measure from the reptilian part of our brain, that structure deepest inside the brain. Awareness of these subtle bodies may also be related to what is called "extrasensory" perception. This is a sense that we all have; but through non–use over hundreds and thousands of years, we have forgotten. Many children however are currently retaining these gifts if supported by loving and encouraging parents. Many adults who choose to live life with full intention and mindfulness are discovering and reclaiming these gifts as our natural birthright. However these gifts or skills are acquired or remembered, they must be used; they are so fragile as to be lost again.

Chapter 7 The Chakra System

It is likely you felt comfortable contacting your subtle bodies in the last process, either having a clear sense or a visual image of the layers of the aura or human energy field. As you do the process repeatedly, you will become more and more aware of these subtle energies. The awareness of these subtle energies is processed in the reptilian brain, a structure deep inside the brain. As a primitive skill, visualization is related to extra-sensory perception, perceptions beyond the five senses that give us information about the world around us. My suggestion here is that extra sensory perception and visual or auditory awareness are not new skills; there is nothing magic or mysterious about them. They are part of our multi-dimensional heritage which we have overlooked. In fact, they are some of the oldest skills we have, but they have not been nourished and supported for thousands of years.

Let me pause a moment here and speak about these skills as present in animals, and the pets around us. Most of us are aware that dogs, in particular, have what we call an "uncanny" (from the word canine) sense of hearing. Because they have not evolved to a higher brain with language, they have developed their perceived senses far beyond humans. Dogs not only have a much more acute sense of hearing and smell, but their vibrational sense is more developed. Many dogs can sense thunderstorms coming a long way off not only because they sense the change in the ozone (through smell) but they literally feel the vibration of thunder.

Cats on the other hand have a highly developed sense of extrasensory perception. If you notice, the structure of a cats eye is decidedly different from ours, from dogs, horses and many other species in the animal kingdom. Cats have the ability to see into other dimensions, or other realities as Fred Wolfe would likely suggest. Have you ever noticed that cats sit very still staring, it would seem, in space, looking and tracking "something." From the mystical and esoteric literature we find the suggestion that cats are tracking negative energies which they absorb into their bodies. Some writers have suggested they are able to track disincarnate beings or spirits floating about in our dimension who are not embodied in form. Perhaps this accounts for many of the old cultures where cats played a major role as palace "guards." I think too that it is no accident that the body of the sphinx is cat form.

All children are born with multi-sensory abilities and unless raised by understanding parents, these specialized visual, auditory and kinesthetic skills are lost. As a society, we have has been hypnotized by some of our leading psychologists into believing that imaginary playmates were just something that would go away. Or, we have attributed these playmates to the child's unrealistic perceptions of the world. Few parents have asked their children to be teachers for them, to be willing to share what they see, and to act as translators of experiences which they have on multi-dimensional planes. It is part of our social conditioning for all of us to be alike. Since the model is that "normal" adults don't see and hear things, we condition these responses out of our children. Obviously, for those adults who do see and hear things, the medical community is quick to label them as schizophrenic and place them on heavy doses of medication to quiet the inner visions and dialogue.

When I was in undergraduate school working on my degree in occupational therapy we were cautioned in our psychology classes not to enter into the world of the schizophrenic. Even then, nearly 30 years ago that did not make sense to me. After I graduated and had about six years of experience I was fortunate to revisit these concepts. I obtained a job in a psychiatric facility working with both adults and adolescents, in-patients and those served on an out-patient basis. I had the opportunity to work with many patients with a diagnosis of schizophrenia. At that time however, I ignored my formal training and I engaged in conversations with my patients -- I asked them to describe their experiences. I reasoned that if I couldn't enter their world, I certainly couldn't expect them to enter mine.

As I reflect on those experiences now, I can see that many of the so called "hallucinations" (both auditory and visual) were rich with archetypes. Some were as terrifying as all the Grecian gods rolled into one -- spitting fire and venom and offering the patient little rest from fear, anxiety, and in some cases, real terror. But as I work with these patients now, I work to acknowledge the visions. The focus is on empowering the individual to control the visions, to acknowledge their presence, to ask if there is any wisdom for the Highest Good and then demand that the archetypes return to wherever they have come from. If necessary, I use guided imagery to call in the angels, to call in images of a higher vibrational nature. I council my clients about whom they can share these experiences with and whom they are best advised not to. I recommend that others not try this unless you have a good understanding of the process of imagery and unless you have a background in both physics and metaphysics. My comments are offered here only to give us a different perspective of human potential.

I have a friend who has been able to see auric fields since she was a small child. Not only was she ridiculed by her peers; her parents placed her in an institution. My friend was able to see the auric fields, but she was not having hallucinations. Because she could "see" not only the energy fields, but had visual images of events in the auric field, most people around her were more than willing to suggest that she was, indeed having hallucinations. Fortunately, she had a wise counselor who supported her abilities, assured her of her sanity and advised her that there would be a time when people would want her skills. Now, she not only has her own business "reading" auric fields, but is able to share with people observations of blockages in the field. More than once, her astute observations served to warn a patient of an impending heart condition, or gall stones. What she sees -- are the blockages or disruptions in the energy field, which signal that there is a breakdown of the subtle body, which is a precursor for the development of "disease."

At this point, a logical question might be: "How does the information from the energy field get into the physical body? To find an answer, we look to ancient languages to find a term descriptive enough, yet a word that has been used in other cultures. We find in ancient sanskrit arts the term *chakra* which means energy vortex. Carolyn Myss, an intuitive diagnostician and co-author of *The Creation of Health* with Norman Shealy, M.D., Ph.D. 1988, suggests it may be helpful to recognize that our biography is crystallized into our biology. In other words, the "stuff" of our lives, the emotional, mental and spiritual content changes into matter in the formation of the body. The physical body then, is a printout of consciousness. I think it is easier to think of the body as the "hard copy."

The energy coming into the chakra from the mental and emotional fields corresponds directly with meridian and acupuncture points. Thus, what occurs at the cellular level in the body is a mirror of the energy in the auric field. The energy field holds information that is not only generated by the individual, as I have mentioned, but information which is held in the collective energy fields, or what Jung may have referred to as the collective consciousness. The energy, regardless of origin, gets stored at the cellular level in the physical body, thereby influencing the information which is stored in the DNA. Although I mentioned this in a previous chapter, it warrants repeating.

The suggestion is made here, that since the DNA transmits genetic codes to the offspring, we inherit some of our belief systems at the cellular level, passed on from one generation to the next. Because we are birthed through the energy field of our mothers, we may also pick up her belief systems. Mothers who nurse their babies, also have a bonding of the auric fields, passing on adult information, sensing, and knowing to the infant child. One could therefore speculate that in order to understand individual health, one would also need an understanding of the social issues at the time and in the space into which one is born. This also implies that some of the belief systems we carry are not ours per se, but are the "stuff" of generation upon generation of years gone by. I trust that these comments assist in accounting for some of the unexplained "knowing" that we experience. Some information may come through the process of intuition, some from dreams, and some through interaction of our energy fields.

It is easier to think of chakras not so much as energy vortices, but as fields of evolving consciousness. For the sake of discussion however, detailed information about location and characteristics of the chakras will be given (See Figure 39 and 40).

As we explore concepts of the chakra system, keep in mind that these perceptions might seem a bit different from any other perceptions of health that you may have. That is because, these are reflections of the holographic body. Each chakra, regardless of its physical location in the body, brings information into the body, and projects information from the body into the astral, emotional, mental, and spiritual fields.

The first chakra is located at the base of the spine. It governs the reproductive organs and the sense of smell. In simple terms, it feeds the physical body information relating to the quality of life. Barbara Brennan, suggests disease is a reflection of existence according to belief systems. The first chakra then, reflects the degree to which we feel connected to the earth or are grounded in our activities. This chakra transmits to the physical body thoughts of time, emotional information relating to biological survival, and mental beliefs which come from the culture and the global consciousness. In essence, this data center contains information about how the self is defined in terms of boundaries relative to the culture. As we examine broader social issues such as abortion, rape and homosexuality, these would be referred to as first chakra issues of social consciousness. This chakra deals with the birthing process, the encodement of gender into form and violation of the physical form.

The second chakra is located midway between the navel and the root chakra, slightly to the right. It nourishes the endocrine system and governs the sense of taste. This energy vortex serves to detoxify the functions of the immune system. Mental and emotional energies through this chakra govern love for the opposite sex and maintain the energetic balance between receiving and giving physical, as well as emotional, mental and spiritual pleasure. In essence, it governs the relationships with everything material and non-material. In terms of energy, this chakra "houses" attitudes about control of material possessions and finances. Thoughtforms which are negative in nature are associated with fear and frustration. Louis Hay, author of *You Can Heal Your Life,* 1984, suggests that low back pain is related energetically to lack of support financially as well as emotionally.

From a sociological perspective, the second chakra is concerned not only with sexuality but gender. It is my opinion that, particularly in our Western culture, we have much confusion about these issues. Gender has to do with the sexual expression in the masculine or feminine form. Sexuality is not only tied to sexual expression, but holds information regarding the assignment of socially sanctioned sexual roles. Historically, the perception has been that that males are dominant,

PHYSICAL FUNCTIONS OF THE CHAKRA SYSTEM

LOCATION		ENDOCRINE GLAND	SENSES	PHYSICAL BODY
7	CROWN	PINEAL	EXTRASENSORY	UPPER BRAIN, RIGHT EYE
6	BROW	PITUITARY	INTUITION	LOWER BRAIN, LEFT EYE EARS, NOSE, NERVOUS SYSTEM
5	THROAT	THYROID	HEARING	BRONCHIAL AND VOCAL ORGANS, ALIMENTARY CANAL, METABOLIC BALANCE
4	HEART	THYMUS	TOUCH	RESPIRATORY SYSTEM, CIRCULATORY SYSTEM, IMMUNE SYSTEM (PROTECTION)
3	SOLAR PLEXUS	PANCREAS	SIGHT	DIGESTIVE SYSTEM, STOMACH, LIVER, GALL BLADDER, PANCREAS
2	SACRAL	GONADS	TASTE	REPRODUCTIVE SYSTEM NERVOUS SYSTEM (PARASYMPATHETIC), IMMUNE SYSTEM (DETOX FUNCTIONS)
1	ROOT	ADRENAL	SMELL	SPINAL COLUMN, KIDNEYS, BLADDER

(Figure 39)

PSYCHOLOGICAL FUNCTIONS OF THE CHAKRA SYSTEM

7	CROWN	INTEGRATION OF TOTAL PERSONALITY WITH SPIRITUAL ASPECTS OF HUMANITY, ENLIGHTENMENT
6	BROW	CAPACITY TO VISUALIZE AND UNDERSTAND MENTAL CONCEPTS, ABILITY TO CARRY OUT IDEAS IN A PRACTICAL WAY
5	THROAT	SENSE OF SELF, WITHIN SOCIETY AND VOCATION, ABILITY TO TAKE IN AND ASSIMILATE INFORMATION, SELF EXPRESSION, CREATIVITY
4	HEART	EGO, WILL TOWARD THE OUTER WORLD, FEELINGS OF LOVE FOR OTHER HUMAN BEINGS, OPENNESS TO LIFE, CONSCIOUSNESS, BALANCE BETWEEN SPIRIT AND BODY
3	SOLAR PLEXUS	INTENTIONALITY TOWARDS ONE'S HEALTH, PLEASURE AND EXPANSIVENESS, EGO, WILL TOWARD OUTER WORLD
2	SACRAL	QUANTITY OF LOVE FOR THE OPPOSITE SEX, QUALITY OF SEXUAL ENERGY, ABILITY TO GIVE AND RECEIVE PLEASURE, ABILITY TO REGENERATE, RELATIONSHIPS WITH ALL THINGS PHYSICAL AND NON-PHYSICAL
1	ROOT	QUALITY OF PHYSICAL ENERGY, WILL TO LIVE, SURVIVAL ISSUES, BELIEFS OF THE CULTURE

(Figure 40)

aggressive and perform a social role as providers. Females, historically, were regarded as nurturing, passive and assumed the social role as the caretaker. Not having a clear understanding the differences between sexuality and gender causes problems when sexuality in the fem- inine is expressed in the masculine gender, in which case we would regard that person as homosexual. Having sexuality in the masculine expressed in the feminine gender may be regarded as lesbian. Yet, we have little understanding beyond the labeling, of why energy is expressed in this fashion nor how to deal comfortably with it in a heterogeneous society. Our society is one where the norm suggests that masculine sexuality must be expressed in the male gender, fem- inine sexuality in the female gender.

The third chakra is called the solar plexus center which is located at the navel in the physical body. It governs the pancreas and the adrenal glands, which, from a psychological perspective, support the "flight or fight" response. This center nourishes the sense of sight, and the digestive system. It energizes self-identity and contributes to personal power. Criticism and judgment originate from this center, both of which are directed toward the self and directed toward others. As criticism is directed toward the self, it creates the sense of guilt. Joane Borysenko, author of *Guilt is the Lesson, Love is the Teacher,* 1990, suggests that guilt, which in simplified terms is repressed anger, is tied to the third chakra and expressed through the second chakra in degenerative processes such as cancer. To treat ovarian cancer, then, requires finding the source of the anger, often tied to repression of personal power and self-worth.

The fourth chakra is located over the heart area. It nourishes the thymus gland and the sense of touch. It governs the circulatory functions and the processing of amino acids which are tied to digestion and immune functions. The heart center is the seat of consciousness, the center which unities the upper three chakras with the lower three chakras. The fourth chakra represents balance. Hence we have a different understanding of the old adage -- *as above so below.* In his book *Vibrational Medicine,* Richard Gerber, M.D. suggests openness of the heart is integral to an individuals' ability to express love. This includes both self-love as well as the expression of love towards others. As we open up the fourth chakra we explore what our boundaries are in relation to the social structure (first chakra), our attitudes about releasing these beliefs (second chakra), and how we can get our needs met (third chakra).

The heart chakra is the seat of forgiveness. One hundred years ago, we knew that forgiveness was healthy spiritually, today we know that forgiveness is a real health issue. Forgiveness clears the bioenergetic fields of the one seeking forgiveness. Forgiveness does not have to be an interactive process. As Christ hung on the cross, we are told his last words were *"Father, forgive them for they know not what they do."* While it was a plea from his human side, this single act of love cleared his energy field that his spirit might be free from the form. This act of love was designed not only to clear mankind for all time, but to demonstrate the clearing process through forgiveness. We have not heeded the message nor have our religious practices come to full understanding of these last words. Instead, we struggle as a humanity with the concept of *sin*, which by example, was redeemed (traded in) more than 2,000 years ago!

The fifth chakra is located over the throat area and is associated with the sense of hearing. It stimulates the thyroid gland which is responsible for balance of the nervous and metabolic systems, regulating body heat and muscular control. The fifth chakra governs our sense of self in relationship to society, and to the larger universe of ideas and concepts. It is from this place that true acceptance of self is needed in the alignment of individual will with the Highest Good in ourselves and others. This requires working through judgments against others, and releasing competition as a mode of "being-in-the-world." As such, it governs our ability to assimilate information, thereby affecting our self-expression through acts of creativity.

The sixth chakra is located at the brow and has been referred to in ancient sanskrit literature as the "third eye." Probably no accident that in Grecian myths, those first created, the Cyclops, had a single eye in the middle of their forehead. Energy from this center stimulates the pituitary gland thereby affecting intuition. It regulates the energy in the lower brain or the limbic system and the left eye. It is directly responsible for our ability to visualize objects, events and happenings in our daily lives as we begin to carry out ideas which come to us in moments of insights. As one opens the third eye, one begins to release defensiveness as judgment against the self is dissolved. In releasing these self judgments, one begins to move into awareness of Divine loving, having a sense of oneness with the universe, and connection with all things.

The seventh chakra or the crown chakra is located at the top of the head. Some persons sense a circle of tingling or having a crown placed on their head when energy is coming into the crown chakra. This energy vortex governs the pineal gland and may be associated with higher forms of intuition that we have referred to as extra-sensory or multi-sensory perception. The pineal gland energizes the upper brain or the cerebral cortex and the right eye. Ancient mystics suggest that this center is associated with enlightenment, with Divine knowing, or having a sense of being one with God as an instrument of service. The word "atonement" from ancient literature literally means *at-one-ment.*

An astute reader can read between the lines in looking for methods to work with the chakra system as an energy system and a system of consciousness. For the rest of us, I will offer little hints as we go along. Initially, I stated there were seven chakras. These are the ones I will focus on as these seven represent the state of mass consciousness. In a later chapter I relate the seven major chakras to musical notes of C, D, E, F, G, A, and B. There are five other minor chakras which would correspond with D#, C#, F#, G# and A#. So there really are twelve chakras. Some writers have suggested the lower seven (including the major and minor chakras) relate more to the physical body, the upper five major and minor chakras relate more specifically with higher vibrations used in developing abilities to manifest energy into physical form and to evolve as co-creators of the planet.

For now, let's stay with the major seven chakra

system. In working with the physical body, it is important to first identify the level of the problem. Second it is necessary to work with consciousness at the same or at least one chakra above the level wherein the energy is blocked. For example, to work with pain, stemming from a second chakra imbalance, my recommendation would be to use meditation and guided imagery (associated with the third and sixth chakras). If one were working with the fourth or heart chakra, one could work with the forgiveness process, or would have to work with a higher vibration. That is, at least the fifth chakra vibration (sound) having to do with alignment of will. I will describe in greater detail in another chapter, the healing processes involved.

Sociological Aspects of Chakras

Now let's expand the perception of the chakras as applied to the physical body and examine this information from a sociological perspective as proposed by Carolyn Myss in her presentation to the American Holistic Health Association is 1992. Our in-depth look will focus on the first three chakras as these are concerned with holding spirit in form and the source of most of the cultural beliefs.

The first chakra holds all the beliefs and attitudes peculiar to a particular culture. It is absolutely bound by time and space. Information is not on a continuum, yet linear time is regarded as a "real" psychological construct. Space, as a psychological construct is something out there, outside of us. The first chakra is generally the first point at which people lose power or relinquish it. If marriage is sanctioned by the culture in which you live, then you have to work through this belief system if you are to have the internal strength to pursue single parenting. At the social level, we see that we have not evolved "single parent" social groups, rather we have an institutional group called "Parents without Partners." This reflects a point of weakness, it does not validate the individual who chooses to balance the masculine and feminine energy in the face of single parenting.

All our institutional systems, our government, our schools, and our universities reflect a first chakra energy. In my own case, I challenged first chakra issues many times, not only in selecting to be a single parent, but in my approach to teaching. I felt that learning was not a competitive activity. Grading was not a reflection of student knowledge, but rather validation that the student was able to reflect what the teacher believes. Thus, I had to work through the traditional values of the university system, until I reached a point where I was no longer willing to take on the "ills" of the system.

Usually, with persons who are on a "path of enlightenment," the energy first affects the heart chakra, where we seek to find a deeper meaning to the process of living. We seek more depth in our relationships and a greater satisfaction in our jobs (second chakra). As we bring forth the heart energy, it affects the third chakra, our sense of self-esteem, and our sense of identity. Suddenly, we are struck with the notion that we are making conscious choices not to be like everyone else.

The moment we begin to challenge the belief

systems which are held in the first chakra, we begin the awakening or remembering process. Yet, most of us have not fully cleared the third chakra, so we begin living our enlightened lives in sort of a schizophrenic fashion -- bouncing, as it were, to opening the fourth, the second, the first, then maybe the third chakra. This can have an unsettling effect on our psyche as well as our physical body. In this instance, we may begin withdrawing energy from transforming those first chakra beliefs and contend ourselves with the belief that the system (outside ourselves) will have to change by itself while we continue our inward journey. Or we may decide that the institution is the best site for us to begin the transformative work, assisting others and the system itself to enliven, reform and transform.

There is no easy path to enlightenment, no pattern of chakra opening that is any easier than another. It is helpful however to think of our own personal evolution as a spiral, not necessarily a straight vertical line. We make a little progress forward, take a step back, grow a little, then become reflective. I have found it personally helpful to study the knowledge associated with each of the chakras so I could track the developing of my own consciousness.

I would however, suggest that the first chakra is not usually where we start the evolutionary process because it holds so much of the collective consciousness. The first chakra holds all the beliefs about our wounds. By "wounds," I mean all those beliefs and self statements we use which keep us in need, lack and limitation. Statements such as: "The reason I have not been able to have a successful relationship is because I have been a victim of incest and rape," "The reason I have lost my job is because my employer discovered I was homosexual." On and on and on.

As a society we are beginning to see change in the first chakra level. The television shows are full of people expressing and raging about their rape experiences, displaying their outrage for social misunderstanding of their sexual preferences, speaking of abuse and neglectful parenting. From the viewpoint of consciousness evolution, individuals are using the energy of self-identity (third chakra), to bring forth changes in relationships (second chakra); however they are bumping into beliefs held in the first chakra. While this process may help to undermine rigidity of beliefs held in the first chakra, it does not promote healing. Using the process just described, we are bringing up the garbage and examining it, but we are not taking it out! Unless discussion contains forgiveness (fourth chakra energy), there will be no release. These discussions only serve as a point of re-creation. Not only do we recreate energy blockages in public displays, we are adding as it were, fire to the fuel of the collective consciousness. In a way, the culture doesn't want healing. It feels threatened. If we as individual members of the society were able to really see the pain expressed in the humanity around us, we would begin to create social reform. Healing would become our jobs, our "religion," our passion!

To begin to heal the culture of which we are all a part seems such an overwhelming job, we tend to sit back and let someone else tackle the problem. We idle away our lives waiting for social or legislated reform. And of course it comes. We are now faced with miles and miles of bureaucratic red tape which attempts to regulate and legislate our social behavior. We have laws which prohibit discrimination on the basis of race, sex, and disability. We have laws protecting ourselves from ourselves and from each other as in the wearing of seat belts, and the metal detectors in airports and public schools. Yet the more we mandate and legislate, the more we feel our freedom eroding. Instead, of our world expanding, it seems to shrink, and individuals sink into despair, fear, anxiety and depression.

Reform on the scale that is needed starts with each individual. All change begins on the individual then moves to the collective, not unlike the hundredth monkey paradox. I sense that it is time for us individually to recognize that we *do not need to share our wounds to transcend them.* If you remember previously, I presented the notion that as we talk about our problems, our woundings, we in fact, re-create them again in each present time and space; so public disclosure is not the healing. It is only talking to a larger audience, so that more and more people are getting the negativity! We must remember that our first chakra energy whether it be viewed individually or collectively, has been designed for biological survival. It is concerned with safety, food and shelter--not health. Further, public discussions are likely to deal only with the needs of the first three chakras, not the needs of all seven. We do not yet have enough enlightened beings on the planet to openly discuss our lives and our culture from a spiritual perspective. Our problems are as old as our entire history itself. The problem comes from the separation of church and state (a first chakra energy). Unless there is unity, the imbalance prevents evolution of the culture.

From a sociological perspective, the second chakra is the seat of weaponry. In the personal body, energy is held around the hips and is closely tied to our sexuality. On a planetary or global level, our energy is tied into our defense systems. The Gulf War is a perfect example of holding energy, in terms of oil. In protecting and hoarding resources, the energy backed up in the form of planetary congestion. In this case, the congestion was so severe, it could only be cleared through eruption of third chakra energy, ego pitted against ego, the outbreak of war, and the raping of the land (a first chakra energy).

Our third chakra concerns our individuality, personal as well as collectively. It seems much of this energy has been used to determine how well we match up to our first chakra cultural expectations. Much of our energy is spent trying to answer the question: "Why can't we love?" instead of saying, we can love (a fourth chakra perspective), "How do we (as a humanity, third chakra energy) go about sharing it (second chakra perspective) with the global community?" My experience is that we live only with agenda. Our third chakra energy is all tied up with first chakra energy which blocks expression of the second chakra. The second chakra becomes blocked usually in areas of sexual expression, so we love "if you will protect me." This is evident in our traditional marriage relationships wherein one is the provider and the other maintains the home for both the provider and the one provided for.

While we hardly speak of love in a sociological perspective, much of our governmental defense systems are geared for protection. Our allies take the stance, "if you will protect me" (a second chakra masculine perspective), "then I will share my goods" (nurture and support you--a second chakra feminine perspective). Yet if one single party, a wife, a husband, or a country stands boldly forth and makes a statement to be alone in the world, this changes the victim--rescue cycle. This was much the position Mother Russia found herself in the year 1994. Yet her position was not validated by planetary first chakra energy; those who choose to go alone (individuals or countries) find there is little support for these choices. The world outside instead, adopts a "wait and see" attitude. We have not assimilated into our consciousness that we are all in this together, we share this planet.

Chakras as a System of Consciousness

Before proceeding, I would like to comment on the interplay between the first three chakras. If we are willing to express our third chakra anger and our second chakra fear as it occurs, we would not store or repress our feelings. In this way, we could escape revenge and avoid pain which results from blocked energy in the second chakra. As we begin to examine our first chakra beliefs and attitudes about health and illness, death and dying, then we can begin to claim the third chakra personal power to heal ourselves. As we begin to reconstruct a world not in terms of first chakra biological survival, or second chakra money and power, but according to the third chakra needs of the self, then we can begin healing ourselves. We can begin to heal the society and the culture of which we are a part.

As the energy from the heart chakra opens up the individual and planetary system, it requires us to figure out what it is that we need, individually and collectively. We are out in a space for which there are no guideposts. Our historical positions have been devoted to being very good about using first chakra energy in figuring out what other people need. We have also used second chakra energy to determine why our needs are not being met. But as we bring fourth chakra loving into our awareness, for the first time we are required to use third chakra energy to figure out how to meet our own needs.

From both the individual and the collective perspective, this suggests that we must go through a restructuring of all relationships with the physical world. Primarily we are working through culturally-held beliefs of the first chakra and our second chakra relationships with all things physical and non-physical. This requires a forgiveness, a reaching into the depth of the fourth chakra energy. While this for the most part sounds good mentally, we have difficulty with this at the emotional level. That is because we have used first chakra energy in our perception of forgiveness. *We have made the assumption that forgiveness frees the one who is forgiven. Energetically it is just the opposite, forgiveness frees the seeker of forgiveness.* It does not require validation of the outside world. It requires releasing our spirit from the illusion that we need revenge (a second chakra characteristic) or that we need our wounds to be shared by the collective (first chakra energy).

It seems we loan our spirit to the energy of the first three chakras so that forgiveness of the heart does not even show up. We suffer the illusion that getting even works (the energy of the second chakra) and that guilt works -- as if there were a universal law suggesting that guilt was the natural payback. To be personally empowered in the individual or the collective, means to give up the authority to hold onto the wounding.

From an individual perspective, we cling to the illusion that at one time (and we are not sure when this occurred in linear time,) we were personally empowered. The truth is, *we have never been empowered in physical form in any incarnation cycle.* We have gotten close to becoming co-creators. Yet each time we realized the omnipotence and the power, it was internalized into the ego state. The power was then used to destroy and control. We therefore carry in our consciousness the remembrance of the destruction of Atlantis and Lemuria. It doesn't matter if we are aware of this on a conscious level. Somehow we have gotten the idea that we are returning to a once healthy state. We are not going backward or even in a full circle. We are moving upward in a quantum way. We are in an evolutionary process of challenging everything we know. One of the strongest challenges may be the seduction of taking our lives personally. I know many enlightened beings who claim to be Isis, Horis, Diana, or Athena. While this may be true, it doesn't matter. In this case, the wisdom of the ages may not lead us forward to a place as yet undefined.

To return to the discussion of energy in the lower three chakras, and to return our discussion to present time, it doesn't matter if we came from a dysfunctional family or not, we still have the perception (which we have judged to be "normal") that it is permissible to judge, to remain separate from each other, and to protect our territory. These perceptions no longer accommodate health. They no longer empower us in achieving a global economy, a global sense of shared goods, a global sense that we share this planet.

From my perspective all of us come from dysfunctional families. All of us have been raped at one time or another. If not in the physical, then in the–non–physical. If you have ever had anything taken from you for which you were not asked permission or did not give permission for, then you have been *raped.* So give it up. It is a collective issue. It is no longer personal. If we continue to blame others for the lack of our advancement, wealth or happiness in our lives, then we have missed the entire point of our being here in the first place.

It is time for us to open up energetically and come to realize that when all seven chakras are open we are in tune with the universe and the cosmic laws. It is then that we create our own reality. This implies we use discernment, not judgment; we release expectations and instead turn the possibilities into probabilities. We give up the need to know why things happen as they do. We give up our need to understand God. To move into the evolutionary cycle toward which we are headed, we move into trust, aligning our will with Higher Consciousness. If we remain with our consciousness tied to the lower three chakras we will continue to do all the "Why me?" stuff. We now have the opportunity to look at events from a higher perspective which suggests we say to ourselves, "Oh, this was set up to empower me."

Let me shift gears a moment and look at consciousness on our planet from a "higher" or at least a different perspective. Planet Earth is God's school. It is that place we volunteer to come to learn lessons of love and forgiveness. It is the only place where we can evolve our spirit while in form. Given this as a background for our scenario, imagine two angels speaking one day:

> Each has agreed to come to planet Earth for a period of embodiment. The angels talk between themselves. One angel says: "I have heard that when you are in form you forget about your Divine heritage, you get really stuck in having a need for houses and cars and lots of money and things like that. I don't know what I would do if I ever experienced separation from God. I don't know what I would do if I believed that the things which I could see and touch were real.
>
> The second angel pondered for a moment and made the following suggestion, coming from a point of loving which is what angels do best. "Let's suppose that I discover that you think your house, your money and all your material possessions are the most important things in your life. I love you so much that I will re–awaken you . . . . I know, I will come and I will burn your house down, thereby causing you to loose your shelter, your money and your personal possessions. And if that doesn't do it, I will begin to take away from you those things which you think 'belong' to you, or are attached to . . . like your spouse and your

children. I will appear as your friend and be the driver of a car in a fatal accident. You will, of course be spared. But I am sure that if losing your house doesn't work, taking the things you think you love will work!"

"Now, all we need to do is to find several more angels who are willing to go on earth assignment at the same time and who will agree to become your spouse and your child." And so the scenario closes.

I love this story which came to me in a moment of lucid dreaming. Whatever the origin, it caused for me a shift in perception that has been one of the most powerful I have ever experienced. It suggests that by grand design, far beyond our ability to perceive from a lower chakra position, the things that happen may be arranged for our awakening. If we fail to awaken through contact with one "angel," chances are we have designed many other opportunities throughout our life span. There simply are no accidents! There is both an implicate and an explicate order in the universe.

The trick is we have forgotten.

For the most part, it is our spiritual field which becomes infused with energy so that our mental fields is the first to really "get it." Then it becomes a journey into discipline, to nurture and care for our emotions and our body. We need to care for these bodies until they become congruent with the mental body. We may want to imagine that our ability to create reality depends on the distance from our mind to our heart.

When we face an issue, we must get into the power of the wounding. Carolyn Myss suggests "we must get to the point of scrapping the truth out of the marrow of our bones." In my own case, when I was first diagnosed with a terminal condition, I had to go into the power of that condition. I had to look around and see whether or not I believed it. I had to experience the reality of it, the sheer terror, the unspeakable fear of beliefs held in the first chakra. Was I willing to give up the illness if the truth which was inside me did not match the truth which was held in the cultural perceptive of my first chakra?

I don't want to claim any magical powers nor do I believe that my actions were any other than those directly guided by spirit. It was spirit which empowered me. It was my upper chakras which transformed the lower ones. That enabled me to hold fast to the belief that I was not going to die because I had not yet done what I came to do. Somewhere in the depths of me, I remembered my life's mission. I remembered, although at the time, not consciously and not with full awareness. I did not know how my life would unfold or what it was that I would do. The illness, the search for meaning, the unquenchable curiosity that led me from one college degree to another was all by grand design.

The keys to unlocking those things which we would regard as unconscious have to do with our willingness to alter our perceptions of time. I have a sense that somehow I projected my consciousness into a future space and brought back those revelations. This would account for my absolute knowing. I also have the belief that as I worked internally, I energetically released the energy from the past. I have repeatedly said I did not get into anger. I did not get into fear--these are all second and third chakra issues. I did not have a sense of guilt which is third chakra energy. Yet on a deeper level, these were issues for me, either in this life or in another time and space. I now know that anger and guilt are located in the same place as the energy which nourishes the sense of sight! Yet since I was unaware of the anger or the guilt, I made the personal interpretation that I created the loss of sight so I could look deeper into my own values, my own purpose, my own being. Guilt and anger were for me, likely carried as soul miasms, memory of other times when I failed to recognize the Divine Plan or in some way resisted it. In many ways, it doesn't matter. The only thing that matters in this lifetime is whether or not I would find, create, or take advantages of opportunities to reconnect with the God–source, to find a deeper meaning for being, to discover that there is a profound inter–connectedness in all things. However the scenario would have unfolded, the process is all that is important. In the process, I created a different identity, one which was connected to the universe instead of one that was separate from it; one which was deeply tied to earth. I created an identity in which I became aware there is no separation between any of us. In the process of forming a new identity, I used the higher energetic fields to transform the lower ones. I used visualization, the energy of the sixth chakra, and with a passion (of the heart) sought relentlessly to find truth for me (a fifth chakra energy).

Holding onto the single belief that I was not going to die, I was then able to take a second step. I looked at whether or not I had any energy invested in the illness. After mind searching and soul searching, I decided that I did not have a need for secondary gains (at least that I was aware of). I made the decision to live my life outside that "as if" zone -- the zone of "we will treat you *as if* you have Multiple Sclerosis." I transcended the second chakra energy of validating myself according to the relationship that I was having with the disease process. As I surrendered to the issues that faced me, I shifted the energy from the lower to the higher chakra centers. That did not mean that I was without vulnerability. No indeed.

As the time of my blindness, I hadn't learned that vulnerability is related to energy in the higher centers. It is the entry into the Heavens, the no–*thing*–ness, a place without form -- the void. At the moment I felt vulnerable and cried out for help, I received it. From the perspective of where I now sit, I regard my ex–husband as the angel who refused to buy into my weakness. His statement: "It's your problem kid" was an empowerment statement. It gave me the strength to continue with the internal growth, transcending the physical, breaking the blockages of energy in the form.

There is another point here I want to make about the de–wounding process. Every time we use our wounding as power for lift off, we must tell ourselves not to do it! The temptation will always present itself for us to return to the collective, to say, "I can't do that because I have a terminal condition." "I should have an abortion because that is what has been recommended for me." Instead, I began the process of living, of energizing every moment. The moment of pondering on the toll bridge whether or not I should use pennies or a quarter was a moment of playfulness. It was en–*spirit*–ed. That moment brought something new into the system. The process is not nearly as difficult as one might envision. Do something different, eat dinner for breakfast, put peanut butter in your soup, take a different route to work each day, contemplate the best shape for an elephant!

Once we start the de–wounding process, rising above the energy blockages of the first, second, and third chakra it can have the illusion of a lonely journey, (unless we can believe we journey with guides, masters, and with the angels themselves)! It means we may have to leave our physical relationships because they are built on wound technology. It is my sense that wound mates are built into our lives for disintegration.

If we are to grow into our spirit, the journey begins with honesty. We need to be willing to say what it is that is in our heart. And it doesn't matter whether or not anyone outside of us changes! We don't need to have our wounds validated, or our feelings, we only need to have the space to express them. It is always our choice what we choose to do about them. We must determine for ourselves how much energy is used for funding ourselves and how much energy we have borrowed from others. If we come to the point of recognizing that most of our energy comes from other's then, it is time to turn the tables. If we are not willing to take this internal look, then we will suffer disappointment, abandonment, betrayal and separation. And it is of our own making.

It is time for each of us to determine personally for ourselves "What is worth responding to that does not cost us our spirit?" Several years ago, I made a very difficult decision. I decided I needed to leave the university setting because I didn't have enough time for all the first chakra wounding. I also gave up the opportunity for marriage as I was not willing to have a relationship with a mate who was not willing to move past the first three chakra issues. I wanted health! I chose health! I chose to be of service. But I would not loan my spirit to another, if that person was still coming from a place of "needing." If however, anyone is willing to recognize his/her own Divinity, then we can move into healing -- the relationship of healing. We can move into sacred time and space in which I serve as a mirror for the other, and the other serves as a mirror for me, out of which each of us will grow.

Perhaps because I am a strong visual processor and learn as much from pictures as from words, let me see if I can offer several diagrams for the process of healing and interacting. As you can see in Figure 41, all of our life experiences contribute to a state of "self."

PERSONALITY MATRIX

(Figure 41)

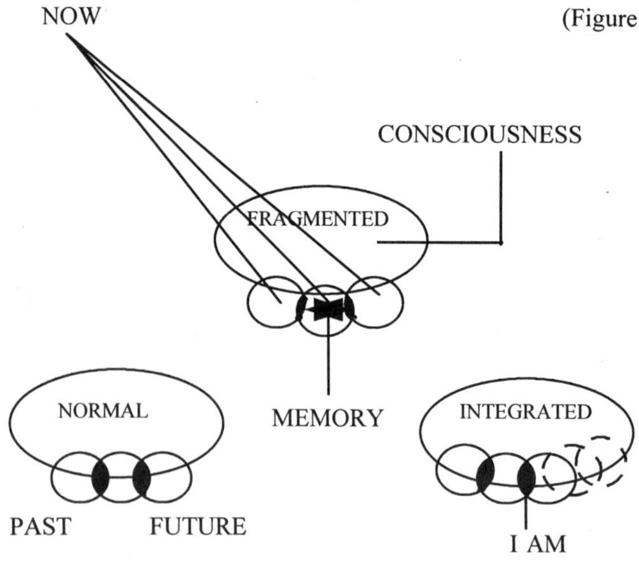

The self is made up of the archetypal echos and genetic predispositions of the past, our instincts and emotions, present and accumulated sensory input which contribute to cellular memory and or bodily needs at any given moment in time. Through the interactive computing of the hemispheres of the brain we send out emotions, thoughts and perceptions which create a state of consciousness we might refer to as the projected self.

In each moment of "now," our "normal" state of consciousness is fragmented. The bits and pieces of our selves are unrelated. As we begin to recognize our deeper connections with self, we begin to recognize that the composite now is made up of both future as well as past images of self. As we begin to integrate this awareness, we literally change the field of consciousness; we create what has been referred to as the "I AM" presence.

Let me back up for a moment. In a fragmented state of consciousness, we may be able to say to ourselves "I am the infant who was held in my mothers arms, the blushing teenager who thought she would never get a date, the risk-taking young woman who ran off to Japan to marry a sailor my parents had never met, a woman who had so little understanding of commitment and intimacy." As we begin to look at the wholeness of our lives, to awaken to the mysteries we may gain another perspective (See Figure 42). I may then be able to be grateful for selecting parents who were kind and gentle, I may bless the events of my innocence during my teen years; I might unravel the notion that intimacy and committment were largely a personal issue not an interactive one. If I had little idea of how to relate to myself, how is it that I could have envisoioned that I would relate to another?

As I begin to look at my pictures of physical reality I begin to recognize that everything that I have, I have obtained for my own awakening (or my own separation/isolation) depending on the choices I have made along the way. If I start each day with a moment of clear intention that I will be loving and gentle; understanding and curious, then I have to trust that each

QUANTUM SELF

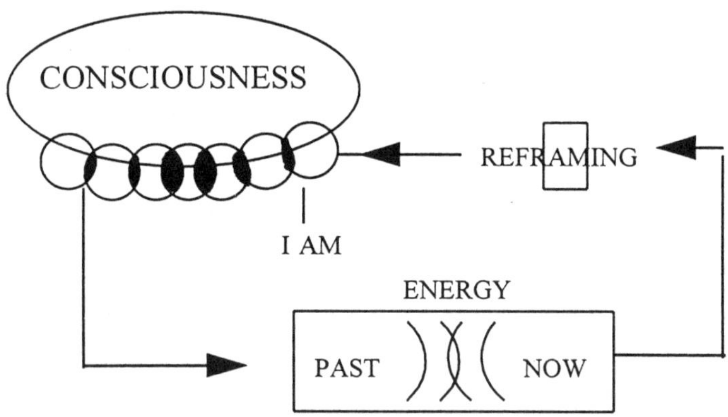

(Figure 42)

decision was made with some sort of mindfulness in that moment. Most of us do not jump out of bed in the morning with an intent that says, "Today I will screw up everything I touch. I will make myself unhappy and anger those around me." This then gives us some power for beginning to look at all of our life events in a different way. We begin to look at events not so much in terms of good or bad but in terms of wonder. "Oh, wow! I really did almost loose that job over a piece of lunch meat! What an absurdity!"

As we string together the events of our lifes, we begin to lighten up. Sometimes using longer and shorter strings between the events, so that we not only ponder the event but the space between! I have often written down all the important events in my life on several index cards. Then I have shuffled them and dealt them out in a random order. Then imagined how it might have been if it had been ordered differently. No matter how many times I do this, I begin to notice that everything occurred exactly in the order in which it needed to occur. I can work backward in time. If I hadn't had children, perhaps I would not have found the joy of nurturing. If I hadn't had an illness, I wouldn't be able to challenge my beliefs as a way of life. If I hadn't married the man I did, I wouldn't have discovered my own inner strength. On and on and on.

If we are willing to work this way, we may be able to claim more of who we are in a single moment of time. This then enlarges the overlap between the segmented parts of self. The greater the selves are related, the larger the "I AM" viewpoint. From a vibrational perspective, claiming all of who I AM sets up a field of coherent energy. This means that when I can be mindful enough to "see" the relationships between the events in my life and my interpretations *of them* (my perceptions) and my reactions *to them* (my emotions), I change the resonance in the entire holographic mind body I AM presence. I, in turn, create a larger memory of who I am. But I must then project that memory into a future time, so that I can recognize who I AM when I get there.

Let me see if I can say this another way from a vibrational standpoint. The weaving of the self happens moment by moment as illustrated in Figure 43. According to Danah Zohar, author of *The Quantum Self,* 1990, as the wave functions of the past overlap with

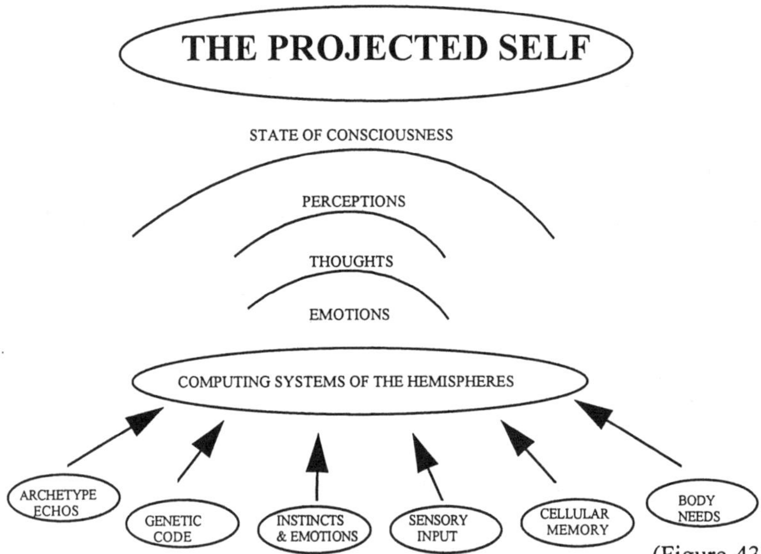

(Figure 43)

wave functions of the present self (or present self to future self), they create quantum memory -- not just cellular memory of facts, events, images or experiences. But rather a *lived* memory, the reaction, interaction, perception and interpretation of each of those events; usually known only to the individual. For example, in working with head injured patients, I have worked with some who cannot tap into cellular memory of the past. That is, they cannot remember specific dates, times, or events. But they can tap into quantum memory, the "stuff" between the events. And it is this "stuff" which needs recognition -- the ability to respond with humor, with gentleness. The wisdom of the reactions to life events are still there! To work with these clients, I think the emphasis need not be on re-creating an entire physical history, but rather the history of the quantum self. My experience suggests that when we say such things as "Can you share with me how you have a sense of knowing that you are loving" will call forth the deeper cellular memory.

Just as meaning is encoded in our lives, it is encoded in our language. You may have noted in Figure 42, that in the process of examining our life events, we engage in a process called "refrAMing"; in this process the intent is to claim the I "AM" self. In Figure 44, I have indicated that it doesn't matter if two life events of a single individual are examined, or if two people interact. In the sacred space between the events, there is the opportunity to release the fear, doubt, anger and guilt. Out of that, comes a different image of self -- a self capable of joy, peace, harmony and love. In the quantum interchange, both events are transformed with new meaning.

I suppose it's time I "fess up." I have an unusual picture of healing, of health. I can identify for a person how the energy is being dispersed in the body, where the blockages are and what the issues are that need to be resolved. Beyond that, unless the individual is willing to journey with me, I am not willing to deny their Divinity by saying, "I will take this experience from you." On the other hand, I will be present as each chooses to go through their de-wounding. I will ask: "What is the meaning of this illness, this experience for you."

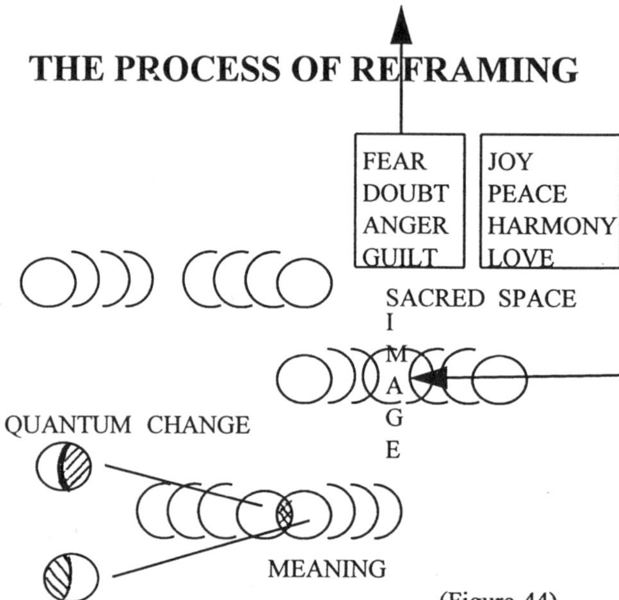

(Figure 44)

But my goal is to stay up in altitude, to work above the waist, if you will. My gifting is to assist in bringing spirit into form. I agree with Carolyn Myss that wisdom lies above the waist, woe below. Angels talk this way you know. I will ask if you want to be separate from your experience or move into the depths of it? Do you want guidance in wisdom or in woe?

These sound like bold statements to make. Perhaps I mean them to be so. They came from a very unusual "gifting." Several years ago when I decided to take unpaid leave from the University to conduct my own workshops on consciousness and health, I discussed these ideas with a friend in Detroit. She in turn talked about me with a friend in New York who had a friend in Arizona with cancer. (The serendipity with which spirit weaves us together continues to amaze me). As it turned out, Susan, the lady from Arizona, came to me for individual sessions. She and her friend, Mary, from New York came and the three of us worked for nearly ten hours a day for four days. We worked with belief systems, with empowerment, with removing the blockages from Susan's body. We talked of God and the encodment of spirit into form. We sang and danced. I grabbed the stereo, put on the William Tell Overture and we laid on our backs under the summer sky and directed the cosmos. We developed a rare kind of intimacy (into-me-you-see) that transcended time and space. We began to explore what love, real unconditional loving was all about. Loving that regards the perfection, the Divinity; love that does not fix or want for more to be brought into the moment. Out of our moments together, each of us experienced a quantum change.

Following our time together, Mary sent me a note that the sessions brought she and Susan even closer. There had been a reunion. They had been college roommates, but separated by time and distance. Susan called me only once; to report that the pain in her back had begun to increase; evidently the cancer had begun to metastasize. Then within only another month, Mary informed me that Susan had died. I grieved and I wept. I wondered why her body had not responded. Had I done every thing I could have? I had no recourse I would think of other than to look for answers inside. It was not that Susan came to me in spirit form, rather the information came intuitively, through thought form. However I can describe it, it was clear to me the nature of our time together. The insights came with so much love and tenderness that tears ran down my cheeks. The sessions were not to heal the body, but to heal the separation between spirit and God. Once the separation was healed, there was no longer need for the form. Susan was released into the angelic essence I always perceived her to be.

Susan was such a gift of courage to me. Throughout our sessions, she willingly talked about her experience with chemotherapy that left her without hair. Her concerns with self image as she started to wear a wig. Her willingness to share with her children (whose pictures held a prominent place on the table where we conducted our sessions). As Susan was one of my first clients I had elected to work with in this way, my sense is that she came to be my guide. To lead me through the process of developing a deep caring relationship -- to reach beyond the confines of the illness. I think it takes a very great soul to have selected that kind of mission. I have no doubt that the blessings were equal for all of us.

Out of this experience, I have concluded that each of us is perfect just the way we are. It is only that we have forgotten. The mission of the healer is to love, to allow each to grow, to reconnect with God, from whom all healing comes. So I share now, what really works for me. The tools of my trade are two things: Prayer and Meditation. Prayer is to ask for guidance; meditation is to listen for the answers, to be willing to follow those impulses, however slight they may be. I think too that it is time to elevate the nature of our prayers. It is unnecessary for us to pray from a first chakra position "show me the way" (a survival issue), because we are always under guidance. We need to learn to pray from a higher perspective, from the fourth, fifth, sixth and seventh chakras. We simply can't sneeze or go to the bathroom without an angel knowing it! So we need to pray for guidance in connectedness (a fourth chakra position), for courage (in the willingness to speak the truth, a fifth chakra position). We need to ask that our visions and our moments of enlightenment be transformed into dense earthly feedback (a sixth chakra position). We need to surrender to the Universal wisdom around us (a seventh chakra position).

Now, for us to share in a personal experience of how energy is expressed in the body, let us go on another journey; this time into the chakras. Into levels of consciousness. A journey to revitalize the body, release emotional trauma, to begin the process of awakening us to our own Divinity.

Balancing the Chakra Energy

Lie comfortably on the bed or on the floor . . . allow yourself to enter into deep breathing . . . breathing in all that is good . . . pleasurable and loving . . . breathing out from the depths of you . . . all that is good, pleasurable and loving . . . breathing in to the count of three . . . and out to the count of 9 . . . into the count of three . . . out to the count of 9 . . . relaxing the body.

You are going to visualize the seven sacred energy centers of your physical body . . . these energy centers are housed in your etheric . . . astral . . . emotional . . . mental . . . and spiritual bodies . . . which monitor the frequencies of energy flowing . . . in and out of the physical body . . . when you imagine the opening of a chakra . . . you are bringing energy into conscious awareness . . . thus preserving and maintaining health in your physical, emotional, mental and spiritual bodies.

Begin with the upper two chakras which are associated with your mental body . . . the crown chakra is located on the top of the head . . . stretch your consciousness to visualize a flower . . . with as many as 960 outer petals with 12 inner ones . . . emitting a violet or white light . . . imagine this white or violet light flooding your crown chakra . . . opening your upper brain and right eye . . . imagine your pineal gland and the sense of "knowing" that goes beyond all senses . . . allow yourself to feel an interaction of your total personality . . . with all of life . . . see what he great painters of the Renaissance saw . . . as they painted the angels, saints and Christ himself . . . see the halo (or hallowed glow) around your own head . . . see the open crown chakra . . . say to yourself . . . "I AM God's wisdom in action . . . the illumination and understanding of the universal laws of creation . . . the discerning presence of my Higher Self . . . manifesting the right choices in my life and all situations . . . for my Highest Good . . . and for enlightenment of the planet."

Now move to the brow chakra which is located between the eyes . . . it consists of 96 petals like a flower . . . imagine now opening this chakra . . . allowing an indigo light to swirl clockwise . . . and have a sense of your lower brain . . . your left eye . . . your ears . . . nose . . . and nervous system . . . embrace your ability to see beyond the beyond . . . beyond the physical illusions . . . seeing real pictures . . . either symbolic or literal . . . see your connection with the earth . . . the planets . . . the solar system . . . sense, see hear and breathe in the wonder of the star that you are . . . the Light emanating from the heart of God . . . say to yourself . . . "I AM opening myself as a visionary . . . and from the stillness of my being . . . I AM on a journey into inner realms . . . discovering the hidden mysteries of life . . . through focusing my energy . . . I AM willing to unleash all the mystical powers of my being . . . opening my ability to see and hear the power and energy . . . behind all creation . . . I AM accepting of my spiritual energy within every cell . . . atom . . . and organ of my body."

Before moving on . . . breathe in the white or violet light of the crown chakra again . . . and the indigo light of the brow chakra . . . allowing this light to fill your awareness.

Now focus attention on the middle three chakras . . . these have been associated with the emotional body . . . place your attention on the throat chakra . . . imagine 16 petals opening with a flooding of blue light . . . sense your willingness to speak the truth . . . putting aside all else . . . hear the whispering of the pines . . . hear the birds urging your awakening . . . hear the sounds of angelic wings unfolding about you . . . flood your awareness with the smells of honey . . . smell the budding of the lilacs in spring . . . the climbing roses of summer . . . the sweet smell of burning leaves in fall . . . the crisp clear smell of falling snow . . . take in and assimilate the seasons of your life . . . and through this have a profound sense of self . . . breathe in the clearest blue of a summer day that you cam imagine . . . filling the throat and flooding into the body . . . giving you a sense of very unique functions you have chosen for participating in the healing of the planet and of mankind . . . say to yourself "I AM expressing the full potential of my creative being . . . allowing myself to flow as freely as a river . . . I AM learning to communicate my ideas . . . and I AM willing to align myself with all that is Divine . . . knowing that I can fully trust myself to protect all that I AM . . . and claim all the power of the being that I AM to fully serve and be playful with all of humanity.

Now move to the middle chakra . . . that energy center in your body . . . which unites Heaven and Earth . . . as above so below . . . imagine now your heart chakra . . . opening it with a flooding of emerald green light . . . opening the 12 petals . . . opening awareness to the uniqueness of this chakra 12 petals reflecting the number of planets in the universe . . . the number of bodily systems . . . the total number of chakras we are evolving into . . . the number of Christ's disciples . . . breathe green light into your heart . . . into the blood and the circulatory system . . . into the thymus gland at the back of your heart . . . which is the opening to the doorway of Higher consciousness . . . sense the profound feelings of love you feel for all other human beings . . . feeling the connection with each whom you come in contact with . . . experience the oneness with creation . . . feel your tie with Mother Earth . . . ask her for forgiveness for the damage you may have contributed to . . . consciously or unconsciously . . . send healing love from your heart . . . back to Mother Earth . . . for the greening of the planet . . . and say to yourself . . . "I AM filled with love and acceptance of all my human qualities . . . as well as my Higher Self . . . I love the earth for the opportunity . . . to learn . . . to serve . . . to master the illusions . . .I AM loving and accepting of my spirit within me . . as I open myself farther each day . . . knowing I AM expanding as I express more love to myself . . . and the world around me."

Before moving on . . . allow your awareness to fill with the blue light of the throat chakra . . . and the green light of the heart chakra . . . breathe in and hold the green and blue light . . . allowing that light to fill and surround your physical body.

The lower three chakras are associated with energy in your physical body . . . move now down the body to the naval or solar plexus chakra . . . sense the energy vibrating through this chakra emitting a yellow color from 10 petals . . . imagine now a flooding of yellow light in this area which sends energy to the stomach . . . liver . . . gall bladder . . . and the nervous system . . . sense your own thinking abilities . . . your own great pleasure and expansiveness . . . and spiritual wisdom . . . be conscious that you are one with the universe . . . breathe in the yellow light and state your intention to care for your body . . . taking care of physical . . . emotional . . . mental . . . and spiritual needs . . . say to yourself "I AM at peace . . . with myself and the world around me . . . I AM radiating energy from the peaceful center of my being . . . harmonizing and healing all my emotions . . . embracing all my feelings with loving acceptance . . . recharged in the loving embrace of Nature and her healing elements."

Now move your awareness down the body finding the sacral chakra which is located in the spleen . . . just below the solar plexus . . . imagine that it has 6 petals pouring out a radiant orange color . . . sense your reproductive organs . . . the giving and receiving of physical, emotional, mental and spiritual pleasure . . . allow your awareness to fill with clear orange color . . . say to yourself . . . "I AM the harmonizing presence . . . balancing my creative male aspect with my feminine receptive aspect . . . I allow myself to experience the balanced union of these poles within me . . . as an unfolding cosmic dance of creation . . . I AM whole and complete with my sexuality . . . I love and embrace all the feelings and emotions . . . that surface from loving and accepting . . . I AM in harmonic union with Heaven and Earth.

Finally, imagine the root chakra which is located at the base of the spine . . . feel the warm red color in this area . . . opening the 4 petals of this chakra . . . allowing red color to flow through your entire spinal column and your kidneys . . . open yourself to your kinesthetic feelings . . . like feeling the shivers . . . or hair standing on end . . . feeling energy running through your body . . . sense your will to love . . . sense and hold the warm red light . . . feeling the vitality . . . sense that your energy is grounded . . . centered and firmly connected to the center of the earth . . . and say to yourself . . . "I AM claiming my birthright to maintain a healthy balanced relationship with my body . . . and the earth . . . I AM using my lie force creatively . . . to receive all the nourishment and abundance that I need . . . I AM claiming my full abilities to act as co–creator of all that I need physically as well as spiritually . . . through the purity of my intentions" . . . scan your body again . . . breathing in deeply . . . breathing in red, orange and yellow light into your physical body through the lower three chakras.

Sink deeply into the wonder of all that you are

. . . flooding your awareness with red . . . orange . . . yellow . . . green . . . blue . . . indigo . . . and violet or white light . . . light beams representing the luminosity, the vibrant being that you are . . . knowing that you are light and are connected to the world . . . knowing that in highest truth you have never left the heart of God.

Chapter 8 **Astrosonics**

> "Study the micro and you'll find the macro reflected in it. Or if we study ourselves thoroughly, we may just find the design of the universe reflected in us" (Itzhak Bentov, 1988).

The term "astrosonics" comes from astrology and sound. It is the study of vibration and its relationship to consciousness, speaking in the broadest possible terms. More specifically, astrosonics is the study of the relationship between planetary motion to the earth rendered as sound vibration (Helius, 1989). Planetary cycles are measured in cycles per year, but we hear in cycles per second, so the octaves of sound have to be raised to audible frequencies. It is just another way of extending our understanding of consciousness into the universe. If we follow the line of thinking suggested by Deepak Chopra, that we cannot separate ourselves from the rest of the cosmos, then our attention is drawn into understanding the nature of our entire universe using a different perspective. Like thinking, personality and consciousness of the heart, the astrological influences also follow a four quandrant model. I offer perceptions of astrology as one method for understanding the evolution of consciousness.

If we envision a circle divided horizontally in half, we would see divisions between the Sun and the Earth (See Figure 45). Raymond Merriman, author of *Evolutionary Astrology,* 1991, suggests that the Sun-Earth relationship is very special to all living beings. It affects how living beings organize their daily activities, from sleeping patterns to eating, working and reproduction.

DIVISION OF THE DAY

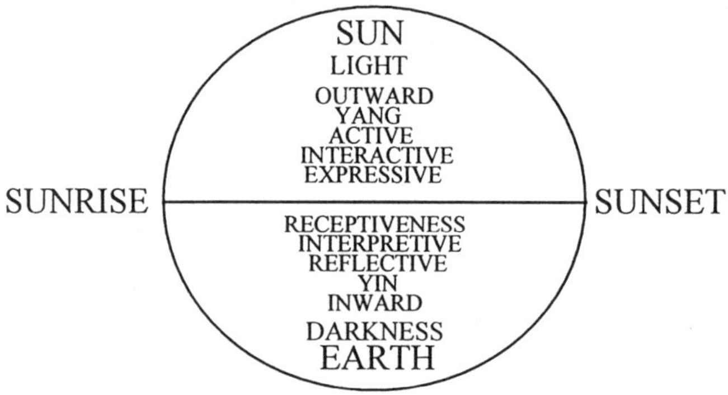

(Figure 45)

The Sun–Earth cycle is associated with lightness and darkness. The symbolism of light refers to the outer physical world while the symbology of darkness refers to that of the inner world. Concepts of light and dark also correspond with ancient Chinese concepts of Yang and Yin. In Oriental philosophy, Yang is active, while Yin is reflective. Some have referred to the Yang as masculine and the Yin as feminine. Hence from Grecian mythology we find reason for the myth of Father Sky and Mother Earth. Activities during the daytime may be loosely interpreted as daily activities which are interactive, nightly activities are interpretive. I suggest that there is also a division between expressiveness and receptiveness. Similarly, the energy is either directed outward (as from the sun) or inward (from the moon).

Generally speaking, those born between sunrise and sunset have a sense of being self-actualized, through interactions with others and through activity in the outer world. Those born between sunset and sunrise are born during the dark part of the day. When the individual receives feedback from others as to what he or she is most like, there may be a sense of surprise, often denial. The "real" me is something that is known only from an inner, subjective point of view.

In addition to concepts of Sun–Earth, or an outward/inward orientation of consciousness, in astrology there is a division between the East and the West. In my metaphorical model, it is represented by the division between right and left. If we look at this model, the right would be associated with the East, the left with the West (See Figure 46). In the natural order of the

DIVISION OF THE HEMISPHERES

(Figure 46)

day, the East is where the Sun rises first, it is that half of the day when the Earth is coming from darkness into greater light.

We could propose that, from an evolutionary perspective the West is evolving toward the East. Or perhaps it is remembering, as civilization of the world occurred in an East–West progression. Perhaps we are just coming full circle--reclaiming the wisdom of ancient civilizations.

In the West, we traditionally hold a perception that "things happen to me" or "I am a product of my environment." Eastern philosophies have a more inward approach. Their collective consciousness holds that each individual makes the life events happen. Their orientation would be "I create the events in my environment." This difference in world views is directly related to different perspectives of the "cause/effect" dichotomy. Similarly, Western cultures seem to spend more energy in responding, often to crisis events, whereas Eastern cultures would hold that their actions initiate events.

Generally speaking, those born between midnight and noon, when the Sun is in the Eastern Hemisphere, find the self through acts of creativity and in understanding that he or she is the cause behind what one experiences in life. On the other hand, those born between noon and midnight, when the Sun is in the Western hemisphere may find that the realm of individual experience is associated with the consequences of its prior actions. One's life may appear to be a series of events brought on by external circumstances which the individual perceives to be beyond his or her control. Life challenges may seem to be repetitive until the individual learns acceptance, and learns to reflect on life's activities and the value of inner control.

As a side comment, imagine how these simple perceptions might affect our understanding of psychology. As we find our deeper connection with the universe, it might be that we could abandon the need to fix each other and move into recognition that we are all part of a grand plan -- more importantly, that the plan for each of us is different. The focus of therapy could be to become more in tune with the universe than with those around us.

As we combine these two models into a four quadrant model, we find that the top of the chart is associated with Mid Heaven or Noon, while the lower chart is associated with the North Node or Midnight (See Figure 47). Sunrise is on the left and sunset on the right. From an evolutionary perspective, movement through the daily cycle matches that of the life cycle--moving from conception through birth, to midlife and to death.

If we were to use this illustration as an emerging model of universal consciousness, we might surmise that we are moving from a perception of darkness into the light. We are finding the balance between Yin and Yang. As the earth moves from greater darkness, through lesser darkness and back into the light, the living organisms are ending their resting state. I propose this is true for individuals as well as for global consciousness. If this model is applied to planetary consciousness, it may be implied that we are moving from a state of void into gestation (from quadrant IV to quadrant I). We are in preparation for a new evolutionary cycle. As the darkness decreases, a state of awareness emerges, a state of en-*light*-enment occurs. In this evolving shift in consciousness there is focused

CARDINAL SECTIONS
OF THE ASTROLOGICAL CHART

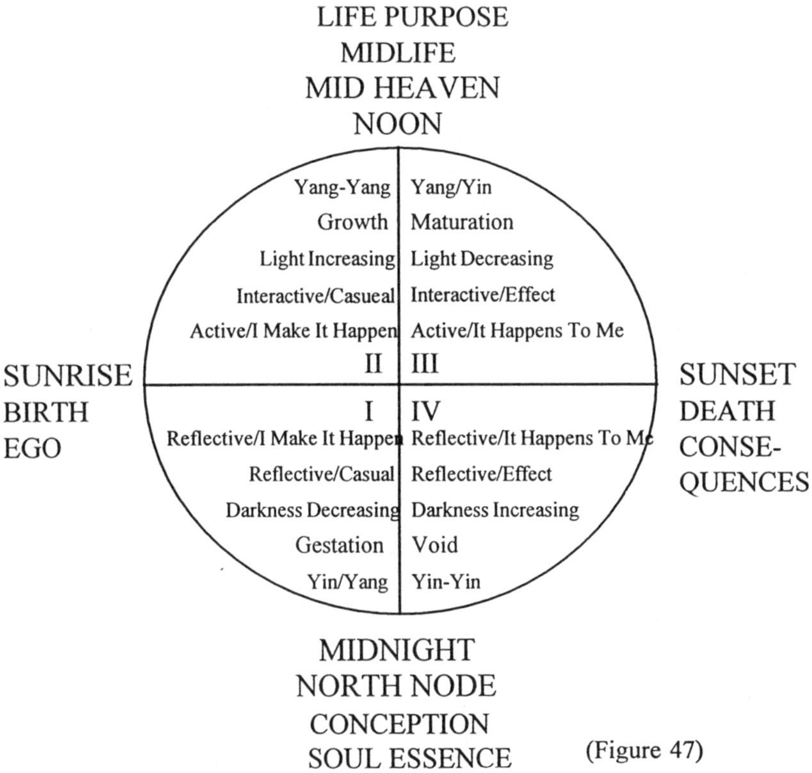

(Figure 47)

attention, like the basketball player focusing all his energy in directing the free throw ball into the net. It is a time of meditation, like the actor rehearsing his lines behind the stage. It is time to go deeper and deeper. Allow more relaxation. Slow the movie down. Enter the state in which there is nothing--no-*thing!* And in that state, there is nothing that is outside of you. There is nothing save that which you create. This is the beginning place of peace, of bliss, of grace. This is the place where we are God-seeded, wherein we are not separate from anything in the physical universe.

Now let's take one other look at an astrological model (See Figure 48). If we focus on each quadrant which might be associated with birth, we would notice in quadrant I that the path of self realization begins with an *awareness.* That small inkling of awareness of connectedness moves into a knowing as each individual claims his or her power as an awakened self-powered

PATH OF SELF REALIZATION

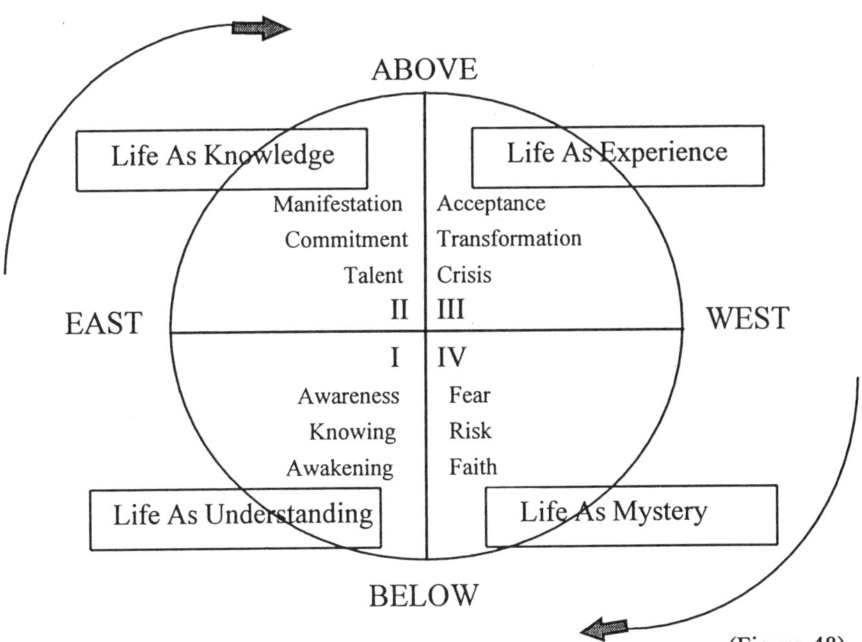

(Figure 48)

being. From the soul level, life is perceived as understanding.

In quadrant II, where the path of self realization is viewed from the perspective of life as *knowledge,* each individual would take that God-seeded talent, infuse it with commitment and move into the realm of manifestation. This individual would be fully involved as a *causal agent in bringing forth change.*

Individuals birthed under the influences of quadrant III, may find that their path of self realization comes *at the moment of crisis.* It may be a crisis of health, loss of job, childhood abuse or a whole host of other causes. However as one moves through the crisis, they may experience a transformation and move into full acceptance of the self. In this instance we might refer to their pre-destined path of self realization emerging from a view of *life as experience.*

Finally, in quadrant IV, those born between sunset and midnight, their path of self realization may come from the *resolution of fear.* They may have had to take risks, to move beyond cultural perspectives, even individual beliefs -- following a path of faith in the process of self realization. For these individuals, the life view may be one of *unfolding mystery.*

We see from this brief journey into astrology that there is an emerging pattern here, far beyond the mere amusement of the daily tabloids. The entire galaxy affects the consciousness of the planet. So we look deeper now for the "wisdom of the spheres." To understand the macroscopic or astrological view of how vibration affects the body, it is necessary to go again back in time.

In general, the propositions by Pythagoras, Copernicus, Kepler and Hans Kayser suggest that these scientists were able to make rudimentary measurements of the distances of each planet from the sun. Kepler suggested that the extreme points of the elliptical orbit of each planet remains nearly constant. He then used these constant points to create the numeric formulas that constitute the Diatonic Tempered Musical Scale that we know today. For example, Mercury is 36 million miles from the sun. When this number is doubled twice, it is 144, and Mars is approximately 143 million miles from the sun. When the distance from Mars to the sun is doubled twice, the number is 484, and Jupiter is approximately 483 million miles from the sun. So it appears that there is some kind of implicate order in the movements of the planets and the ratios between those distances which match the musical scale. The conjecture might be that the movements of the planets constitute an octave of sound and that the human brain or the mind/body complex in some way replicates these patterns.

Let's look at precisely what Pythagoras found. Counting backward from earth to the outermost sphere of fixed stars, Phythagoras noticed a fixed musical interval as follows:

> From the earth to the moon was a whole step, from the moon to Mercury a half step; Mercury to Venus another half step; from Venus to the sun was a minor third, which is equal to three half steps; the sun to Mars, a whole step; Mars to Jupiter, a half step; Jupiter to Saturn a half step; Mars to Jupiter, a half step; Jupiter to Saturn a half step; and from Saturn to the

sphere of the fixed stars another minor third (James, 1993).

Thus, the musical scale, the so called Pythagorean Scale was C, D, Eb, E, G, A, Bb, B. If you were to play this scale, it would not sound very musical!

The seventeenth century astronomer Johannes Kepler, attempted to find a cohesive unity in the universe. He studied the planets in terms of their mathematical relationships to physical man. According to Jamie James, author of *The Music of the Spheres,* 1993, Kepler was not especially interested in the motions of a few planets and stars, but wanted to explain the very structure of the cosmos. He tried to make sense of the planets, their distances and velocities and wondered whether it was accidental there were just six of them, (at that time the seventh planet, Pluto, had not been discovered). Kepler was certain there was a rational and eternal plan in the cosmos that drove everything.

While teaching a class on plane geometry Kepler drew a figure with a circle encircling a triangle, which contained yet another circle (See Figure 49). What

KEPLER'S GEOMETRIC FIGURES

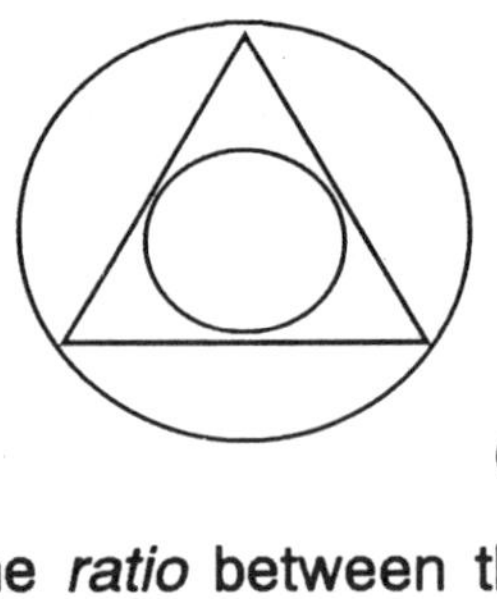

(Figure 49)

struck him was the *ratio* between the orbits of Saturn and Jupiter in *relationship* to the triangle, the first figure in geometry. Next he inscribed a square representing the interval between Jupiter and Mars, then between Mars and the Earth a pentagon, between the Earth and Venus a hexagon.

According to James, Kepler was struck by the finding (coincidence?) that the five perfect solids were just the number of figures needed to describe the intervals between the six planetary spheres (See Figure 50). He then suggested that the ratios between the

GEOMETRIC FIGURES
PLANE FIGURES

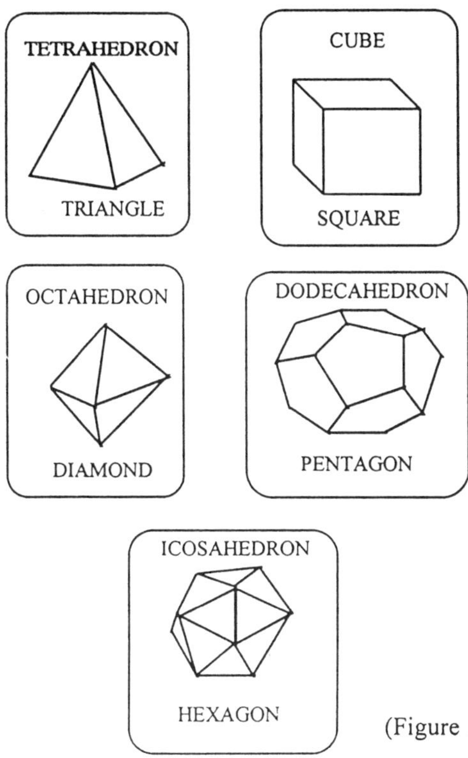

(Figure 50)

heavenly spheres could not be described as plane figures, but were themselves three dimensional. So that the ratios between them *had to be described by solid figures*--the tetrahedron (pyramid), the cube, the octahedron, the dodecahedron and the icosahedron.

It would be much later, after the creation of the table of periodic elements that it would be discovered that the configuration of the platonic solids are represented in the molecular structure of the elements which make up the physical body. Not only are there mathematical relationships between the planets and molecular structures, but in the geometry of the body itself! A recent text titled *Nothing in This Book is True, But It's Exactly How Things Are* by Bob Frissell 1994, depicts the geometrical findings of Leonardo da Vinci in his geometric representation of the body (See Figure 51).

OUR EXTERNAL CHAKRA POINTS

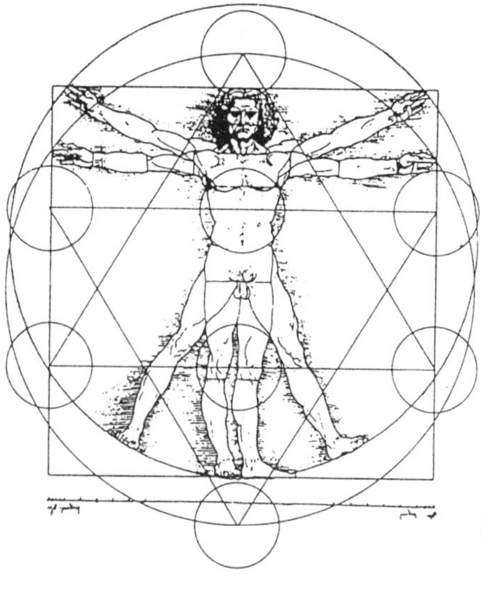

(Figure 51)

The geometry of the body is contained in a figure which contains all of the geometric shapes of the platonic solids when they are superimposed on each other (See Figure 52).

THE TOP VIEW OF HOW MALES AND FEMALES FIT INTO THE STAR TETRAHEDRON

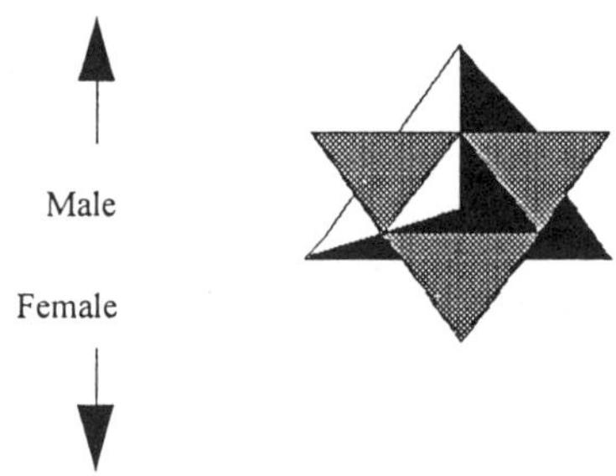

(Figure 52)

In terms of music, the mathematical relationships suggested by Kepler are critical in understanding the half-step intervals between planetary bodies and the eventual construction of the Diatonic Tempered Musical Scale composed of 12 notes (See Figure 53).

DIATONIC TEMPERED MUSICAL SCALE

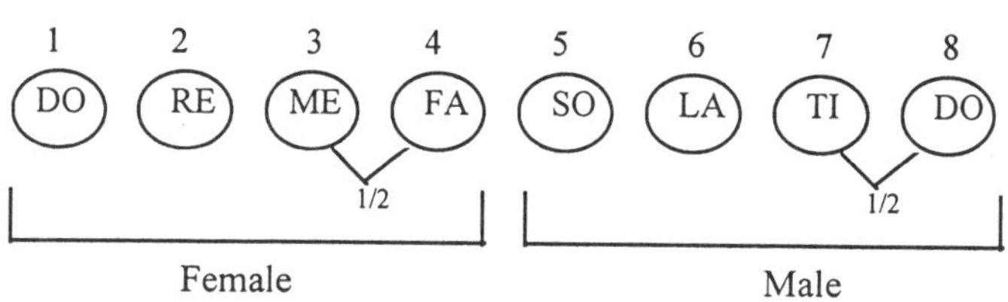

(Figure 53)

In Kepler's model where WH means a whole step and HS means a half step, his scale was comprised of WH WH WH HS WH WH WH HS; in other words, C, D, E, F, G, A and B.

Referring to a keyboard analogy, Gerber stated that octaves of musical notes are seen as similar to octaves of electromagnetic energy (See Figure 54). The

PIANO KEYBOARD ANALOGY OF HUMAN FREQUENCY SPECTRUM

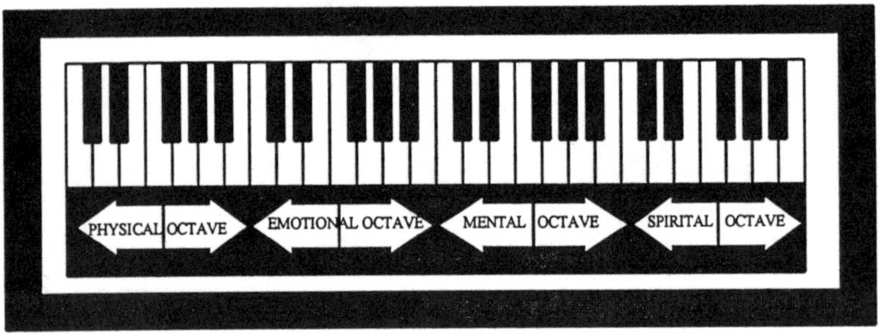

(Figure 54)

lowest octave corresponds to the physical spectrum of frequencies and also to beta brain wave patterns. The next octave is composed of matter and frequencies associated with emotions and alpha brain waves. Next are frequencies associated with theta brain wave patterns which constitute the mental octave. Finally, there is an octave corresponding with delta brain wave patterns which we might call the spiritual aspect, which coincidently correspond with genetic codes. Each of these octaves of sound can be measured and are believed to relate directly to the physical and subtle bodies.

Let me back up a moment and explain the relationship between the musical scale, frequencies and &brain wave patterns. There is an entire range of frequencies from 261 to 493 Hertz (Hz) or cycles per second, representing the note of Middle "C" on the piano. Each octave below middle C is simply one half of the previous frequency. This means that the note of "A" at Middle C has a frequency of 440 Hz. That same note, the note of "A" one octave below middle "C", has a frequency of 220 Hz, two octaves below middle C, "A" is represented by the frequency of 110 Hz. Going three octaves lower, "A" has a frequency of 55 Hz; four octaves lower still, it has a frequency of 27.5 Hz. At that level, the vibration matches beta brain wave patterns (See Figure 55). In a previous chapter when I was describing some of the characteristics of sound, I used the example of a guitar string. I suggested that there were interval patterns which created waves as we plucked a guitar string. It would seem then that when we hear a note of "A," our bodies also respond through the process of sympathetic vibration in the respective brain wave patterns.

As early as 1929 Hans Berger, a German neurologist, began measuring brain waves or the electrical patterns emitted by the brain. His work was important in the development of electroencephalography (the EEG) that we use today in tracking brain wave patterns. Only recently have we discovered that brain wave patterns match musical notes.

So it seems that the things that we have known all along are being unraveled. We have always "known"

BRAIN WAVE MUSICAL SCALE

(Figure 55)

C-8	C-7	C-6	C-5	C-4	C-3	C-2	C-1	MID C	NOTE
X	DELTA	THETA	ALPHA	BETA					
1.021	2.043	4.087	8.175	16.351	32.70	65.40	130.8	261.63	C
1.082	2.165	4.330	8.66	17.323	34.64	69.29	138.5	277.	C#
1.147	2.294	4.588	9.176	18.353	36.70	73.41	146.8	293.	D
1.215	2.434	4.869	9.722	19.445	38.89	77.78	155.5	311.1	D#
1.287	2.575	5.150	10.30	20.601	41.20	82.40	164.8	329.6	E
1.364	2.728	5.456	10.91	21.826	43.65	87.30	174.6	349.2	F
1.445	2.890	5.78	11.56	23.124	46.24	92.49	185.9	369.9	F#
1.531	3.062	6.125	12.25	24.5	49.	98.	196.	392.	G
1.62	3.244	6.489	12.97	25.95	51.91	103.8	207.6	415.3	G#
1.71	3.437	6.875	13.75	27.5	55.	110.	220.	440.	A
1.820	3.641	7.283	14.56	29.135	58.27	116.5	233.0	466.1	A#
1.929	3.858	7.716	15.433	30.867	61.73	123.4	246.9	493.88	B

that music could be irritating (non-resonant) or it could be soothing (resonant and coherent). We have known for a long time that music has an effect on the way we feel. Considering what I have just presented, sound and vibration have more than a casual relationship to what goes on in the physical body. Yet we have just begun to unravel what happens in the body in reaction to sound.

Neurologists suspect that beta waves are given off by the brain during normal attentive consciousness, alpha waves are produced in a state of restful awareness or meditation, theta waves are produced in a near sleep state and delta waves are normally found in deep sleep (See Figure 56). Beta waves are also associated with structural components like the skeletal and musculoskeletal systems. Alpha waves are associated with digestive and emotional states. Theta waves, while associated with intense mental activity are also associated with the biochemical states. Finally the

BRAIN WAVE RELATIONSHIP TO MUSICAL OCTAVES

Octave	C-8	C-7	C-6	C-5	C-4
Brainwaves	Delta-X	Delta	Theta	Alpha	Beta
cps	1-2	2-3	4-7	8-15	16-30
Function	Genetic	Bio-electrical	Bio-chemical mental	Bio-nuritional emotional	Neuro-muscular physical

(Figure 56)

upper ranges of Delta waves are associated with bio-electrical balances while lower Delta waves may be concerned with genetic encodments.

The slower the frequency the more subtle the influence, as in the delta wave correlation with genetic components. Mid-range frequencies (from four to seven octaves below middle C) correlate with maintenance of form or structure. Frequencies which are seven or eight octaves above Middle C would begin to fall in the inaudible range of human capacity.

For us to really understand how music or particular frequencies affect molecular structure and brain wave patterns, we need to understand another property of sound. Suppose you had a room full of clocks and you set each pendulum just slightly different for each clock. Interestingly enough, in a few days you would notice that all of the clocks were beating with the same frequency. This phenomena is called *rhythm entrainment.* It seems that nature finds it more economical in terms of energy to have periodic events that are close enough in frequency to eventually come in phase or in step with each other.

This is precisely the phenomena that occurs when we play notes on a musical scale or when the brain emits particular wave patterns that are close to the frequencies of the elements in the body. Eventually the musical waves and the brain waves become in phase or in sinc with the natural occurring elements needed to maintain the body. Or perhaps, the natural elements in the body respond to the environment around us. Using the later train of thought we might begin to have an inkling about how it is the human body begins to break down in the process of disease, aging, and death. Not only does the body respond vibrationally to our thoughts and emotions, it responds to the environment around us. The body is contstantly bombarded with the sounds and vibrations we experience daily through rock music, high tension wires, radio and television waves, to say nothing of microwaves and a whole host of other environmental interferences.

At this point, let's imagine that we could go on a journey through the body with a super microscope. If we could magnify sections of muscles, tissue and bones we would eventually see whole sections of molecules vibrating regularly, in constant but orderly motion. With more magnification, we would see atoms characterized by electrons moving in eliptical orbits about a seemingly solid nucleus. With more magnification even the nucleus seems to loose its solidarity. What we would soon witness is vast empty space filled with oscillating fields. Yet if our instruments were sensitive enough we could see that the tiniest vibrational change in one field carries over to the others. Conversely, when a strong harmonizing rhythm is applied to this matrix of interlocking fields, the resultant effect will be more orderliness in the system. This comes about because of the way with which the universe (both within and without) organized and modulates itself.

At room temperature a nucleus of an atom vibrates at about 10^{22} Hz, an entire atom at 10^{15} Hz or about a million billion times a second. Molecules vibrate at about 10^{9} Hz, and cells vibrate in the 10^{3} Hz range (Bentov, 1988). At we look at these differences we notice the modulating effect of vibration as structures combine to make larger and larger systems. It is apparent then, that when sound is used in a systematic manner, working from the most dense to the least dense in terms of organization, it affects organ functioning, cellular structure, molecular coherence; indeed, even atomic vibration.

As I have just demonstrated, each organizational level of the body is characterized by particular vibrational patterns. If we were to take a laser beam and shine it through a tumbler of saline solution, in which we have isolated a single element of the body, say magnesium, and pass that light through a prism, we would be able to determine the vibration of that molecule of magnesium (See Figure 57). In fact, science has done precisely that.

SPECTRUM ANALYSIS

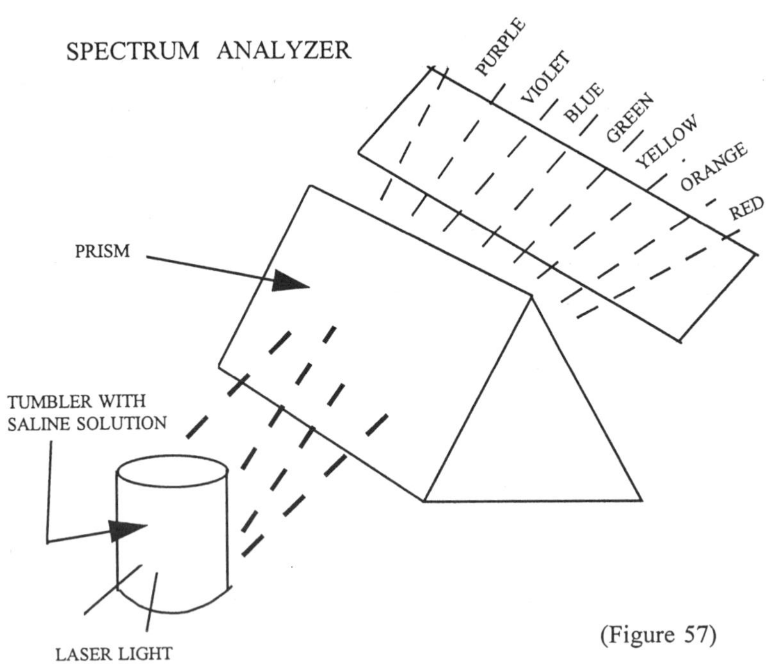

(Figure 57)

The laser light is measured by an instrument called a spectrum analyzer which measures vibration (or color) in angstrums. Angstrums are the mathematically converted into hertz, the frequency measurement for sound. This means that we can literally create all of the known elements of the body with sound! (See Figure 58). Colors are also related to the elements in the body, but then, I am getting ahead of myself.

COMMON ELEMENTS OF THE BODY MEASURED IN HERTZ

Oxygen	15.999	Sodium	22.981
Sulfur	16.032	Magnesium	24.312
Zinc	16.342	Chromium	25.950
Chlorine	17.726	Manganese	27.469
Germanium	18.147	Lithium	27.764
Florine	18.998	Nitrogen	28.013
Potassium	19.551	Phosphorus	30.972
Calcium	20.040	Iodine	31.726
Boron	21.622	Copper	31.672

(Figure 58)

Measuring the vibration of elements should really come as no surprise considering that for years our scientists have been able to find precious metals such as plutonium using geiger counters. What they are actually measuring is the vibrational pattern put out by the plutonium. While we don't measure vibration of the body using a geiger counter, there are other ways in which vibration of the body can be measured. The important thing is that when we look at the elements of the body, we find they are ordered in a particular way having to do with their atomic weight, and their resultant frequency.

Because information comes to me in holographic fashion, it seems I have to keep circling forward and backward in order for me to share with you how sound, vibration, color, and even planetary bodies all affect our states of consciousness. So rather than take all this terribly seriously, I ask you to read all this information playfully. I am just, and I think sometimes this is mostly for my own amusement, putting together the pieces of a cosmic puzzle. It might not even represent "truth," but it seems to me a fun way to begin to look at our place in the grand scheme of things.

I have had the fortunate opportunity to work with both Sharry Edwards and Robert Lloy both of whom are masters in inderstanding sound and its effects on consciousness and its potential for balancing the body. The wonderful thing about using sound as a tool for balancing the holographic body is that from a philosophical position each individual is regarded as unique. There is no comparison to something regarded as "normal."

In using sound, the focus is on examining the relationships between physical, emotional, mental, and spiritual states of being. The intent is to balance the whole person, not diagnose pathology. In fact, in using sound we are not looking for disease, but rather for balance. This means there is no conceptual difference, no separation between physiological states of being, our feelings, our thoughts and our spiritual nature.

For example, when something irritating enters our awareness, whether it be an improper food substance, a disempowering comment from another person, or a thought of self-doubt; it is processed as stress. These events over time, cause a disruption in the vibrational patterns of the body. In a congested or underactive system the energy does not flow freely. Energy which is blocked can result in tiredness or anemia at the physical level. It may result in an emotional state such as loss of self-confidence. At the mental level, an underactive system may reflect depression. Sometimes, blocked energy causes us to feel a separation -- not only from our selves but from the rest of humanity. At extreme levels, blocked spiritual energy can result in a sense of being separate from God. This is most often experienced as a deep sense of yearning for meaning in our lives and a wanting to find a deeper connection.

At other times, an overactive system has too much energy. This can be expressed in the body as nervousness, anxiety, or high blood pressure. We might seem to fly off the handle with very little provocation if energy is stressed in the emotional area. We might find ourselves in a situation where it seems we think about the same events over and over, like a record which is stuck in a groove. An overabundance of spiritual energy may leave us in a state of not wanting to be fully present in our daily living, in which case we deny the physical body of its natural tendency to seek pleasure. In this case, we may neglect the expression of love; instead, remaining in a state of being closed to receiving affection and attention from those around us.

In using sound to balance the body, the human voice serves at the output system for the body. The senses -- vision, hearing, smelling, tasting and touching serve as input modalities. The voice energetically carries a "sound print," as individual as a finger print. In viewing the body energetically, there are no judgments as to right or wrong, good or bad, healthy or ill. We simply look at how the energy is expressed, where the system shows an over-abundance or a scarcity of energy. *Once this is identified, vibrational patterns can be altered through sound, as sound IS vibration. In other words,* sound is used to affect vibrational patterns at the sub-atomic level. We know this in turn, affects cellular structure, organ formation and hence system functioning. This implies that changes through sound balancing occurs at a subtle level, but changes are long lasting, if not completely transformational.

I have earlier made the conjecture that our musical scale is based on the mathematical ratios of the planets to the earth. Let me now make an even more direct relationship between planetary bodies and astrological signs. If we take the four quadrant model presented earlier and divide it into the twelve astrological signs and match them to an expanded musical scale, with their respective color coordinates, we would come up with a model similar to that shown in Figure 59.

Research conducted by Sharry Edwards suggests that persons often experience stress related to the birth note or the note opposite (Aries/Libra, Taurus/Scorpio, Gemini/Sagittarius, Cancer/Capricorn, Leo/Aquarius or Virgo/Pisces. Can it be that when we are not aware of our purpose for being on the planet, when we are not mindful of the deeper connection to the universe, that the body responds with stress? Or that if we live our lives in the denial of who we really are, we cannot escape the deeper meaning? My conjecture is yes, so that the stress in any of the subtle bodies (physical, emotional, mental or spiritual) is expressed when we are not aware of our universal connections.

MUSICAL AND COLOR CORRELATES TO ASTROLOGICAL SIGNS

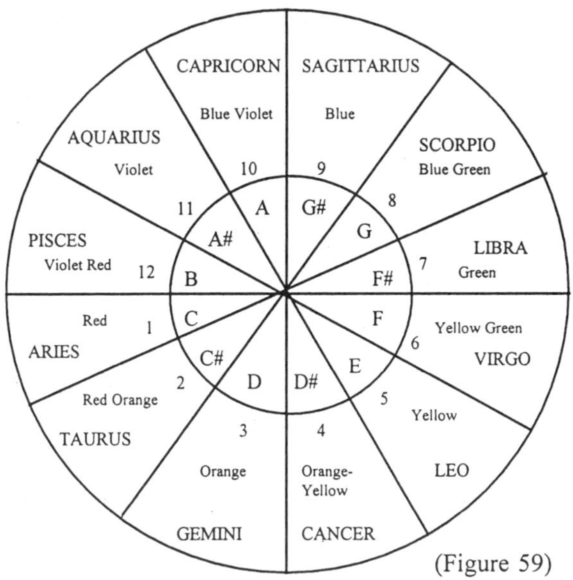

(Figure 59)

I think it also interesting that Edwards found that *stress in the physical body* is expressed as a disruption in *color vibrations* (red/green, orange/blue, yellow/violet) while *stress in non-physical areas* (emotional, mental or spiritual) is expressed in *light complements* (red/green-blue, orange/blue-violet, yellow-violet/red). (Notice that light opposites are polar opposites offset by 1/12. Again, this should come as no surprise as color is tied to pigment, it is a form of matter. It is a vibration that is denser than that of light. So not only may there be a disruption in the, what I call the "birth note", but there may be the corresponding disruption in the polar opposite (either by color or by light). And yet again, it should come as no surprise that disruptions may be expressed in polar opposites as this universe has a primary code of opposites: light/dark, day/night, yin/yang, male/female and so forth.

In looking at Figure 60 where I have made the correlation between color, astrological sign, musical notes and brain patterns, the clients I have worked with often are able to identify their own notes in stress relative to specific months in which negative life events occurred. Similarly, several have reported that following periods of intense stress, there was often an urge to buy clothes with a different color scheme.

Let's again bring this information into our real practical daily lives. Have you ever wondered *why* you selected a particular dress or shirt to wear for the day? I know, you say it was the only clean garment. No. Remember there are no accidents. The choices you made the preceeding days influences what you select in each moment of now, or what you select today. I know many women who state, "I needed an extra boost of energy, so I picked this bright yellow dress today." I myself have often felt the need to feel "grounded" so I am likely to pick beige and brown tones. Sometimes, I feel a need for greater connection, so I pick green, a heart chakra color. Just an accident? Or could it be that the wisdom of the body suggests that the vibration of yellow, brown, or green was needed, the vibration which corresponds with the third, first or fourth chakra? Can it be that our internal "knowing" seeks to balance the vibrational fields in a simple act of dressing?

COLOR, ASTROLOGICAL SIGN, BIRTH NOTE AND BRAIN WAVE PATTERNS

COLOR	ASTROLOGICAL SIGN	NOTE	BETA	ALPHA	THETA	DELTA
Red	Aries (March 23–Apr 22)	C	16.35	8.17	4.05	2.04
Red–Orange	Taurus (Apr 23–May 22)	C#	17.32	8.66	4.33	2.16
Orange	Gemini (May 23–June 22)	D	18.35	9.17	4.58	2.29
Orange–Yellow	Cancer (June 23–July 22)	D#	19.44	9.72	4.86	2.43
Yellow	Leo (July 23–Aug 22)	E	20.60	10.30	5.15	2.57
Yellow–Green	Virgo (Aug 23–Sept 22)	F	21.82	10.91	5.45	2.72
Green	Libra (Sept 23–Oct 22)	F#	23.12	11.56	5.78	2.89
Blue–Green	Scorpio (Oct 23–Nov 22)	G	24.50	12.25	6.12	3.06
Blue	Saggittarius (Nov 23–Dec 22)	G#	25.95	12.97	6.48	3.24
Blue–Violet	Capricorn (Dec 23–Jan 22)	A	27.50	13.75	6.87	3.43
Violet	Aquarius (Jan 23–Feb 22)	A#	29.13	14.56	7.28	3.64
Violet–Red	Pisces (Feb 23–Mar 22)	B	30.86	15.43	7.71	3.85

(Figure 60)

I trust that you can intuit for yourselves the twelve chakra system as it follows the same scale as the musical, color, and astrological chart, beginning with the note of "C" and the color red, reading counter clockwise; counting the note of "C" as the first chakra as illustrated in Figure 61.

The seven chakra system matches the primary notes so that the first chakra corresponds with the note

CHAKRA COLOR MUSIC SYSTEM

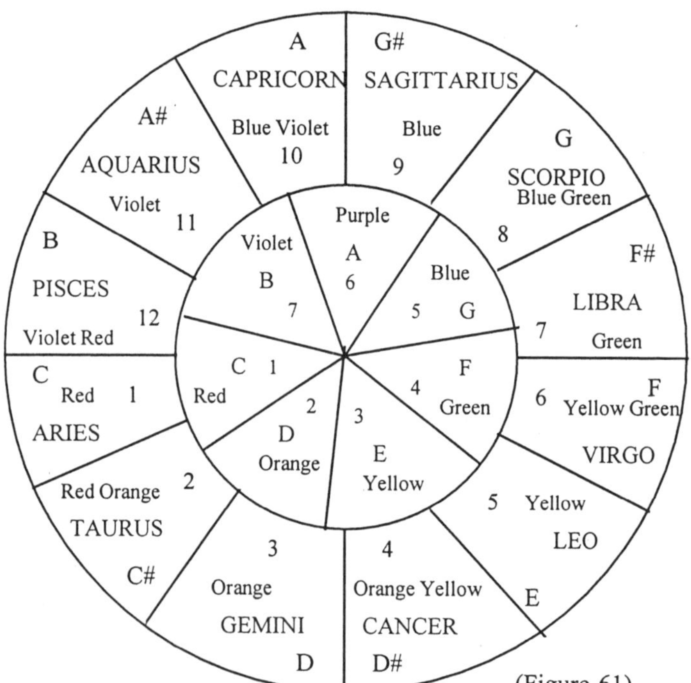

(Figure 61)

of "C" and the color red. The second with "D" and orange, the third with "E" and yellow, the fourth with "F" and yellow-green, the fifth with "G" and green-blue, the sixth with "A" and blue-violet and the seventh with "B" and violet-red. Notice that in the seven chakra system the notes of C, D and E correspond with the lower three chakras, notes below the horizontal line on the astrological chart. They are mostly concerned with maintenance of the form, concerned with matter. In the seven chakra system, the upper notes of the body, the G, A and B correspond with light, not color frequencies. These would be associated with non-physical states -- the emotional, mental and spiritual states according to light. In the 12 chakra system there is equal representation of color and light associated with the notes and signs of the Zodiac. The seven note chakra system is exactly the musical scale proposed by Kepler which matches the white or whole notes on a piano keyboard. The black notes or the half tones, in either the seven or the twelve chakra system, represent the fine tuning of the system.

As I began gathering information for this book, I found sources which matched planets with their respective astrological signs. The work of Edwards made correlations between musical notes and planetary signs. As I looked into medical astrology texts, searching for planetary influence on the endocrine glands, organs of the body and physical structures and then referenced this back to information on the chakras, I found some very interesting paradoxes. I won't attempt to explain them, but will present what I found (See Figure 62).

In short, I found that there was not always a perfect match. So the conjecture that I make is that as

VIBRATORY ASPECTS OF PLANETS ON THE PHYSICAL BODY

PLANET	SIGN	GLAND	ORGAN	STRUCTURE
Sun	E Leo		E Heart	G Thoracic
Jupiter	G# Sagittarius		F Lungs	D# Sacrum Femur
Neptune	B Pisces	B Pineal F Thumus	B Lymph glands	C Foot bones
Uranus	A Capricorn	A Pre-Pituitary	A Gall Bladder	D Patella
Saturn	A# Aquarius	A# Parathyroid	C# Tibia	
Mars	C Aries	D Adrenals		B Cranium
Pluto	G Scorpio	D Ovaries Testes	D Colon Prostrate	E Upper Pelvis
Mercury	D Gemini		F Lungs	A Shoulder Arms
	F Virgo	D# Pancreas	D# Spleen Intestines Liver	F# Abdominals
Venus	C# Tarus F# Libra	G Thyroid	G# Adenoids D Kidney	A# Cervical F Lumbar
Moon	D# Cancer	A Post-Pituitary		G# Sternum Ribs

(Figure 62)

vibrations are "stepped down" into this physical plane, octave by vibrational octave, there are some very interesting harmonics going on in the body. This serves to reinforce the idea that when examined holistically, the tampering with a single part disrupts more than just the vibration associated with it -- it harmonically disrups the whole.

I can't even imagine and leave this for those with computer or mathematical skills far greater than mine to begin to conjecture what happens not only when we look at the astrological sun sign, but when we begin to examine the effects of the ascending and descending planets. Add all this to information I presented previously about the infinite variety of cognitive processing and personality traits that are possible. Then add to this the variety of cultures, perceptions, values and life experiences that we each have. As I begin to let these images float in my mind I am filled with absolute wonder. You may just come to the conclusion, as I have, that there are no two of us alike on the planet! Just as I asked a previous question about the existence of God in the space between the sub-atomic particles, I now ask: Can it be that each of us is so unique we hold a "God-space" that no one else does? Further, when all of the pieces come together, can it be that then we will recognize God -- for it is in each of us. These thoughts are important, and are dependent on whether or not each of us can open ourselves to this awareness. I happen to think that playing on this level is much more fun and exciting than worrying if I have placed the flap on the toilet paper in the right direction or ponder whether or not I want to get involved in the neighborhood gossip!

Before I end this chapter, I would like to present, a table which attempts to translate "meaning" of the various vibrational frequencies associated with the primary energy fields. This meaning has been derived from the functions of organs and chakras, again looking for the deeper meaning (See Figure 63). I present this information because the intelligence is in the body.

OCTAVE MUSICAL INTERPRETATION

	PHYSICAL		EMOTIONAL
C	Gross circulation/heart	C	Self Awareness/Denial
C#	Cellular Oxygenation	C#	Frustration or Stubborness/ Adaptability
D	Digestive organs	D	Self Approval/Disapproval
D#	Metabolism	D#	Fear or anger/joy or happiness
E	Cjonduction/Respiration	E	Empowerment/Self Sabotage; guilt
F	Immune System	F	Love/Hate
F#	Filtration	F#	Avoidance/Repression
G	Neurotransmitters	G	Peaceful/Depression
G#	Enzymes, Vitamines	G#	Defensiveness/Openess
A	Minerals	A	Prioritize Feelings/Frustration
A#	Body Regulation	A#	Self/Others More Important
B	Nervous System	B	Willful Giving/Martyrdoom

	MENTAL		SPIRITUAL
C	Beliefs of the Culture	C	Recognition of Divinity
C#	Quality of Life	C#	Self Power
D	Relationships, Money	D	Flow with the Universe
D#	Acceptance/Denial	D#	Service to Self/Others
E	Belief in Self/Ego	E	Align Will with Higher Will
F	Consciousness	F	Connectedness with the All
F#	Action/Procrastination	F#	Willingness to Forgive
G	Creativity	G	Speak own Truth
G#	Defensiveness	G#	Devotion
A	Intuitive Thinking	A	Insight, Guidance, Clarivoyance
A#	Judgment/Competition	A#	Consecration
B	Rational Thinking	B	Universal Knowing

(Figure 63)

If we can accept that each cell at the sub-atomic level has a particular vibration and that like tissues come together to form organ structures with a higher vibrational pattern, then this suggests that there is an "internal intelligence" in the body. The heart *knows* how to circulate blood, the liver *knows* how to filter fluids, the stomach *knows* how to digest food. The brain *knows* how to make neural connections.

Some systems have a higher "intelligence" than others. So if we feel uncomfortable in the pit of our stomach without reasonable explanation, then it would be well for us to honor the wisdom, because the gut has not evolved to the same level as the brain. The stomach has not yet learned about self-doubt. Since the body functions holographically, we must look at the relationships between the functions of the subtle bodies and the chakras. For example, I have stated that the liver *knows* how to act as a filtration system. Yet at the same harmonic frequency in the other subtle bodies, it may be that on an emotional level we are struggling with avoidance and repression. Perhaps in our life choices, we (with good intent) filter the problems of everyone else through our body when we listen to their problems. Perhaps we do this in the vain hope that we won't have to look closely at what is going on in our own lives; in other words, perhaps we are avoiding self-examination.

It would be no wonder then, that caretakers of the terminally ill often feel a sense of repression. It may feel as if they have taken on the weight of the world. My sense is when they open the heart chakra (associated energetically with functions of the liver) and begin working on their deeper connections, they will have an awakening of their own consciousness and come to the realization that they do perform a service. But it must come from a place of deep love, rather than from a sense of duty and sacrifice.

If we pause for a moment to take a deeper look at Figure 62, we note the paradoxes I mentioned. Notice that the vibratory frequency associated with the kidney is the note of D. If we were to remove it, not only would there be the corresponding harmonic destructive interferrence in all of the other subtle bodies (as described above) but there may be more profound influences. Because the kidney is under the influence of Libra, an F# frequency, the removal of the kidney or the D harmonic may affect other systems, say the thyroid, a G frequency. I could speculate that there may be harmonic distrubance of the F frequency associated with the lumbar vertebra (which is the same chakra system as the kidney). I suspect that for persons with chronic and multiple problems, the primary causal agent is that we keep tinkering with the system, so that instead of fixing it, we are causing more and more disharmony. At least that is my thinking in working with an aging population, it offers speculation as to why people may experience diabetes and arthritis, or kidney/heart failure. My conjecture is that the more tinkering we do, the more we disrupt the natural harmonic vibrations of the whole.

Let me give another example. Since there is no separation between physical, emotional, mental or spiritual states of being, instances of imbalance tend to "spill over" from one subtle body to another. The note of D, for example, has a different meaning in the physical expression from that in the emotional, mental or spiritual expression. By looking at the holographic meaning of this note, it is not difficult to determine that if we are having difficulties with our relationships or our finances (a second chakra mental activity), it often can lead to a state of disapproval or self-doubt (a second chakra emotional disturbance). If stress persists, it may manifest in digestive problems or imbalances in the kidney or liver (the physical expression). In combination, this can lead us to being out of touch with the flow of the universe (a spiritual phenomena).

Now let me for the moment make a quantum leap to tie astrology to a medical perspective, getting some of these insights grounded, as it were. If we look at the physiology of the body we would recognize that we make a new stomach lining every five days, a new skin once a month, a new liver every six weeks, a new skeleton once every three months. What would happen if we meditated and sent loving energy to the planet which influences the disease process associated with a particular body part? Could we influence the healing process? I certainly think so and in fact I would encourage it.

It also seems to me that if surgery is warranted, then the patient should at least be given the opportunity to participate in the healing of his or her own body. As we make the tie back to astrology, let us consider that your physician has recommended that you have open heart surgery. Previously I mentioned that the heart, at the level of brain wave multiples, resonates with the frequency of the note of F. The note of F in turn corresponds with the planet Mars. So if Mars is ascending, the outcomes for surgery at that time might be much greater than if completed when Mars is retrograde. If this is too far a stretch for us to make, then we could at least play particular pieces of music in the surgical suite or in the recovery room to aid the body as much as possible, to come back into balance.

As outrageous as these basic principles sound, I can't seem to stress enough that we cannot separate ourselves from the rest of the cosmos. It is time to begin finding the threads which connect physics with medicine, astrology with physics, medicine with education. As we move into awareness that there is only One consciousness operating in the universe, the potential is here to harness individual as well as planetary consciousness, to bring new information into our bodies which can be channeled into regeneration at the cell level.

I have stated that the mind is omnipotent, it is everywhere, it is nonlocal. The individual mind is connected to a larger perspective, that of consciousness. But in order to reform that which is generally held in the collective consciousness, we must first be willing to look at thinking, to look at our minds from an individual level. As long as we are tied to the perception that we are limited, and not part of a larger whole, our thinking can create problems over and over as we talk about them. Our thinking can create illness or disease at each instant in time that we give negative attention to the thoughts that arise. If I get up in the morning with pain, and say to myself, "Oh, that is my arthritis again," at that moment I create the arthritis. I attach the negative thought about pain to my feelings of discomfort and further attach the thought–feeling energy to a culture belief system having to do with the nature of arthritis. As I place emotion on a perception, the limbic system is triggered which acts to encode information into memory. Not only do I have individual thoughts and emotions which are tied to my personal experiences to contend with, but I also have thoughts that are part of a larger mind field of information.

Most of us are completely unaware of the hypnosis of social conditioning. As we watch television, we see the ad extolling the virtues of Advil over Tylenol and Excedrin, but we fail to see the underlying message. The message is that you cannot deal with your arthritis pain *unless* you take one of these medications. The message is that the relief for what is happening in your body is found by resorting to something outside your body which is artificial. It is no different than telling our divorce stories to persons outside ourselves. If you ignore the pain, that doesn't help either, because in truth, it is not unlike the example I gave you about not thinking about the red pen. Unless we are willing to begin working on the cause of our illnesses and diseases, medical management will remain at the symptom management level. It will remain as a bandaid approach. We must break down the barriers between the mind/body system. We must open up the body for internal dialog. We must seek to find the universal wisdom that is stored in the body.

This is not as difficult as you may think. Researchers at Harvard Medical School have been demonstrating for years that when a person engages in deep breathing and focuses on a single object or a word, that the body goes into what has been called "the relaxation response." In this state, blood pressure normalizes, there is a balancing of brain chemistry, an increase in oxygen absorption at the cell level and a triggering of the immune system. The relaxation response can be coupled with guided visual imagery as it taps into the right hemisphere of the brain, into site receptors which contribute to our sense of oneness with the universe. The sensations that are experienced will be unique to each individual just as the chemical make-up of the body is different for each individual.

As suggested in an earlier chapter, try visualization for a moment. Visualize a meadow . . . . For some of you this will be experienced as a grassy place. Others may see flowers although my only cue word was "meadow." Still others will see a clearing bounded by trees because "meadow" means "clearing" rather than "field." This points to a very fundamental problem with medical intervention that supposes that all persons will have a similar response to a medical treatment. In other words, traditional medical intervention does not honor the uniqueness of each individual. You can be assured that visualizing the inner workings of the body, or connecting the body part to a planetary body, is just as easy as visualizing scenes or events outside the body. One does not have to have a degree in anatomy or physiology to be able to talk to the body. We just have to be willing to open up the channels of internal dialogue. We can engage in imagery processes which expand our field of awareness to foster a deepening connection with the universe.

We have an incredible pharmacy right here in the body. Haven't you noticed that when you were really scared or angry, you didn't experience these feelings just in your heart or your head? In real fear, even your big toe gets scared! The entire body gets into the act without you needing to send an invitation! When you are sad your body makes the equivalent of valium and it depresses the entire system. When we are excited or happy we produce norepinephrine or acetocoline. In short, we make happy, jittery, joyful molecules throughout the whole body. So each of the bodily systems not only has its own set of specialized functions, each can respond cooperatively with all others to produce those overwhelming feelings of sadness or happiness.

It might be important here to make a comment that the physical body is very concrete. As I have said, it is the print-out of consciousness. It doesn't discriminate the source of information coming into it. While each part of our body does have its own intelligence, it is not an intelligence of a higher order. The cells of skeletal system are not as evolved as the cells of the nervous system. The cells of the peripheral nervous system are not as evolved as cells of the brain. This does not in any way make them less responsive.

When the cells in the muscle tissue "hear" that they are doing pain, they feel bad. They get depressed! They slow down, become uncomfortable, they are not at ease. They suffer "dis-ease." They cease to function. They die. If enough of them die and it comes to our awareness that the pain is unbearable, we might create an emergency. We create the possibility of an *"emerge-and-see"* condition. An emergency condition is meant to take us out of the world of time, to create the opportunity for us to lie quietly. The body already knows the wisdom of the relaxation response whether or not you acknowledge it. The body knows how to care for itself, if we are reasonable caretakers. And it will do all that it can to awaken you to a different way of relating to it. The body wants a different kind of dialog. It wants attention. It wants all the love and affection that it can hold.

The human body is the vehicle of consciousness. It is the bodymind and the mindbody at the same time. To understand what is going on in the mind, one only has to look at the body. Does it radiate joy and happiness? Does it move with grace and ease? Is it playful and spontaneous? Is it en*spirit*ed? My experience teaches me that we must become aware of all our thoughts and feelings. We must trace the origin of our thoughts to our own truth, separating them from the collective consciousness. It is time we start acting like the traffic cop or the symphony conductor. It is time we go deeper to obtain the understanding that we are the thinkers of the thoughts. We are the feelers of the feeling, the doubters of the doubt, the skeptic behind the skepticism. We are the mystic behind the mystery.

Chapter 9 Entering the Silence

Birthing of a Soul

In my previous chapters, we have talked about the energy fields and the chakra systems in terms of how energy is expressed in the physical and the subtle bodies. We have pushed our understanding into realms of physics and astrology. A broader application, a metaphysical application, is now appropriate. It seems I am about to take a quantum leap here because I want to approach a subject around which we have a lot of emotion -- the subject of abuse. Yet I wish to approach it from a soul level perspective.

Each soul contracts with a particular set of parents who have the genetic traits most necessary for learning those life events which will likely serve to evolve the soul. Most biological parents have a contract with the birthing soul. Occasionally, by mutual consent, the birthing soul will elect biological parents for the desired DNA encodements, yet not choose those parents for the process of parenting and raising. Thus from this perspective, we have a very different sense of the adoption process. This suggests that some biological parents may have only a short term contract with the soul. Hopefully, if one were to adopt this point of view, the biological mother could eliminate her sense of guilt in giving up her child for adoption. Perhaps biological and nurturing parents could come to a different understanding of their mutual interests in the child, and value the contributions made by each, however different.

As we look at birth anomalies from a soul perspective, we can again gather other pieces of wisdom. Children who are born handicapped as result of prenatal or birth trauma have contracted for the experience on a soul level. Usually the lesson that the soul has chosen is one of learning to receive love and nurturing. What greater opportunity than being totally or partially dependent! In a similar way, parents of these children are often learning lessons of unconditional loving.

As we continue in this vein and look at the dynamics of child abuse, we again gain a very different picture of reality than one that is generally held in the consciousness. The moment of birth is the soul's second most profound experience to be engaged in during an incarnation cycle or a biological cycle (keeping in mind those of you who are not comfortable with the idea of reincarnation). Not only is the child separated from his mother's womb, the moment he or she draws the first breath, the child may experience a profound sense of separation from God, from Source. For this viewpoint to have meaning, the underlying assumption is that the breath IS the connection with Source. Yet, paradoxically as we draw the first breath, it is the first moment of awareness of that which is the Self (the God–seed) and that which is the not self (the personality biological "lived in" state of being).

Occasionally, the moment of birth is so traumatic for the infant, that the first levels of awareness which are imprinted on the infant may be feelings of profound separation. The soul of the infant may sense that he or she is being terribly punished for being sent so far away from home –– from God or Source. This sets up a negative energy field which attracts to it a reinforcement of negative belief systems. Thus, it is the infant who attracts the verbal and physical abuse, which in turn, reinforces the notion of unworthiness. My sense is that it is usually a very great and loving soul who takes on this mission. A soul of this nature very often takes on this mission as one of great service to the abuser, to sacrifice the body for the connection of spirit.

As with any health issue, whether it occurs at birth, during childhood, or in adulthood, in our willingness to work through the trauma that has occurred, we in turn, clear the consciousness from humanity. From the perspective of the abused, the soul not only yearns for the connection with the abuser, but for all souls who have contracted for similar experiences. The intent is to learn forgiveness -- forgiveness that clears the energy patterns of the abused, not the abuser.

From the perspective of the abuser, my sense is that this soul is in transition from lower planes of living. In order to make the transition, the soul must learn that what he or she does to another is really an infliction upon the Self. It is a denial of the Divinity, an attachment to ego, it is a stance of external power and control. The lessons to be learned often involve surrender to a higher power.

I have said that the moment of birth is the second most profound experience we encounter in an incarnation or biological cycle. Birth deals with separation, abandonment, and desertion as viewed from a soul perspective. But the most profound experience is the return to Source. The experience of reconnection is often so exquisite and profound that it cannot be matched by any other human experience. It is an internal process. Abused children, may, through their own choices, realize at some point in time that forgiveness heals the wounds. It also opens the door to their own Divinity. Other times, this revelation is not accomplished until the death process when the soul returns to God.

Traditional therapies have dealt with cases of abuse strictly from the personality level. For the most part, abusers have not been regarded as victims of their own unawareness. Instead, focus has been placed on those who have been abused. Further, whether dealing with the abused or the abuser, the efforts in treatment have been related to fixing, rather than using the experience for internal growth. When the time of awareness or awakening comes either to the abused or the abuser, this is the time real healing begins.

The Process of Creation

Let's now look at the process of creation and use both our own internal processes as well as a developmental down-to-earth perspective. In our daily lives we continually go through the process of creation although we may not have called it creation. Pause for a moment and look around at the possessions that you have. For discussion purposes, let's say you have a new car. That you have it, began with just an inkling of an idea, a seventh chakra inspiration. Then likely after that first inspiration, you began to visualize it. You began to bring that energy into the sixth chakra; you may have even pictured yourself in the car or dreamed about it. You may have begun to sense how your life would change with it. You may have found yourself saying: "I will be able to take my children on camping trips with this extra room." In other words, you may have begun to communicate about it, to speak about it, to creatively play with the notion of ownership of that car -- a fifth chakra position.

Likely then, you had to decide how you felt about it. Your real love of the color blue rather than red may have come from the fourth or heart chakra (although love of a color is not a particularly high vibration). As you thought about how a new car would affect your identity, you were evoking the third chakra. You may have said something like, "I will be able to pick up my clients in a car that looks more respectable." That kind of statement is reflective of self-esteem, self-identity, perhaps even ego. Then comes the real test moving the energy into the second and first chakras. The second chakra as I mentioned earlier is associated with finances, with possession of things physical and non-physical. So usually after you have "consciously" considered the new car (using the data banks of processing on different levels), the real test of seriousness about ownership is determining whether or not you could afford it. If you can, then of course, it is birth into your possession, a first chakra function. It is also likely that if you decided you could not afford it, then it is likely that the entire idea was aborted (also first chakra energy).

I have found this model particularly useful with every new prospect I have undertaken, whether it be to look at the use of my energy for the purchase of a car, changing my career, or dealing with health issues. This suggests that the miracle of creation is not relegated to the birth process alone, it is a miracle that happens all the time! This is the way we manifest on Planet Earth. Because we use this process so often, it is terribly *ordinary.* We have just not conceptualized creation in this way. In not thinking about miracles in this way, we do not recognize that *we are the creators of everything that we have.*

This model of creation also helps me in my own thinking to bridge the gap between the subjective (the ideas and feelings that we have, but cannot see) and the objective (the objects, relationships and events that occur in our lives). The model speaks to the encodement of spirit into form, expanding our realities to include the "non-real" as well as the real. It allows us to look at how we, as creators, are also unable to have what we want. If there is something that we want and we are unable to manifest it, or obtain it, it means that somewhere along the way we have blocked the energy.

I stated in the car example that if we cannot afford something, it does not become manifest in our reality, usually related to blocked energy in the second chakra. The second chakra holds not only the energy associated with finances, but is the energetic source for the *relationship* with all things physical and non-physical. How many times have each of us gone through the entire creative process only to get blocked when we thought that other people would not approve of the idea? Or how many times have we aborted the idea at the third chakra level, because we felt we did not deserve it? Perhaps we have put off changing our careers because we have not honored our own self worth. We have instead fallen back into traditional roles, allowing our own needs to be put on the back burner.

Before moving on to a developmental perspective,

I would like to go deeper into concepts of creation, specifically the creation of the physical form. My orientation for this discussion stems from the belief I have said before, that we are spiritual beings having a human experience. When we can understand this perspective, then the spirit can be used to transcend and transform the limitations of the form.

From a Hindu perspective, Anodea Judith, in her book *Wheels of Life,* 1992, suggests that the first chakra is the point at which energy is first converted into matter (See Figure 64). Within the void of "no-thing-ness,"

LAW OF CREATION

CHAKRA	CHARACTERISTIC	ELEMENT	ASTROLOGICAL SIGN
1	Mass	Earth	Feminine: Taurus, Virgo, Capricorn
2	Movement	Water	Feminine: Cancer, Scorpio, Pisces
3	Interaction	Fire	Masculine: Aries, Leo, Sagittarius
4	Relationship	Air	Masculine: Gemini, Libra, Aquarius
5	Vibration	Sound	
6	Color	Light	
7	Consciousness	Thought	

out of the void
Mass = Oneness
Mass + Movement = Duality
Mass + Movement + Interaction = Energy
Mass + Movement + Interaction + Relationship = Love
Mass + Movement + Interaction + Relationship + Vibration = Communication
Mass + Movement + Interaction + Relationship + Vibration + Light = Image
Mass + Movement + Interaction + Relationship + Vibration + Light + Consciousness = Oneness

(Figure 64)

whether we speak of the formation of galaxies or single cells, there is a focus. Since the void is a non–material intelligence, we can say there is a focus of consciousness, a focus of energy, or a focus of a primordial substance. We could even call the focus Love. The language we use to describe the process is largely a matter of choice. It is the fabric of space–time.

The point of focus causes the energy to shift into matter, waves into particles. Matter comes when there are enough forces of a similar nature and direction to reach critical mass. "Critical mass," a term borrowed from physics, is the first stage of manifestation. Form, once created, then shapes the space around it and in turn is re–shaped by the space. This would support notions offered by Rupert Sheldrake concerning the morphogenetic field which shapes all living bodies, and in turn, influences the energy field surrounding the form.

Out of the "no–thing–ness" of spirit prior to conception, comes the "some–thing–ness" of form. That which is solid, whether we view matter as the point of conception of a human being, or conception of a single cell, or the galaxy itself; the process follows the same universal laws. Form, once created, is then subject to the forces of gravity. We may wish to look at the force field of gravity around the earth as being similar to the etheric template of our own physical bodies. It is the template of consciousness for the planet.

Thus, the Mother Earth draws to her the consciousness of her own creation, transformed by her own energy field. It is one of two co–dependent relationships that has been sanctioned on this planet. The second co–dependent relationship is the oxygen–carbon monoxide exchange between the Plant and Animal

Kingdoms, which is related to the first chakra issues of biological survival. If I deviate for a moment, I really want to make a clear statement about these relationships.

We need Mother Earth for our very survival and paradoxically, she needs us. The original plan of creation was that we were to serve as caretakers, and in turn, through the process of reciprocation (exchange of energy), the planet would support, shelter and nurture us. Somewhere over eons of time, we forgot this deep connection. We began to pillage and burn, we forgot the sacred ties with the earth.

It should come as no surprise then, that the first chakra is most often referred to as the Earth chakra. Some individuals live their entire lives or more specifically, develop their personality subject to first chakra energy. These persons are likely to have characteristics of resolve, practicality, prudence, obedience and a love of material possessions. Their orientation will be toward maintenance of form. As we move from an individual to a planetary chakra system, we notice that from an astrological perspective, there are groups of people who manifest Earth tendencies. The astrological signs associated with earth are Taurus, Virgo and Capricorn.

I have suggested that out of the Earth Chakra the form is created (Figure 65). As form is subjected to the forces of gravity, there is the creation of movement. Movement is bi-polar in nature. Thus, the notion of dual-ity, the movement away from spirit occurs the moment that energy is transformed into matter. This then is the paradox. The separation from God is encoded in the very DNA structure that we inherit from the moment of conception!

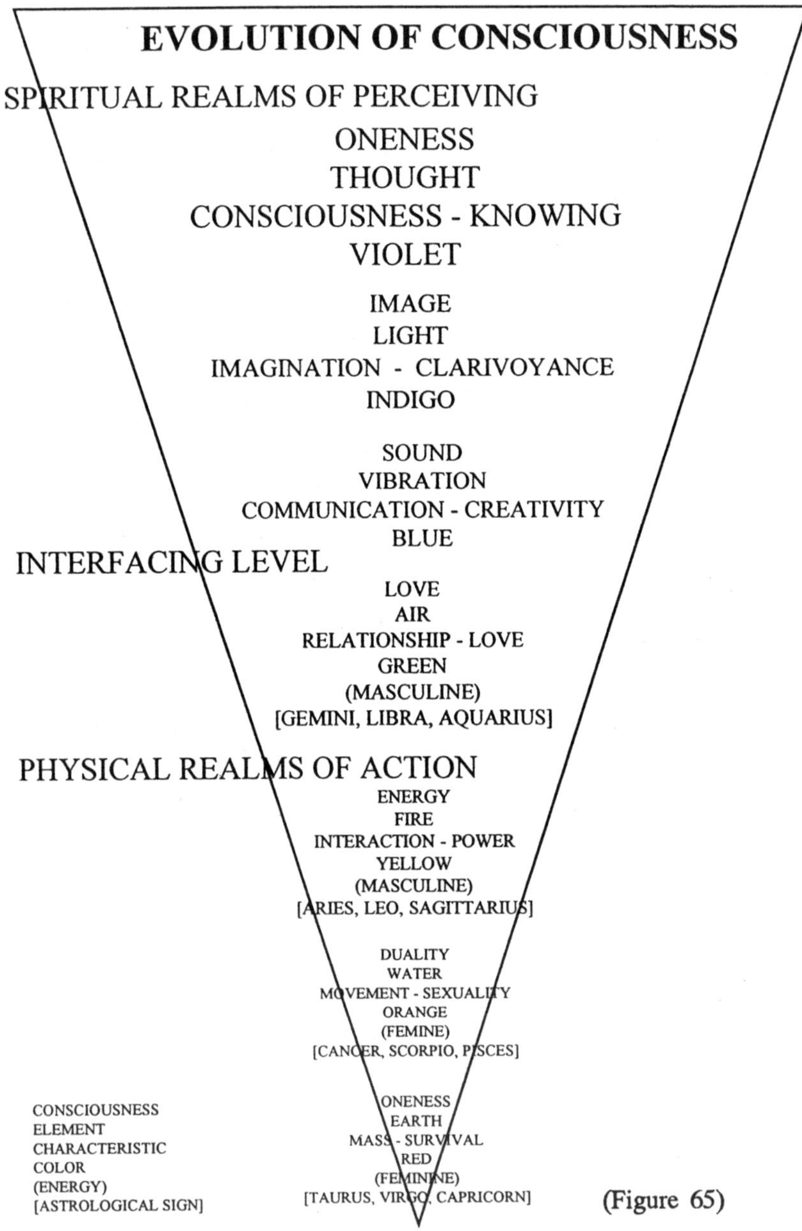
EVOLUTION OF CONSCIOUSNESS
SPIRITUAL REALMS OF PERCEIVING
ONENESS
THOUGHT
CONSCIOUSNESS - KNOWING
VIOLET
IMAGE
LIGHT
IMAGINATION - CLARIVOYANCE
INDIGO
SOUND
VIBRATION
COMMUNICATION - CREATIVITY
BLUE
INTERFACING LEVEL
LOVE
AIR
RELATIONSHIP - LOVE
GREEN
(MASCULINE)
[GEMINI, LIBRA, AQUARIUS]
PHYSICAL REALMS OF ACTION
ENERGY
FIRE
INTERACTION - POWER
YELLOW
(MASCULINE)
[ARIES, LEO, SAGITTARIUS]
DUALITY
WATER
MOVEMENT - SEXUALITY
ORANGE
(FEMINE)
[CANCER, SCORPIO, PISCES]
ONENESS
EARTH
MASS - SURVIVAL
RED
(FEMININE)
[TAURUS, VIRGO, CAPRICORN]
CONSCIOUSNESS
ELEMENT
CHARACTERISTIC
COLOR
(ENERGY)
[ASTROLOGICAL SIGN]

(Figure 65)

Duality is expressed in our consciousness as opposing forces, most of which are present in human form -- masculinity/femininity, yin/yang, darkness/lightness, positive/negative and so forth.

The duality of nature is the primal characteristic of the second chakra. Since we speak of opposites and understand that there is an attraction between them, the creation of movement is therefore fluid. Again, stretching our interpretations, it should come as no surprise that water is associated with the formation of the second chakra. Likewise, the second chakra influences all bodily functions having to do with liquid movement, our circulation, urinary flow and other bodily fluids.

Thus, we see the creation of the second chakra is the site of emotional interactions with all things physical and non-physical. The second chakra is particularly susceptible to the influences of the limbic system, which encodes and decodes emotional information for storage and retrieval at the cell level. It is important to remember that feelings rise out of the form and are the foundation of emotional response. If feelings are suppressed, we essentially have insufficient information to clearly identify the emotional content -- so the emotional content is stored, as it were, with a distorted energy field. This literally produces a short circuit in the body. As we continue over time to invalidate feelings, we create a field of tension, hence, we have the human experience of pain. Pain arises out of the imbalance of the second chakra and is one of the key reactors for letting us know that the body is out of balance or "out of flow."

Working backward in time, if we can translate our emotions back into specific *feeling states* we can unlock the mysteries of the mind/body link. Once we have unlocked the mysteries, we can then with intention reframe our experiences. In other words, we create a new reality picture which supports our Divinity. We transcend the duality of the separation at birth. In this process, we move back into flow of the mind/body system. The key is to remember that pain is an indication we are going in the wrong direction. We are out of sync with the internal and external universe. *Pain is not, as we have been led to believe, an indication of pathology of the system!*

I have associated the first chakra with mass and the second chakra with movement. With movement, there is interaction. Physicists would look at interaction as a result of particles which interact and repel and thereby change each other's nature. Interaction, then, is the energy of the third chakra. With extremes of interaction, there is combustion, there is the emission of energy. Hence, from a Hindu perspective, we find the third chakra association with fire. It is the energy of transformation. It is the point at which matter is transformed into heat and light (the principle energies of the fourth and sixth chakras respectively). Heat and Light in turn, transform the inertia of earth and water into action. The momentum created by this transformation, transcends the duality which is held in the second chakra.

The third chakra, as a point of action, has been regarded as the first level of intellect. In fact, the third chakra has been associated with the very same characteristics as the thinking processes of the left hemisphere of the brain -- specifically the rational, logical and factual aspects of thinking. "Facts" are the consciousness of things which are tangible and tied to form (the energy of the first chakra). "E–motions" are the tie between facts and feelings (associated with the second chakra). Thus, the third chakra forms the emergence of how the facts and emotions relate, the point out of which our identity as a personality evolves. If we look to our larger universe of knowledge, we find that the fire element has been associated with the astrological signs of Aries, Leo and Sagittarius. The personality traits which have been associated with these particular signs include activity, vitality, enthusiasm and ambition.

The interaction which is produced by mass and movement then begins to form patterns we might call relationships. If we view both the subatomic level of bodily systems and the planetary system, we note that there is movement of the particles and planets around a particular focal point or nucleus. Particles and planets cannot go beyond a particular orbital path as there are equal and opposing forces which keep them directed. The relationship between movement and attraction to the core or focal point which then creates a state of dynamic equilibrium, a state of balance or affinity. In human terms, we call this relationship "love." It is represented in the body in the fourth chakra. It represents reflection (giving back to the universe, the energy it has taken in) and assimilation (receiving from the universe the energy it has released). The heart, then, is the point of connection between spirit and matter, mind and body, heaven and earth. We call these connections the formation of consciousness. Hence there is the notion that consciousness comes from the heart and not the head.

As we go back now to our physics and our perspectives gained from astrology, we notice that particles and planets are confined by the parameters of their relationships. These forces which dictate the orbital path are equal and opposite to those forces which would disrupt motion. This then sets up a field of vibration, a field of sound. At this recognition, we begin to unravel the mystery, the miracle of vibration as related to the organ systems in the body. We begin to understand that sound, in terms of hierarchical organization of the chakra system, corresponds with the fifth chakra. This vibration is not of the body per se, but contributes to the construction and maintenance of the form.

It has been said that the temples in Egypt were constructed with toning or sounding chambers in which an individual would stand or sit and tone. Toning was believed to be a major source of balancing and healing the body. Unfortunately, we rarely tone any more; seldom do we sing to the body. Sound, when used appropriately, may become the source of healing in the next decade. Since it is characterized by vibration, it is no wonder that the fifth chakra has been associated with speaking and creativity. This is a process which externalizes the form, transferring energy from one individual to another.

In moving up the chakra system, the energy becomes less dense, it moves at increasing speeds, hence when we are speaking of "higher consciousness." It is still part of the mind/body system, but begins to move out of the confines of matter. At higher frequencies, the vibrating mass of particular fields can be seen as electromagnetic radiation perceived by the consciousness as light which has been associated with the sixth chakra. Our consciousness perceives light, according to Anodea Judith, through the sense of sight and records these patterns in the form of symbolic images, stored holographically in the brain. At this point we begin to unravel the human experiences of clairvoyance. We also begin to understand how guided visualization can aid in unlocking the mysteries, or should I say, the miracles of the form.

Light according to most physicists is represented in the physical body as a massless particle or wave form called a photon. (See Figure 66). A photon can be either

PARTICIPATORY UNIVERSE

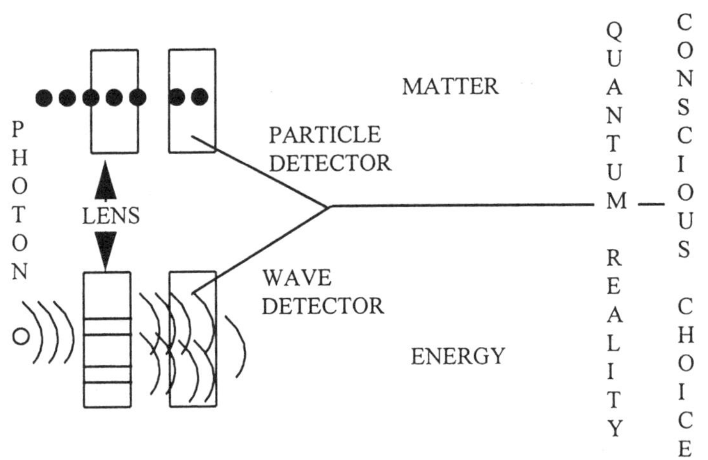

(Figure 66)

a wave or a particle but not both at the same time. If a photon is converted into energy at the cellular level, it is used in the regeneration process. If it is converted into a particle, it is used in the creation of the form, specifically the creation of cells. What then determines whether this massless photon will be converted into energy or particles? I propose that it is our free will, our choices which arise from the third and fourth chakras.

As one becomes aware or chooses a path of enlightenment, one feels a connectedness with the universe. It is this awareness which calls forth the use of higher vibrations in healing the form. In other words, positive loving thoughts convert photons into energy, not only used for transforming mental and emotional fields, but at the cellular level in the physical body. Negative thoughts arising out of the consciousness of the third chakra (which are ego based and tied to form) change the photons into particles which leads to the thickening of the cellular membrane making it more difficult for the cell to enter a natural state of cell division. Cells then become rigid. They go into entropy, they collapse on themselves, they die. Thus, we have inherited an unenlightened form full of belief systems recorded at the cellular level. If no enlightenment occurs during a lifespan, the form goes through the process of aging, death and dying. The causal agents are constructs of consciousness, not constructs of reality!

As we move up to the seventh chakra which is the culmination of mass, movement, interaction, pattern, vibration and light, we move into the realm of pure-consciousness. At our most transcendental states there is no form, and we enter again into the void. We become pure spirit; and the cycle starts again. Since it is a continual cycle, not bound by time and space, there are infinite possibilities for resurrecting the mind/body system. We have infinity encoded in our cellular structure! Over and over again, with each breath we take, with each action that arises from the form, there is the opportunity for transforming the form.

Developmental Perspective of Soul Evolution

I started this chapter talking mostly about the birth process, so it seems appropriate that I now shift and talk about the entire developmental process using the model of creation that I have just presented. The soul enters the physical body shortly before the birth process, once it has decided that it has a habital host. It is my belief that infants are seventh chakra beings. They are pure love, unconditional love. Developmentally, it has long been recognized that humans develop cephalocaudally -- from head to tail, from seventh to first chakra beings.

Sometime before the advent of language, at about 18 - 21 months, the soul descends into the sixth chakra. Responses, both physical and emotional, are generally guided intuitively. We might say that toddlers are right hemisphere beings. They are busy putting together their sensory motor world. They explore with their hands as well as their mouths. There are no rules. They stare at objects for a long period of time, forming the construct or idea of the object.

As the child begins to acquire language and speak in simple words and sentences, the soul enters the fifth chakra. In the initial stages of language, the energy is devoted to labeling objects, using language specific to the culture. There may be remembrances carried on at the cell level, of the connection to Source. This is evident in the absolute faith on which children accept answers to questions such as: "Why is the sky blue, mommy?" Parental roles at this time are therefore critical. I want to deviate a moment here and speak about the development of children up to about school age. Many of these children have remarkable clairvoyant abilities -- they may "see" angels, devas, even disembodied spirits. We have, however, as an adult community preferred to call these experiences "paranormal," rather than recognize that they are part of our normal spiritual heritage which we have neglected to foster. Instead, we have suggested that children engage in too much fantasy, they have imaginary playmates, or they have not acquired adult perceptions. Indeed, they have not acquired adult perspectives! Most adults don't see or relate to the angels anymore. But that does not make them any less real from my perspectives. In fact, it is my belief that children are gifts to us, they are sent to continually remind us of our spiritual heritage, of the gifts that we have all been given, but gifts which with our emphasis on materialism, we have chosen to ignore. This then, is perhaps one of the greatest tragedies of humanity. We can't see the miracles anymore. We can't see that they occur daily as ordinary cornerstones in the lives of our children.

The time period in which children acquire language is critically important. In reinforcing language, many parents mimic back to their children the very words that the child says. While reinforcing language, unknowingly, this can also reinforce the separation from Source. For example, I had the occasion to observe a father interacting with his two year old child. As she reached for her pacifier, she said "mine." While tickling her, and putting the pacifier in her mouth, the father playfully said: "mine, mine, mine." On initial observation, it might be concluded that the father was reinforcing language. But on a deeper level, he was also teaching object "belong-ing-ness." This is a far different perception from mine which suggests that since planet Earth is God's school, all objects seen and unseen belong to God. They are just on loan for us to use as part of our evolution.

The problem with very young children learning that objects are "mine" is that it makes it difficult for the concept of sharing to emerge about six months later. Concepts of self and others begin to develop as the soul descends into the fourth chakra. If the word "mine" is used for all objects and toys used by a two or three year old, then it gets very confusing for that child when the parent takes away an object at the age of three or four, insisting that the child "learn to share." From the child's perspective, having an object taken away and given to another child seems a form of punishment. It is a violation of universal laws. The "Self" (the Divine self) is not given to the not "self" (or the personality); the not self is included in the Self. If however, there is no attachment to physical objects in the first place, then there is no denial of the Self in the act of sharing.

These are critical concepts which influence the development of self identity as the soul descends into the third chakra. Self identity emerges at about age five and continues throughout the life span. In the Western culture, it seems little time and energy is spend nourishing the uniqueness of individuality and the connectedness with all other parts of reality.

In my role as a single parent, I can remember enrolling my son in a T-Ball team. I expected that this would enable him to learn "game rules," sharing, taking turns and team spirit. I was very disappointed to observe that competition was the name of the game. Enculturation of the male had begun. Winning reared its ugly head. I used to think I was too much of an idealist; now I know I have always been driven by my spiritual nature. I believed six year olds needed to be applauded each time they hit a ball, regardless of the team to which they are assigned.

As a youngster, my son was not the most well coordinated child. But he played with such a great deal of heart. He wanted so much to play, so much that giant tears would trickle down his face when he wasn't picked to play one of the major positions. This single event is just another example of setting kids up to believe they are not good enough. A pattern which, if not interrupted, continues into adolescence and adulthood. A pattern which leads to striving for perfection rather than recognizing we are each perfect just the way we are. I think these early childhood patterns of negative reinforcement create a personality pattern which invites stress. By continually striving for an ideal that has been man made and not related to our Divine Heritage, it is something that is never attainable.

It is my sense that the soul descends into the physical body to activate the second chakra during the pre-adolescent and adolescent years. This perception suggests it is no mystery that sexual activity and interest become heightened at this time -- there is the infusion of a great deal of energy! I suggest too, that the second chakra doesn't get all the attention it should in most metaphysical or soul discussions. We seem to want to focus on the upper centers. The second chakra holds not only the energy associated with male and female gender, but the energy associated with sexuality and the expression of masculinity and femininity. In most families where there *is* open discussion, there might be discussion of sexuality, but only from the point of social expression or physical protection. As a society, we rarely engage our teens in discussions of ways of demonstrating masculinity or femininity. We have failed to recognize that these are human qualities, not gender qualities. We tend instead to blindly fall into traditionally sanctioned social roles. Unfortunately, we rarely engage in discussion until there is a breakdown of the system.

It has only been in the last several years that cancer centers have been willing to talk about repressed feelings and the lack of self-worth felt by many who have a diagnosis of cancer. Males, largely through the work of Robert Bly, are just beginning to discover their own capacities for nurturing, for sensitivity, and for reconnecting, often with their own gender on a deeper level. To this end, it would seem, many males are seeking to find the wholeness with the recognition of their own femininity. Likewise, the majority of persons attending self help seminars on assertiveness training are women -- seeking to find the wholeness in the calling forth of their own traits associated with masculinity.

Lest I belabor the point, I do want to suggest that the second chakra, although we may not relate to our bodies or levels of consciousness in this way, needs more discussion. This is the energy center for the formation of relationships with *all things.* Other people's opinions fall in this category. As a humanity, we seem so influenced by others, so unable to honor another's point of view without abandoning our own. Our social structures are founded on the manipulation of this energy field. Since I am in the health field, I will confine my comments to health rather than politics. In this counry, more than any other, we have a illness management system, not a health care system. Physicians, pharmaists, therapists, nurses, and other types of care givers are all supported because of illness. We focus on the illness, and what is wrong with the body, rather than on the wholeness and the holiness. Body systems engage in sickness in the very act of a simple statement by a physician: "Take the prescribed medication and call me in a week or so if you do not feel better." The implication is clearly that the medication will help and if it doesn't, it is only the physician who can help. Thus our "health care system" is a disempowerment illness-generating system.

Ironically, the second chakra is not only the data bank of consciousness for other's opinions, but is the energetic source for financial management. So to talk about reduction of welfare to offset the strain on the Medicare system is like trading apples for apples. It is just shifting around the energy at the same level! To reform any system, one must go the next higher level or above. If we were to gather together as communities and talk about how we could be better integrated, more loving of our elderly, more inclusive of their involvement, they might feel better and have less need to access the illness reimbursement system.

As stated in an earlier chapter, the first chakra is concerned with biological survival. While all beings have energy in this center from birth, spirit is given the opportunity to fully descend into form usually as the adolescent declares parental independence. Survival issues would at that time likely focus on the need for food, shelter, warmth and safety. Yet all too often in our Western culture, where the focus is on materialism, we seldom teach our children how to become grounded -- how to sit quietly holding spirit in form. Unless specific to religious practices, we do not teach our children to meditate, to be still -- to come to an understanding that the body holds spirit out of which all creation flows. Instead, our youth go off to college under the illusion that education brings knowledge, knowledge brings skills, skills bring accomplishment, accomplishment brings money and money brings security.

At this point, it seems important that a point of clarification be made. At the moment of birth, infants are spiritually seventh chakra beings, yet they have sufficient energy in the first chakra to maintain the form. It is the energy in the form which gives rise to the concept of the inner child. The inner child has needs relating primarily to biological survival such as the need for safety, food, warmth and security. These needs, as a biological being, are present throughout the life cycle. The needs are largely concrete, in other words, they form a construct of what we call "reality." If at any time these needs are not met, it can interfere with the full manifestation of spirit into form.

Again, let me go back to the discussion of abused or neglected children. If abuse is of the nature that the needs for security, safety and nurturing are severely absent, the spirit may have difficulty descending into the lower bodies, particularly working its way through the third and second chakra energy fields. In these cases, the biological form is maintained and energized largely through the sixth chakra limbic system, the phylogenetically older brain system. Since this is the seat of emotional processing, the abuse incidents may have a higher probability of being encoded into the biological cellular memory, even the DNA. This then gives some rationale for the occurrence of abuse from one generation to the next. This is particularly true if the cycle is not interrupted by spiritual enlightenment.

Enlightenment can breakup the abuse cycle and release the cellular memory so that it cannot be transmuted to the next generation. This perception then lends importance to the need for healing the inner child. The real intent is to bring forth the cellular memory for clearing, for release, and for forgiveness. This suggests that it needs to be an internal process, it does not have to be an interactive process between the abused and the abuser.

Before presenting a visual imagery process for healing the inner child, I would like to suggest that by cultural design, all of us are abused, even those of us who have been raised in loving and supportive families. We are abused because we have not been nurtured in maintaining the spiritual connection. Some have been raised, perhaps with religious affiliation, which is not the same thing. Most of us have not been raised to align our will with a Higher Power; we have not been raised with unconditional love. Most of us have not had a self-identity supported which would engender our own Divine Heritage. In our Western culture in particular, we have not been raised with the notion that material possessions are not ours, but are the gifts of creation for the evolution of our souls. While it may be true for some raised in Christian homes that it is appropriate to honor our father and mother, the emphasis has been on honoring our biological parents, not our Creator nor Mother Earth.

In my frame of reality, I view God, or Source as prime Creator, the embodiment of both the masculine and the feminine. Earth I view as feminine, that part of creation which gives birth to all types of form. Although I earlier presented a visual imagery which suggested evolution of the form through lower forms of life, the intent was to open up our perceptions to a connectedness with all life. While I concur with a few of Darwin's perception of evolution, my sense is that it is only the form which is inherited. I suspect there was a quantum leap between ape and man in which man was God-seeded. While the form may have evolved through the Animal Kingdom, the form was infused with the Divine Spirit in the formation of the human species. I don't believe there is a missing link. I am not pulled into the polarity of the need to separate the concepts of Darwin from the Creation stories.

Depending on whether or not you choose to look for clues in our language to find a deeper meaning, you may find it interesting that the word "human" comes from ancient Sanskrit writing which refer to "hu" meaning God, "man" referring to the human species. As "humans,"we are therefore God-seeded. Just as I find it amusing to believe that humans *descended* from monkeys, I am sure monkeys would find it amusing to believe they *ascended* from humans! A little "whimsy" seemed important here, as we enter the process of healing the inner child.

Healing the Inner Child

Lie down on the floor or if you like . . . or sit on a chair . . . changing your position from when you worked with the physical body . . . breathe in deeply . . . and exhale slowly and gently . . . feeling safe and secure in your physical body . . . know it will teach you and be there for you as you heal . . . your emotional body.

Before continuing . . . imagine a giant screen in front of you . . . like a TV screen or a movie theater . . . on this screen you will place particular images, feelings, symbols or sounds of your life.

Now go back in time . . . back to one of your first memories as a young adult . . . pick one single event that seems representative of that time . . . and sense who was with you at that moment . . . what were you doing . . . where you were . . . and from that point in time make an interpretation of what you were learning or what messages you received from that experience . . . then let that image shrink in size . . . or if you cannot retain the image . . . create a feeling, sound or symbol that has meaning for you so that you can store this time as a young adult on your screen . . . then shrink that image, feeling, symbol or sound down to a size of 2" X 2" and place it in the bottom right corner of your screen.

Now go back to a single time when you were a teenager . . . pick an event that you remember as being representative of those ages . . . again look to see who you were with . . . what you were doing . . . where you were . . . then look again to see what you were learning . . . or what messages were there for you . . . as before create an image, feeling, a symbol or a sound representative of that time . . . and let it shrink to a size of about 2" X 2" and place this to the left of your previous one at the bottom of your screen.

Now go to a pre–teen time . . . a period of being 8 or 10 . . . select a single event that may be representative of that time for you . . . look around to see who you are with . . . where you are . . . and what you are doing . . . when you have a clear sense of what was happening . . . look at that situation to see what you were learning . . . or what messages you received . . . as before, create an image, a feeling, a symbol or a sound which represents the pre–teen time . . . let that shrink to a 2" X 2" size and place it to the left of your previous ones at the bottom of your screen.

Go back once more . . . to a time when you were 3 or 4 . . . get a clear image of the child you were . . . make the image of who you were as a child seem very real to you . . . now enter into this image . . . clearly seeing you as the adult you are now . . . with the child you were then . . . sit with this child under the arms of a vast oak tree . . . surrounded by a field of daisies or in a forest . . . which- ever is the most comfortable and safe for you . . . hold this child and ask if there is any fear or pain . . . hurt or disappointment . . . listen carefully to this child . . . and as you are listening . . . be aware that this sweet child may want to crawl into you lap . . . or may want to cry . . . allow that to happen through you if it seems right for you . . . now listen to this child, looking deeply into his or her eyes.

Breathe deeply . . . if you have a sense that this small child needs loving . . . calmly tell the child that you cannot undo what was done . . . but that you can from now on take better care of this child . . . imagine stroking the hair of this child . . . rocking gently back and forth . . . ask this child to forgive you for any harm you may have caused consciously or unconsciously . . . encourage this child to forgive anyone else for any harm he or she may have done . . . consciously or unconsciously . . . acknowledge this beautiful child . . . for the implicit trust he or she has in you . . . smile from your heart of this child who is you . . . and say to this child: "I accept you just as you are . . . you are very special to me . . . I love you and I care deeply for you."

Now ever so gently . . . imagine that you are once again this child . . . feel the love and warmth that flows from the adult you . . . let the caring permeate you the child . . . until your child can regain a sense of being deeply loved . . . tell this child that you are going to take a picture of him or her so you can remember this very moment in time and space . . . then take this image (or make it into a feeling, a symbol or a sound) and shrink it down to a size of about 4" X 4" . . . larger than the other pictures, symbols or sounds . . . and place this to the far left corner at the bottom of the screen . . . now invite the child who is you to come on a journey with you . . . a journey through time and space.

Imagine now that you are going to retrieve the image, feeling, symbol or sound of you when you were 8 or 10 . . . let that fill the screen . . . and let it come back to life now . . . then while holding onto the hand of your small child who loves you and who is deeply loved by you . . . look at what was happening when you were a pre–teen . . . see if there are changes in the image or if new messages come from that time . . . a time you now see through the eyes of a healed child . . . then the two of you are to thank this pre–teen child . . . let the screen fade . . . so that you no longer have either a large or a small image, symbol, feeling or sound at the bottom of the screen of this time.

Continue on your journey holding the hand of yourself as a small child . . . and come to the time when you were a teenager . . . retrieve that image, symbol, feeling or sound and allow it to fill the larger screen . . . like watching a movie . . . let the screen unfold . . . this time look again at what was happening through the eyes of a healed child . . . see what messages are there for the two of you . . . then the two of you are to thank this adolescent child . . . let the screen fade . . . so that you no longer have either a large or a small image, feeling, symbol or sound at the bottom of the screen of this time.

Continue holding the hand of the child that is you and come to the image, feeling, symbol or sound that was you as a young adult . . . let this fill the screen and let it come to life . . . again view this larger screen through the eyes of a healed child . . . see what images or messages appear for you . . . now the two of you are to thank this young adult . . . and let the screen fade . . . so that you no longer have either a large or small image, feeling, symbol or sound on the screen except for the one of you as a small child.

Breathe in the Light and breathe out the Love . . . turn now and look deeply into the eyes of this small child who is you . . . acknowledge the need for playing . . . for unbridled enthusiasm . . . bouncing back from some of life's lessons . . . provide assurances that you want to keep in contact . . . and that you will place the needs of this child in your awareness . . . thank this child who is you for being a guide for you on this journey through time . . . then let this image, feeling, symbol or sound shrink to a size of 2" X 2" . . . retain it in the lower left screen that you may always have it in your consciousness.

Now . . . come back into the adult that you are . . . with a renewed innocence, wonder and joy . . . when you are ready come into full conscious awareness.

Chapter 10 Transposing The Ordinary Into Miracles

The human heart can go to the lengths of God.
Dark and cold we may be, but this
Is no winter now. The frozen misery
Of centuries breaks, cracks, begins to move,
The thunder is the thunder of the flows,
The thaw, the flood, the upstart Spring.
Thank God our time is now when wrong
Comes up to face us everywhere,
Never to leave us till we take
The longest stride of soul men ever took.
Affairs are now soul size
The enterprise
Is exploration into God.
What are you making for? It takes
So many thousand years to wake,
But will you wake for pity's sake?

Christopher Fry
A Sleep of Prisoners

So far, I have presented a model of cognitive processing of the brain, evolutionary perspectives of the body, consciousness of the heart, and astrological perspectives along with concepts of the human energy fields and the chakra system. A discussion of the descent of spirit into form from the seventh to the first chakras has been presented. The course of enlighten–

ment as well as healing begins at this point. While we have been looking at an unfolding plan that seems to have both implicate as well as explicate order, it is now time to talk about the process of ascension or resurrection. We may similarly talk about this in terms of the spirit rising from the first to the seventh chakra.

This is a process of awakening, of remembering -- a process of reclaiming our Divine Heritage. Since I draw heavily on my own experiences, it seems appropriate that I share more of my interpretation of my own experience. It is based not just on my interpretation, but my insights, the reading in many fields of information from astrology to physics, psychology and medicine. Most importantly, information comes from the "lived experience." If I had to make a single conclusion about my life, it would be to urge all of humanity to begin to break down the barriers we have created between fields of information. We need to be willing to expand what it means to be normal. If we continue to place unexplained events into a category of the "paranormal," we may never discover what it really means to be human. We need to be willing to let go of our labels us of other, labels that separate people, nations, cultures and countries, labels that separate experience from the deeper meaning of our lives.

I have stated that the energy in the fields beyond the emotional field is very fine; it is subtle, yet the most powerful. That energy is not exactly expressed in the form of layers as I presented. Instead, it is swirling around, interweaving like the ebb and tide of the oceans. At the outermost realms of our energy fields there is the *cosmic band* or a field of energy which connects our personality with our Higher Self and with universal consciousness. We have however, been conditioned to believe that up until now, all this information has been unavailable to us, it has been called the "unconscious." From an energy perspective there is nothing unconscious at all! This is a myth of our social conditioning. We have been led to believe over eons of time that while we live in our bodies, we cannot access all that we are. We have instead empowered the psychologist and the physician with the responsibility for our mental and our physical health. We have given up our authority to trust in our own decisions. Since we gave this power away a long time ago, we now feel as if we are pawns in a game we no longer have interest in playing. Yet for many people who have not had the opportunities for education, and who have not had role models to challenge the system, it seems there is no way out of the morass.

I think that this is why the timing is right for my story. It's time for me to stand in my own truth. It's time for me to say that our lives are guided by a Grand Design, perhaps too subtle for us to understand. Yet at the same time, we must surrender to that guidance. We must be willing to let go of all that we know -- for our knowledge of the world, our place in it and how it works certainly is not helping us as a humanity evolve! So I now share with you my insights, my interpretations, and my understanding which come from years of reading as well as being willing to listen to the inner guidance. It's O.K. if it doesn't make sense to you because it is my story. I invite you to stretch yourself a little, to be open to a different view of the world.

I believe that the outermost band of energy, the karmic band of energy began pushing other energy fields into my awareness. initiating experiences which, at the time, I could only interpret as illness. Long after my symptoms had gone away, and long after I was aware that I really was on a soul journey, I continued to see other evidence of how spirit was working in my life. There was nearly a twenty year interval between my first symptom and an incident which was like the final piece falling into a puzzle. The incident happened only several years ago. I was at the home of a friend taking a course on the "Middle Pillar Healing Technique" which is associated with the sacred Kabbalah. At the time, my friends were planning a trip to Egypt. As I leafed through the flyers and brochures on Egypt, to my astonishment, I came across a picture of the Temple of Saqquara. It is a step temple, the exact replica of which I had made into a logo for my business cards only six months previous to seeing this picture! My friend, Dan Chesebro, a gifted psychic and healer, casually said to me, "Of course it looks familiar. You have been there. The temple of Saqquara is the place of soul initiation for those who lived during that time."

Following these words, I did some library research. Then I followed this with a period of deep meditation. I have enough practice with meditation and have worked extensively with hypnotherapists, so that I can now enter into a state with focused awareness. What came to me was that I was indeed in that temple! I had climbed into the Sarcophagus, which is like a large coffin. It was used as we would use a sensory deprivation chamber today. The intent, in ancient Egypt, was to eliminate sight, sound, feeling, taste and smell to allow the soul initiate to enter into the space of *no-thing-ness.* It was proposed that while in that space, it was easiest to remember the connection with Source. This revelation accounted for my unshakable sense of *knowing* that there was *no-thing* wrong with me.

From my reading and research, I have stated that the one of the outer-most layers of our energy field contains a karmic band (in addition to the cosmic band). it is this energy that serves as a blueprint for how we will meet the challenges and life obstacles that we have contracted for in this life time. It is also the band which contains in capsule form, the energy relating to all other lifetimes. Since this field is energy, made up of electrons and protons whirling in space, there is no reason to assume that it is unreal. I suspect that when I had an X-ray taken of my head, the particular life time I spent in Egypt came in direct alignment with the center of my head. The picture of what was a tumor, the whited-out area on the X-Ray was really nothing more than a picture of a past life experience, represented in negative form as a blur of white, mistaken as a tumor.

I was then presented with the opportunity of deciding what I would do about it -- would I believe in the pathology, or would I look for other interpretations? At the time, I did not know how important our choices are, nor did I really know anything about aligning our will with a Higher Will. I just lived my life in an ordinary way, unmindful that there were miracles in the making.

It is my understanding that this outer energy field corresponds with the seventh chakra. It is through this chakra that intuitive processes originate, processes which are predominately right hemisphere related. This would explain my intuitive knowing *that I would not die!* This would also account for the strange language that I used in my own recognition that I would not die. My words that "I would not die because I had not done what it was I needed to do on this planet" implies some kind of *knowing* about incarnation, a *knowing* about soul assignments, a *knowing* that I was a volunteer in this time and space.

My experience also represents tapping into universal knowledge, where all souls evolve through different experiences, in other times and places, other constellations, galaxies, and other planetary systems in the solar system. My language would suggest a *recognition* of life beyond this planet. ven as I use the word "recognition" now, it means to "re-cognize," to re-think, to come to a different understanding. My experience, in short, was to recognize my own soul essence!

The times when I was working with visualization in clearing the symptoms of Multiple Sclerosis would imply my having some kind of knowledge of the energy associated with the sixth chakra, although it was nearly fifteen years before I discovered this information and this terminology. The ability to visualize, to use the third eye, to look through the obvious to create a different kind of reality would be functions of the sixth chakra. The sixth chakra has also been associated with the celestial energy field, the realm of angels. I suspect that I had great assistance from angels, as my reaction to both the tumor and the Multiple Sclerosis, was one in which I held no fear and no anger. There was just a *knowingness* that somehow my experience had a different meaning, a deeper reality.

It has been said that the celestial field and the sixth chakra are associated with soul awareness. I imagine as I accepted that the symptoms were not "real" for me, I surrendered to the opening and descent of my own soul into my body. It was as if a higher power encouraged this awareness. That Higher Power brought full descent of spirit into form. Although I don't remember feeling that it was a time of spiritual growth, I did maintain a "light hearted" attitude. This was evident the time I was driving to the neurologist and pondered whether or not the toll bridge would accept twenty-five cents in pennies or in a quarter.

The energy that seemed the driving force throughout my illness as well as the enduring years that followed, may be regarded as energy from the fifth chakra. This energy seeks to align personal will with the Divine Plan. The energy field associated with the fifth chakra has also been called the spiritual field. (I recognize this may seem a bit confusing, as I think all the energy fields are of spirit). Yet using that terminology, my spirit simply would not be dampened, not in the face of death, terminal illness, nor in facing abortion of my own daughter. I continued to search for that which was true for me, hanging onto, it seems only threads of intuition. I wanted to speak my truth as it was emerging, but I didn't yet trust my own wisdom. I was stretching my boundaries beyond the limitation of the five senses as the time I had a paraconscious or preconscious sense of the two men who would be helpful to me and who could be trusted, before I jumped my car over the curb, having lost in an instant, all visual processing.

As the energy descended through my mental field, it served as the impetus to continue with the questioning, the searching, long after all symptoms had passed. It seems I was blessed with the use of both hemispheres (although I used to think I was right hemisphere dominant). The *"what if"* questions are indicative of right hemisphere thinking. "*What if* I created the illness? *What if* I could uncreate it? *What if* I don't have an abortion? *What if* I did? I think perhaps spirit was attempting to balance my right hemisphere in a Western dominated left hemisphere culture. My spirit was teaching me to trust in the face of all odds. I am aware now that I used my left hemisphere in logical and analytic thinking, looking for a pattern, looking for what it was that was true for me, using discernment and critical thinking. The times when I noticed that ten opinions from ten doctors did not yield the same results, are an example.

The mental field has been associated with the fourth chakra, with the heart and with the sense of loving. Just as I would use my mental processing for answering questions, for conducting the self-dialogue, there were also many moments when I felt incredibly connected with all of the universe. Those moments when I transcended the illness to appreciate the greenness of the grass, the blueness of the sky, I was expressing a Higher Consciousness. This was the expression of my connection to the Universe. I have a sense now that the fourth chakra was activated through my sense being fully aware that I was in my body, but that my body was not the totality of who I really was.

I remember the constant shifting back and forth. My shifting from awareness of the upper chakras to the lower chakras, from Heaven to Earth is much like the perceptual shifts one experiences as one looks at a picture of a vase. With a slight shift in perception the vase can be two faces in profile looking at each other. My experiences were like that. With the energy of the fourth chakra I was able to love my body enough to feel absolute delight with feeling and touching, with hearing and smelling. I could feel the sheets on the bed, and had a knowing they could feel me. This is just a single instance of feeling a different kind of connectedness, sensing and living with a continual perceptual shift that I did not understand.

Previously I stated that the fourth chakra is associated with the expression of Higher Conscious–ness. Although I have not considered myself religious, I have been a student of the great religions of the world for many years, even before my illness. It has only been in the last few years that I have been courageous enough to want to regard myself as mystical. Yet all through my illness I had images and remembrances of other times and places. Sometimes it seemed so strange to hear myself chanting, "I AM healing, I AM grace, I AM in tune with the universe." I didn't tell anyone about these experiences because they did not fit the "norm" of human understanding at the time. Few would understand that the chanting was part of me. I didn't share these experiences because knew, that part of me would not be recognized by the world in which I lived. I remember now that I had training from my early experiences with my mother, to "hide" the sacred parts of me. Since I have recently spent much more time reading the esoteric, sacred and mystical literature, I know that the words "I AM" are the most powerful in any healing or consciousness–raising process. They are patterned after Christ who said: "I AM the way, the truth and the Light. Be to state to the Universe: "I AM that I AM" from a Buddhist point of view is to recognize one's connection with God.

Previously, I also mentioned that the emotional field is connected with the third chakra, the seat of our self-identity. The manner in which a new identity is formed follows the descent of spirit through the fifth to the first chakras. My absolute faith that the knowledge inside me was that which constituted *MY truth* (a fifth chakra energy). As that energy descended and I listened to my heart (a fourth chakra energy), I was able to honor the shifts of perception. In other words, my spirit was transforming the energy in the second chakra, I was in the process of transcending the opinion of others. As I worked through giving-up the opinions of others, this higher energy was used to transcend the beliefs of the culture, which is a first chakra energy. It is my understanding now that the purpose of my illness was for me to form and reclaim a new identity (to transform the energy of the third chakra). The process involved forming an identity made-up of all things I believed to be true for me regardless of whether or not they were true for anyone else -- then to be willing to stand and honor that truth.

As I took a closer look at third chakra energy, long after my recovery, I was suddenly struck with the information that the third chakra contains the energy which nourishes the visual system. So again, by shutting down my visual system (which was likely a soul contract), my spirit was gifting me with the opportunity to develop my own identity -- a spiritual identity that was not bounded by the perception of others. I was developing an identity that transcended time and space -- one that was constantly evolving and changing. I needed an identity that flowed with events, without ever believing what was happening was "personal," nor "real."

It was as if my spirit was teaching me never to doubt that I could overcome all obstacles.

The moment in my blindness when I was teaching at the University of Kansas and discovered that learning was not a competitive activity and translated that into the recognition that living was not a competitive activity either, serves me now as evidence of working through the energy of second chakra. Once I was willing to give up competition, I was not only able to come to a new identity, but to relate to my students on a far different level. I was able to move into relationships of the heart.

In retrospect, I know many of my experiences with illness were to open me to the possibility of trusting my own intuitive abilities. I therefor prefer at this point in time to regard myself as a mystic rather than a psychic, because mysticism has a higher vibration than astral projections, although I have to admit to my own psychic experiences. When the physician told me the results of the myelogram were negative, I already knew that! I had seen them! At the time I did not know there was a difference between clairvoyance and lucid dreaming. And I do know that I had other psychic or precognitive experiences. The perception that I could trust the two young men on the street as I jumped the car over the curb, could be regarded as psychic phenomena. My "seeing" the space between the cars on my right, as I entered a left hand turn, could also be regarded as an instance of extrasensory perception. My ability to design a logo representing a step pyramid on my business cards before I had seen actual pictures of the Temple of Saqquara would be another example.

But for the most part, most of my healing was concerned with releasing the energy of the first chakra, which holds the beliefs of the culture. There was a part of me that would not give up my spirit to the diagnosis of the physician. I clung to the truth that I was not having "symptoms," I was just not seeing. I clung to the belief that I would not die even in the face of a terminal diagnosis, because for me, it just wasn't real. I clung to the knowing that I could bear a child and she would be fine even if it was believed by the culture and the medical profession that such an advent would increase the symptoms of Multiple Sclerosis.

At this point, I want to make a special note. It is hard to explain one's life journey. My journey into healing may be different from anyone else. The point is, that we must awaken ourselves, we must find the miracles within. I am awakening to the miracles. I am becoming acutely aware that they are the stuff of our ordinary lives! Yet we have to look for them. They come in the definition of our experiences, the meaning we assign to the events that "happen" to us. I know that I have always been under guidance. I have traveled this path with angels. I AM God-seeded, just as each of you are, when you awaken to the deeper meaning for being on earth. Our spiritual nature is light hearted, blissful, and joyful. WE ARE ON A JOURNEY OF HIDE AND SEEK. WE JOURNEY BE TO FIND THE HIGHER SELF. THE MIRACLES, THE COINCIDENCES, THE SERENDIPITY OF SPECIAL MOMENTS ARE THE ANONYMOUS FACE OF GOD!

I invite you now to enter into a special guided visual imagery process. It is one which connects us together, unites us with Mother Earth, and gives adoration to our Creator. It is a process which expands our perception into the realm of being multi-dimensional beings, no longer limited by the five senses. For me, it serves as recognition that healing does not come from outside us, it comes when we open ourselves to the healing -- when we remember our own Divinity, when we connect to the God-Source inside us.

There is the deeper meaning to life, *always the deeper meaning.* I do know that we are entering a new age, a new millennium, a time of great awakening. The human spirit is yearning to be free. We see this in the fall of communism, the Berlin Wall tumbling down, in a war stopped dead in its tracks which could potentially have triggered a Third World War. The human species is caught in the act of evolving. Even as we speak, the membranes between the cerebral hemispheres and the limbic system are dwindling. The duality is resolving, a Oneness is emerging. From the very depths of the human spirit there is a crying of the need for social reform, for economic reform, for health care reform. It will not come from the systems themselves. Reform will come from awakening souls. The children in our schools cry out in their desperate turn to drugs. They know at some level of the deeper experience. Change is everywhere -- it is inescapable because it is global, it is planetary, it is universal!

Information and wisdom come to us as we open ourselves to guidance -- to connection with each other, those in bodily form and those not in form. To separate ourselves from the rest of the cosmos is simply an artifact of our social conditioning. To be open to the wisdom, to trust the truth is the beginning of the journey. We must be mindful of the power of our choices (See Figure 67). Our choices can cause a life shift when we are willing to engage in self-awareness at each moment of time. All we need is a willingness to experience all that life has to offer us. The willingness invites its own opening.

Although I am not Jewish and have no awareness of a capacity to know foreign languages (ooops, perhaps I have just forgotten), I find myself chanting: "Kodoish, Kodoish, Kodoish Adonai Tsebayoth/Sabayoth." It just comes to me naturally. My understanding is that this is Hebrew. It means "Holy, Holy, Holy is the Lord God of Hosts." According to J.J. Hurtak, author of *The Keys of Enoch*, it is a glorious salutation given to the "Lord of Hosts" by those conscious of their dominions of the Living God.

Journey Into All That Is

Lie down in a comfortable position . . . and begin breathing deeply . . . breathing in the breath of all who have gone before . . . Buddha . . . Khrisna . . . Jesus, The Christ . . . breathing in the body of Leonardo de Vinci . . . Michelangelo . . . George Washington . . . Abraham Lincoln . . . Henry Ford . . . Babe Ruth . . . John F. Kennedy . . . Ella Fitzgerald . . . John Lennon . . . John Glenn . . . George Wagner . . . breathing in the breath of all beings for all time . . . and as you exhale . . . breath out into the universe all that you are . . . loving . . . compassionate . . . trusting . . . whimsical . . . and joyous . . . sharing your soul with the Universe . . . breathe in to the sacred count of three . . . the trinity of Father, Mother and Holy Spirit . . . breathe this essence into your body . . . and exhale out to the count of seven . . . letting go of all that you are . . . enlightenment . . .

vision . . . truth . . . loving . . . identity . . . relationships . . . beingness . . . sustaining and nurturing all beings for all time.

Imagine going now . . . to a field of daisies and lie down . . . breathing in the pure gold essence . . . the Christed essence of Light and Love . . . feel yourself part of the field of daisies . . . feel yourself as part of the nurturing planet . . . breathe now as you did as a child . . . in tune with the Mother . . . gently caressing each breath . . . loving each atom, molecule, tissue and organ that represents your being in form.

Hear the soft whisper of the fawn . . . as it shakes loose its wetness from the birthing . . . flood this small being with your love . . . as you do all creatures of the forest . . . guide the steps of the scampering squirrel . . . hesitate with each hop of the rabbit . . . as do the angels guide your own footsteps . . . breathe aloft with each bird that soars into the Heavens . . . ground yourself in greenness . . . breathing into each blade of grass, the grace of flowing with the wind . . . sing your heart song into the flowering of each blossom.

Hear now the sound of the babbling brook . . . the stream of water . . . not unlike your own stream of consciousness . . . imagine now rolling over and over . . . gently descending into the stream . . . until you feel you are one with the water . . . flowing . . . lapping against the shore . . . floating . . . moving gently . . . touching and caressing the form of the Mother Earth . . . seeking sustenance . . . moving now swifter and wider . . . into your own beingness . . . into giant streams . . . transforming the landscape with your flow . . . uniting all that would seem to be an undertow in your gentle movement . . . stretching now to the far sides of the river bank . . . sweeping to the depths . . . washing clean the algae . . . the rocks . . . expanding from a stream into a river . . . a river into a lake . . . holding and supporting the many forms of fish that yearn for life from you . . . pausing to support and nurture them.

Now expanding . . . from the lake into the giant gulf stream . . . being drawn ever deeper into the life of the coral . . . the myriad forms of life . . . the dolphins . . . the whales . . . hearing their yearning calls for awakening . . . allowing and accepting that for eons of time these magical creatures . . . the whales and dolphins have served mankind by absorbing negative thought forms . . . release now your striving and fear . . . release these feelings to the dolphins . . . the water . . . flowing into expansiveness . . . feel yourself touching the sides and bottom of the oceans . . . as a vast being . . . absorbing and supporting . . . releasing and flowing . . . into the ocean . . . the cleansing . . . the vastness of flow . . . you . . . the water . . . the Earth Mother are One.

Slowly in your watery form . . . you surrender . . . you surrender to the Sun, the Source, every molecule . . . every atom . . . into the air . . . into the ethers . . . you rise above the earth . . . into the atmosphere . . . expanding . . . nurturing all life forms . . . you move into *The All That Is* . . . transcending time and space . . . floating . . . beyond this planet . . . into the cosmos . . . into the *no–thing–ness* . . . you are consciousness . . . ever present . . . expanding past the moon with her feminine energy . . . her capacity to relate to your instincts . . . your habits . . . something deep inside you stirs your imagination . . . your receptivity . . . your impressionability . . . your desire for the freshness of each experience . . . you feel a nurturing awakening . . . you feel the depths of your emotions . . . acknowledge your mood swings . . . a profound sensitivity wells up from the very essence of your cellular being . . . you feel an incredible sympathy for the suffering of mankind.

Into the vastness of space you pass . . . you see Mercury . . . and know that it represents the messenger planet of the Gods . . . it represents your mind . . . the link between spirit and matter . . . between soul and personality . . . you recognize that from this place comes your power of communication . . . your ability to interpret and reason . . . to gather facts and perceive relationships . . . your mobility and adaptability comes from this planet . . . you caress this being in your passing.

Once gain you feel yourself in the vastness of space . . . floating in the black velvet . . . guided by the stars from which you came . . . embracing all that you are . . . moving until Venus appears before you . . . and in your own being you acknowledge the receptive side of your emotional nature . . . you feel the power of her love . . . the power of attraction and cohesion . . . the power of quiet gentle persuasion . . . you feel her balancing and harmonizing effects . . . her eternal desire to act as peacemaker . . . you absorb her affection . . . and in so doing acknowledge your own sense of sympathy . . . romance . . . pleasure . . . and you bless the beauty of your own soul . . . touching and holding the vast expanse of Venus . . . in the palm of your hand . . . you release her and journey into the beyond.

Breathing in your ever-expanding state . . . you sense you are coming into the energy field of planet Mars . . . the opposite of Venus . . . you sense the positive outgoing masculine energy . . . you feel the deep desire of this planet . . . the need for action . . . it stirs all that is in you that is physical . . . you sense the assertiveness in the very marrow of your bones . . . the aggressiveness held in check . . . the courage . . . the self that is inspired by this tiny red planet . . . and it sparks your dreams of adventure . . . you smile in your passing . . . eager to move still farther.

The giant planet of Jupiter looms before you . . . you float around her like a satellite . . . exploring the vast consciousness of this floating body . . . you sense that this planet is symbolic of your own expansion . . . it triggers your higher mind . . . the deep wisdom of benevolence and generosity . . . you sense that from this planet the urgency to examine all your experiences . . . to learn from them . . . the urge to improve the state of things . . . and from inside you comes a deep knowing that Jupiter is your center of opportunity . . . reward and abundance . . . tolerance and charity . . . faith and justice . . . loyalty and extravagance . . . you have a profound sense that this marvelous shimmering planet is your protector . . . yet it magnifies all aspects of your life that you might learn . . . it is your place of inspiration and counsel . . . with reluctance you allow yourself to move past this great planet . . . knowing how profoundly it affects you . . . you move on . . . into the cosmos . . . reaching further and further out into the galaxy.

The rings of Saturn intrigue you more than this orange ball floating in space . . . the ice crystals which form the rings give you an eerie feeling . . . this planet is far different than others you have passed . . . there is something etheric about this being . . . you have been here before . . . sitting on the seat of High Council for the Universe . . . you have a sense that this planet assists with deep introspection and meditation . . . it fills you with unconditional love to work out your karma in the process of evolution . . . you feel the seriousness of this being . . . the sacredness . . . the deep caring and responsibility . . . the strength of ambition wells inside your breast . . . yet you have a sense of restraint . . . of caution . . . of perseverance . . . you feel a need to bless this place . . . and in so doing a joyfulness comes over you . . . and you see this planet in transition . . . a knowing comes to you . . . soon this vast planet will pass on the mantle of Universal Governance to the small planet Earth . . . your home planet . . . which will become the seat of High Council . . . you sense the awesomeness that this entails . . . you pass now through her outer rings again . . . once more finding yourself entering the *no-thing-ness* of space.

Uranus looms before you, one of the largest planets in the solar system . . . matched nearly to the size of your expanded self . . . you feel the mental power of this planet as you draw near . . . you become aware of the awesome power of this being . . . this planet pulls at you, tugs at each part of your being . . . urges the claiming of your freedom . . . you notice that without words . . . this planet contains a force which destroys the old to allow room for the new . . . it breaks up the crystallizing force of Saturn . . . it displaces and overthrows the established attitudes which have outlived their usefulness . . . you feel her rebellion . . . it rises within you . . . you waken to the sense of invention that flows from her energy fields into your own . . . you sense the detachment that comes from intuitive knowing . . . yet there is something deeper here . . . you dare to float . . . scanning the surface . . . you embrace the planet . . . and hear her urgent whispers to awaken your own Christ Consciousness . . . to begin to move in flow with Spirit . . . to transcend the limitations of form . . . the awesomeness of this being seems almost overwhelming . . . you cry out in tears of release and joy . . . with reluctance you release yourself from this energy field.

You float again . . . without form . . . now with focused awareness . . . you are in the realm of consciousness . . . eternity . . . in a space two million miles from where you started . . . the vastness of the universe presses upon your soul . . . you feel yourself being drawn into the energy of Neptune . . . you sense it has a higher vibration than that of Venus . . . it is a vast loving being . . . you feel the receptivity . . . as if she welcomes a small child into her bosom . . . nurtured and held close . . . you open to the awesomeness of this gentle being . . . for this planet influences the highest evolution you can achieve in a single embodiment cycle . . . your idealism soars . . . you become hypersensitive . . . aware of all things for all time . . . creativity flows not just into form but feelings . . . and visions . . . you put aside all need to be practical . . . you move into awareness of the depth of compassion . . . time and space collapse . . . and in some ancient Grecian memory you remember Neptune as the God of the Oceans . . . you feel a sense of being washed clean in your passing.

You find yourself out now into the farthest reaches of our solar system . . . no body . . . no form . . . no energy . . . just a point of focus . . . you move in this expanded state . . . having a sense of amusement as you come to the tiniest planet of all . . . Pluto . . .

representing all that has not yet been integrated into the collective consciousness . . . the unseen path this planet leaves in space is so erratic . . . it is as if Pluto is not yet in tune with the rest of the solar system . . . you sense this little rascal planet represents the urge to transform and regenerate . . . to bring rebirth . . . to bring cleansing . . . to assist in healing . . . with a gentle breath you steady her course . . . that her wisdom may infuse the solar system.

You pause in your journey . . . gazing at the vastness of the Milky Way . . . as if God had taken a handful of stars . . . in a giant game of jacks . . . and flung them across the sky . . . for the sake of amusement . . . and yet from this place it is like peering out of a peephole of an egg . . . into worlds and worlds beyond . . . you stand on the brink of infinity . . . instantly dwarfed by it all and yet part of it all . . . you amuse yourself with the notion that you could crawl right into the lap of the big dipper . . . hang your feet over the lip of those stars . . . and rock back and forth . . . as if you were in a giant rocking chair . . . and from there you could contemplate the constellations of Leo . . . Orion's belt . . . and wonder if it would be large enough to girth your own being . . . so vast you have become . . . you pinpoint Acturus . . . Andromeda . . . The Pleiades . . . other sister star systems . . . without words . . . or explanation . . . you know some of these places . . . you have been there . . . some of you have originated from there . . . these are the homes of other beings who urge your remembering . . . a part of your consciousness yearns to return . . . to the stars from whence you came.

But there is a calling . . . you feel a drawing to Earth . . . you feel yourself descending through time and space . . . passing each planet in the cosmos . . . reaching out and taking part of the essence of each . . . weaving these golden threads into a giant spiral . . . you sink past Neptune and Uranus . . . Saturn . . . Jupiter and Mars . . . weaving and weaving threads of consciousness into the fabric of your own being . . . building and transforming your very DNA structure . . . building infinity into the fabric of your being . . . transposing your cellular body . . . from a two helix to a twelve helix model . . . you feel as you did in the beginning . . . yourself as spirit descending into matter . . . taking on form . . . coming through the ethers of planet Earth.

You draw your awareness back to form . . . from the universe that you contain inside your being . . . through the universal consciousness of your energy fields . . . back into your celestial field . . . your spiritual field . . . descending through the mental and emotional fields . . . drawing in your astral field . . . containing your vastness . . . weaving and re–weaving a new etheric template . . . restructuring your physical body . . . breathing in the sacred breath of life into your own form . . . having the profound sense that you are not separate from the rest of the cosmos . . . it is contained in you . . . and you in it . . . as the planets influence your daily and monthly cycles . . . so to do you influence their endless travels in space . . . you who are God–seeded . . . you are being called . . . called to become a co–creator . . . to create this Universe with your awareness. . . with your love . . . with the Light you are.

Breathe now . . . containing all that you are in bodily form . . . wiggle your toes and your fingers . . . listen to your breathing . . . feel as you have never felt before . . . the endless rivers flowing in your form . . . the mountains and valleys of your own being . . . the fire in your heart . . . feel the floor with your hands . . . and allow the floor to feel your hands . . . absorb all the love and goodness that Mother Earth sends into your soul . . . your being . . . your physical body.

Come into full awareness . . . out of the altered state of consciousness . . . perceive with a new focus . . . the vastness of who you really are . . . love the *miracle* of yourself . . . and know in your own *ordinary* way . . . that you are one with God.

LIFE SHIFT

WILLING TO EXPERIENCE

EXPANSION

TAKING CHARGE

CHOICES

OPINIONS

ASSUMPTION

BELIEFS

MOVEMENT TOWARD LIVING, DOING, LOVING

I AM
EXPERIENCING
SELF - AWARENESS
NOW

FEAR
GUILT
JEALOUSY
ANGER
RESENTMENT
REJECTION
DOUBT

CHOICES

CONTRACTION

GIVING UP

NOT WILLING TO KNOW

Bibliography

Chapter 1 My Story

Lana J. Ford, *I'm Just That Kind of Woman*, New York, Carlton Press, 1982.
Formal citations of poetry in this chapter were first published in 1982.

Chapter 2 The Physical Body

Jean Houston, *The Possible Human,* New York, J.P. Tarcher, 1992
The reference to the kinesthetic body came from my work with Jean in Mystery School of 1991 as well as this text.

Jean Houston & Robert Masters, *Listening to the Body,* New York, Delta Books, 1978.
Other insights regarding the kinesthetic body were taken from this text by Jean and Robert, who based their work on the Alexander technique and the Feldenkreis method.

Thich Nhat Hanh, *The Miracle of Mindfulness,* Boston, Beacon Press, 1987.
The concept of Mindfulness and a direct quote was taken from Thich Nhat Hanh's Manual on Meditation.

Jean Achterberg, *Imagery in Healing,* Boston, Shambhala Publications, 1987; and audio tape by same name from Boulder, Co, Sounds True, 1991.
For information on imagery, citations were taken from Jean Achterberg's work -- both her book and her audio tape.

Robert Masters, *Masters Psychophysical Method,* Chicago, Il, Mythic Theatre, 1991.

The guided imagery incorporated into the section,"Alignment of the Physical Body" was influenced by Robert Masters in a workshop I attended in Chicago in 1991. His work can be explored in depth through this audio series. The philosophical background behind working with the mind/body in this fashion comes from the work of Feldenkrais. Although not referenced, Feldenkrais' older text *Body and Mature Behavior* (New York, International Universities Press, 1975) is worth investigation. For information on the Feldenkrais Method, and national workshops, readers may wish to contact the Movement Studies Institute, 1832 Second Street, Berkley, Ca 94710.

Lana J. Ford, *What Color is Your Brain,* Paw Paw, MI, JLM Enterprises, 1988.

Information contained in the process titled "Entering the Brain-Body Temple" was adapted from a text I published as part of my doctoral dissertation. It is available from me, that text was influenced by the work I completed with Ned Herrmann in his professional workshop called Applied Creative Teaching and Learning (ACTAL) in Lake Lure, NC.

Chapter 3 Thinking Styles of the Brain

Ned Herrmann, *The Creative Brain,* Brain Books, Lake Lure, NC, 1988.

Formal citations on the four quadrants of the brain came from Ned Herrmann work's as well as his workshops I attended, cited above.

Adatol Brillard in Jeanne Ackterber's audio tape *Imagery in Healing* Boulder, Sounds True, 1991.

Adatol Brillard was the New York editor who made the comment regarding "being on the edge of being."

Stuart Dimond, Performance by split brain humans on lateralized vigilance tasks, *Cortex,* 15, pp. 43-50, 1979.

Functioning of the left and right hemispheres of the brain was gathered from this article. Although not specifically cited, other works related to hemispheric preferences can be found in W. Lowen's *Dichotomies of the Mind* (New York, John Wiley & Sons, 1982); S. Sringer and G. Deutsch's text *Left Brain, Right Brain* (New York, W. H. Freeman, 1981) and Tony Buzan's *Use Both Sides of Your Brain* (New York, E.P. Dutton, 1974).

Charles Hampden-Turner, *Maps of the Mind*, New York, Collier Books, 1982.

Charles Hampden-Turner offered the most exquisite tracking of theoretical positions regarding the mind.

Edward de Bono, *Lateral Thinking: A Textbook of Creativity,* New York: Harper & Row, 1970.

Edward De Bono's books are confusing because of the differences in American and British titles. His text on lateral thinking is titled *Lateral Thinking: A Textbook of Creativity*. Although not cited directly, background information was gleaned from his text *De Bono's Thinking Course* (New York, Facts on File Publications, 1982). The story of the merchant's daughter came from *New Think* (New York, Avon, 1971) by De Bono, but was quoted from the version offered in the Hampden-Turner text.

Charles Panati, *Extraordinary Origins of Everyday Things*, New York, Harper & Row, 1987.

The reference to the origin of toothpaste was found in this text.

Paul MacLean, On the evolution of three mentalities, in Silvano Arieti and Gerald Chryanowski's text *New Dimensions in Psychiatry: A World View,* Volume 2 (New York, Wiley, 1977).

Reference to the concept of the Triune Brain was taken from Paul MacLean's above work. However, the formal citation was taken from Jean Houston's book, *The Possible Human* (New York, J.P. Tarcher, 1982). In pursuing my doctoral studies I completed a major work on the details on brain functioning in a paper titled *Each to the Tune of a Different Drummer* (1988). It was a lengthy volume with over 387 references, citing all that was known about the neurophysiological functioning of the brain at that time. It can be requested from me or a copy may be reviewed at the library of The Union Institute, Cincinnati, OH. I also published a paper titled "Investigation into clinical reasoning as a cognitive/phenomenological process," available from me as an unpublished manuscript completed at Western Michigan University.

Jean Houston, *The Possible Human,* New York, J.P. Tarcher, 1992. Concepts of evolution of the brain were taken from this text.

Although not referenced directly, the reading of several other books no doubt influenced my knowledge base. I refer the serious reader to tackle Charles Laughlin, John McManus and Eugene G. d'Aquili's work: *Brain, Symbol and Experience* (Boston, Shambhala, 1990). The master of them all is perhaps Robert Ornstein. My favorite is *The Evolution of Consciousness* (New York, Prentice Hall Press, 1991) and his earlier work with David Sobel, *The Healing Brain* (New York, Simon & Schuster, 1987).

Figures 1–4, 6–7, were adapted from my text *What Color is Your Brain,* (Paw Paw, MI, JLM Enterpreises, 1988); these were used with permission from Ned Herrmann from his handouts in the Applied Creative Teaching and Learning workshop in Lake Lure, NC. Figures 5, 8, and 9 were my original illustrations.

Chapter 4 Personality Types

Michael Patton, *Qualitative Evaluation Methods,* Beverly Hills, CA, Sage Publications, 1986.
Formal citation referring to the story about Halcolm was taken from this text.

Ingri & Edgar D'Aularie, *Book of Greek Myths,* Garden City, NY, Doubleday, 1962.
Much of the information on the Grecian myths was adapted from this text.

Charles Hampden–Turner, *Maps of the Mind,* New York, Collier Books, 1982.

Comments on Grecian mythology were taken from the work of Charles Hampden-Turner. He also offered insights into the work of Jung I found particularly insightful.

Anthony Andrew, *The Greeks,* New York, Knopf, 1967.
The funeral oration quote from Pericles was taken from this source. Additional background on Greek myths was gained from Edith Hamilton's *Mythology* (New York, Mentor Press, 1959) and G.S. Kirk's *The Nature of Greek Myths* (New York, Penguin Books, 1976).

Carl Jung, *Psychological Types,* New York, Harcourt Brace, 1923 and *Modern Man in Search of a Soul,* New York, Harcourt Brace and Company, 1933.
Information on the work of Carl Jung was gleaned from Jung's own work *Psychological Types* and *Modern Man in Search of a Soul.* Background information was taken from Jung's *Collected Works,* (Princeton, NJ, Princeton University Press, 1970).

David Keirsey & Marilyn Bates, *Please Understand Me: Character and Temperment Types,* Del Mar, CA, Prometheus Memesis Book Company, 1984.
The quote under the section "A Deeper Look at the Wisdom of Jung" was taken from Keirsey and Bates' text.

Isabel Myers & Mary McCaulley, *Manual: A guide to the Development and Use of the Myers Briggs Type Indicator,* Gainesville, FL, Center for Application of Psychological Type, 1985.
Information regarding type theory based on Jung's typology was selected from Isabel Myers & Mary McCaulley's work.

Additional information was gleaned from Isabel & Paul Myers' *Gifts Differing* (Palo Alto, CA, Consulting Psychologists Press (1980). The workshop I attended on the Myers Briggs Type Indicator was sponsored by the American Association for Higher Education; Pat Battle Associates is a Human Resource Management Consulting Company in Columbia, MD. A serious reader wanting to explore personality theories might want to explore Steven Maddi's

Personality Theories, (Georgetown, Ontario, The Dorsey Press, 1980). Although not directly quoted, other information about Carl Jung was gleaned from Joseph Campbell's *The Portable Jung* (New York, Viking Press, 1971).

Figures 10–18 were computer converted from my original illustrations. Figure 19 was adapted from Isabel Myers & Mary McCaulley's *Manual: A Guide to the Development and Use of the Myers Briggs Type Indicator* (Gainesville, FL, Center for Application of Psychological Type, 1985). Figure 20 was used with my permission from my text *What Color is Your Brain* (Paw Paw, MI, JLM Enterprises, 1988).

Chapter 5 Beyond the Brain into Consciousness

Jean Houston, *The Possible Human,* New York, J.P. Tarcher, 1992.
My references to multi-tracking experiences came from this text as well as Mystery School of 1991 with Jean.

Deepak Chopra, *Quantum Healing: Exploring the Frontiers of Mind Body Medicine,* New York, Bantum Books, 1989.
Formal citations were taken from this work regarding evolution from five sensory humans to multi-dimensional humans. Readers are also encouraged to read *Ageless Body, Timeless Mind,* New York, Harmony Books, 1993 for additional insights into the quantum alternative to aging.

Candice Pert, The wisdom of the receptors: Neuropeptides, the emotions and the bodymind, *Advances,* 3, p. 8–16, 1983.
The role of neuropeptides was interpreted from this article by Candice Pert.

Rupert Sheldrake, Cause and effect in science: A fresh look at ten years of consciousness research, Sausalito, CA, *Noetic Sciences Collection,* p. 74–82, 1991.
Information on the morphogenetic field was found in this work.

Deepak Chopra, *Magical Mind, Magical Body,* Chicago: Nightengale Conant Corporation, 1990.
I have been most influence by this audio tape series by Deepak Chopra, I find it equally as important as his books.

Bertrand Babbinet, *The Bioenergetic Matrix,* Kalamazoo, MI, 1991.
Information about how consciousness of the heart works was taken from this workshop with Bertrand Babbinet.

Albert Camus, *The Myth of Sisyphus,* New York, Knopt Publications, 1955; and *The Rebel,* New York, Vantage Press, 1971.
The reference to "sickness unto death" is a reflection of Existentialism taken from these two works by Albert Camus.

Gary Zukav, *The Dancing WuLi Masters*, New York, Quill, 1979.
The reference to the new physics was taken from this work. Serious readers are encouraged to read his second work *Seat of the Soul,* New York, Simon and Schuster, Inc., 1989.

Figures 21–24 were my original illustrations.

Chapter 6 The Vibrating Universe

Itzhak Bentov, *Stalking the Wild Pendulum: On the Mechanics of Consciousness*, Rochester, VT, Destiny Books, 1988.
Formal citations regarding the physics of vibration were taken from this most invaluable resource.

Barbara Brennan, *Hands of Light,* New York, Bantam Books, 1987.
Information on the human energy fields was gleaned from the work of Barbara Brennan, a US astronaut turned healer.

Richard Gerber, *Vibrational Medicine: New Choices for Healing Ourselves,* Santa Fe, NM, Bear & Company, 1988.
Formal citations on the human energy field were taken from this text. Written by a Detroit physician, it is highly recommended not only as a resource on healing ourselves, but the nature of consciousness.

Jerome Frank, *Persuasion and Healing,* New York, Schocken Books, 1961.

Reference to the placebo effect was found in Jerome Frank's first work *Persuasion and Healing.* For a more thorough study, it is recommended that the reader review his more recent work, "The faith that heals" *(The John Hopkins Medical Journal,* 137, p. 127–131, 1975).

Fred Wolf, *The Dreaming Universe*, New York, Simon & Schuster, 1994; and *Parallel Universes: The Search for Other Worlds,* New York, Simon & Schuster, 1988.

Specualtion about the nature of dreams, the formation of reality, and perspectives of alternate realities were gleaned from these two sources.

Marlene Mhyer, Personal communication, Sedona, Arizona, 1995.

Marlene not only served as my publisher, but offered comments regarding the nature of dreams.

Figures 25–32 were adapted from Itzhak Bentov's *Stalking the Wild Pendulum: On the Mechanics of Consciousness* (Rochester, VT, Destiny Books, 1988). Figure 33–36, 38 were my illustrations translated into computer graphics by Karla Mullennix. Figure 37 was a computer illustration adapted from Fred Wolfe's *The Dreaming Universe* (New York, Simon & Schuster, 1994).

Chapter 7 The Chakra System

Norman Shealy & Carolyn Myss, *The Creation of Health,* Wolpole, NY, Stillpoint Publishing, 1988.

Formal references on the creation of health for this chapter were taken from Norman Shealy and Carolyn Myss's book. Additional information on the chakra system was found in Barbara Brennan's work *Hands of Light* (New York, Bantam Books, 1987).

Louise Hay, *You Can Heal Your Life,* Santa Monica, CA, Hay House, 1984.

Information on negative thoughtforms was taken from Louise Hay's hallmark book. She also offers other insights into the origin of nearly all disease processes.

Joane Borysenko, *Guilt is the Lesson, Love is the Teacher,* New York, Warner Books, 1990.
Comments about guilt and the origin of cancer were taken from this text. Joane also offers much insight into the origin of other disease conditions and imbalances of the body. Her first book *Minding the Body, Mending the Mind* (Addison–Wesley Publishing Company, Reading, MA, 1987) is equally important for understanding the mind–body relationship.

Richard Gerber, *Vibrational Medicine,* Santa Fe, NM, Bear & Company, 1988).
In addition to references on the chakra system, this was the only text I found which introduced the concept of miasms.

Carolyn Myss, *Intuitive Diagnosis,* Sounds True, 1992.
Sociological perspectives of the chakra system was gathered from the work of Carolyn Myss in her presentation to the American Holistic Health Association in 1992, her audio tape presentation was called *Intuitive Diagnosis.* It was also from that tape that I found the quote about "scrapping the truth out of the marrow of our bones."

Paul Tillich, *The Eternal Now,* New York, Charles Scribner's Sons, 1963.
Although not formally cited, concepts of the eternal "now" were no doubt influenced by the work of Paul Tillich.

Danah Zohar, *The Quantum Self: Human Nature and Consciousness Defined by the New Physics,* New York, Quill, 1990.
Concepts about the quantum self were gleaned from Danah Zohar's work *The Quantum Self.*

Although not formally cited, one might want to review Richard Bandler and John Grinder's book *Reframing: Neurolinguistic*

Programming and the transformation of Meaning (Moab, Utah, Real People Press, 1982).

Figures 39-40 were original tables; Figure 44 was an original illustration. Figure 41-43 were adapted from Danah Zohar's *The Quantum Self: Human Nature and Consciousness Defined by the New Physics* (New York, Quill, 1990).

Chapter 8 Astrosonics

Itzhak Bentov, *Stalking the Wild Pendulum,* Rochester, VT, Destiny books.
The formal quote at the first of the chapter was taken from Itzhak Bentov's work. The citation regarding vibration of cells and atoms was also taken from this source.

Michael Helius, personal communication, 1994.
The relationship between planetary motion and the earth was taken from Michael Helius' article "Reconnecting with the cosmic bearings of life through the right use of sound" (printed in the January-Febuary issue of *The Journal of Borderland Research,* Santa Fe, NM, 1989); notes on the translation of sound from planetary cylces to cycles per second were taken from Michael's work called "The astrosonic generic tapes" (July-August, *The Journal of Borderland Research,* Santa Fe, MN, 1989).

Raymond Merriman, *Evolutionary Astrology,* W. Bloomfield, MI, Seek-It Publications, 1991.
Astrological references and a deeper understanding of their influence was found in this self-published text.

Frank Capra, *The Tao of Physics,* Boulder, CO, Shambala, 1975.
Although not cited directly, background information on the Yin/Yang was gained in the reading of Frank Capra's work.

Sharry Edwards, Sound Signature Works, Athens, Oh.
Reference to the propositions of Pythagorus, Copernicus, Kepler and Kayser were obtained in a workshop I attended on "Sound

Signature Technologies" with Sharry Edwards in 1992.

Jamie James, *The Music of the Spheres: Music, Science, and the Natural Order of The Universe,* New York, Grove Press, 1993.
References to the Pythagorean musical scale was quoted from this source. It is excellent for understanding both the mechanics and physics of music and vibration.

Bob Fissell, *Nothing in this Book is True, But It's Exactly How Things Are,* Berkley, CA, North Atlantic Books, 1994.
Comments on the mathematical relationships between planets and molecular structures was taken from Bob Fissell's book. His work was based on a workshop we both attended called the "Flower of Life" by Drunvalo Melchizedek located in Flagstaff, AZ.

Robert Lloy, Sound Energy Research, Oxnard, CA
The reference to my work with Robert Lloy is through the training I have taken with him; he is the Founder and Director of Sound Energy Research in Oxnard, CA.

Herbert Benson, *The Relaxation Response,* New York, Avon Books, 1975 and *Beyond the Relaxation Response,* New York, Times Books, 1984.
Reference to the relaxation response was taken from these two sources.

Although not cited directly, I found the work of Skye Alexander, *Planets in Signs,* West Chester, PA, Whitford Press, 1988 to be very helpful. Additional resource reading was completed from Mario Paltrinieri and Elena Rader's book *The Book of Practical Astrology* (New York, MacMillan Publlishing Company, 1981). Another text not cited, but no doubt of influence in my writing was Alan Orken's book *Soul Centered Astrology* (New York, Bantam Books, 1990).

Figures 45–47 were adapted from Raymond Merriman's text *Evolutionary Astrology* (W. Bloomfield, MI Seek-It Publications, 1991).

Figure 48, 50, 56-59, 61-63 were original illustrations developed for this text. Figures 49 and 53 were adapted from Jamie James' *The Music of the Spheres: Music, Science and the Natural Order of the Universe* (New York, Grove Press, 1993). Figure 51 was taken from handouts given during Drunvalo Melchizekek's Florwer of Life workshop I attended in Dallas in 1992. Figure 52 was adapted from Bob Fissell's book *Nothing in This Book is True, But It's Exactly How Things Are* (Berkley, CA, North Atlantic Books, 1994). Figure 54 was adapted from Richard Gerber's text *Vibrational Medicine: New Choices for Healing Ourselves* (Santa Fe, MN, Bear & Company, 1988). Figure 55 and 60 were adapted from information received in the Sound Signature Workshop with Sharry Edwards, 1992.

Chapter 9 Entering the Silence

Anodea Judith, *Wheels of Life: A User's Guide to the Chakra System,* St. Paul, The Llewellan New Times, 1992.

Citations for this chapter were taken from Anodea Judith's work *Wheels of Life.* Not directly cited, but none-the-less an important resource for me has been Gary Zukav's *The Seat of the Soul* (New York, Simon & Schuster, 1990).

Figures 64-66 were taken from my own drawings and tables and transposed into computer text.

Chapter 10 Transposing the Ordinary Into Miracles

Christopher Fry, *A Sleep of Prisoners,* Dramatists Play, 1953.

The poem at the beginning of this chapter was taken from Cristopher Fry's play.

J.J. Hurtak, *The Keys of Enoch,* Los Gatos, CA, The Academy for Future Science, 1977).

A direct quotation was taken from J.J. Hurtak's work.

Not directly quoted, but other resources for the serious student include Steven Locke and Douglas Colligan's work *The Healer Within: The New Medicine of Mind and Body* (New York, E.P. Dutton, 1986); David Peat's work *The Philosopher's Stone: Chaos, Synchonicity, and the Hidden Order of the World* (New York, Bantam Books, 1991), Michael Talbot's *The Holographic Universe* (New York, Harper Collins Publishers, 1991); Steven Levine's book *Healing into Life and Death* (New York, Doubleday, 1987); and Kenneth Pelletier's new work, *Mind as Healer, Mind as Slayer* (New York, Delta Books, 1992).

About the Author

Research Associate and Clinician, Holistic Healing Arts, Sedona, AZ
Regional Chairperson, Occupational Therapy Department, Texas Tech University Health Sciences Center, Amarillo, TX
Owner, Lanajean Stain Glass Studios, Amarillo, TX
Private Sabbatical and Research in Quantum Physics
Founder and Director, Sound Health Center, Rochester, MI
Fellow, American Occupational Therapy Association, Rockville, MD
Ph.D. Neurocognitive Behavior, Union Institute, Cincinnati, OH
Consultant, Commission on Practice, American Occupational Therapy Association, Rockville, MD
Associate Professor, Western Michigan University, Kalamazoo, MI
Consultant, Army Medical Specialists Corps, Surgeon General's Office, Washington. D.C.
Assistant Professor, Medical College of Virginia, Richmond, VA
Federal Research Project with Severely Handicapped, Akron Children's Hospital, Akron & Louisville, OH
Director, Child Find Project, Duval County Schools, Jacksonville, FL
Academic Consultant, Retardation Program Office, Jacksonville, FL
Director of Psychiatric Therapies, St. Vincent Hospital, Jacksonville, FL
M.S. Education, University of Kansas, Lawrence, KS
Instructor, University of Kansas, Lawrence, KS
Private Practice with the elderly in Extended Care Facilities, San Diego, CA
Owner/Operator, Black & White & Beautiful (art gallery), San Diego, CA
Craft Instructor, Yokuska Naval Base, Yokuska, Japan
B.S. Occupational Therapy, University of Kansas, Lawrence, KS.

In 1995 Dr. Ford formed a partnership with Dr. Rita Ward. Both serve as Associates of Natama Institute for the Research, Education and Balance of Subtle Energies.

Dr. Ward is the creator of the **Harmonic Wave Table** developed to assist in self-healing sessions by promoting relaxation within a safe environment. The table allows the body to reach a state between conscious and unconscious relaxation, promoting alpha and theta brain wave patterns. By allowing the conscious mind to actively participate at this stage in healing, the opportunity is presented to recode old habits that are no longer desirable, thus allowing the body, mind and spirit to balance and attune to higher individual vibrations.

Harmonic Sounds facilitated by Dr. Ford, is based on an individual voice sample which is analyzed by a computer generated spectum analysis process. The intent is to determine harmonic frequency overlay between the subtle energy bodies and how they are expressed in physical form. These frequencies are then reduced to beta, alpha, theta or delta frequencies (which correspond with physical, emotional, mental and spiritual states of being) and are played during a session or transferred to an audio tape for at-home use. This allows the brain to enter a process of "entrainment" in which new neural pathways are created, thus balancing the body from within.

Inquiries regarding telephone and clinical services may be directed to Holistic Healing Arts, 40 W. Cortez, Sedona, Arizona, phone 520-284-0196. Dr. Ford and Dr. Ward are available for seminars and workshops in your area.

About the Artist

Gene Falk is a world renowned photographer, known for creating magical images on film that communicate the realities of nature's inner world, expressing itself through crystals and minerals.

For over 15 years he has communicated with nature through the medium of film. His visionary work suggests that crystals hold the images of earth and mankind as a living library, recording the joys and sorrows throughout the entire evolutionary cycle. His photographs provide viewers with a look into a once invisible dimension of the living world inside crystals and minerals.

Gene constructed a unique optical bench with lenses inherited from his father, a telescope enthusiast. By refocusing the lenses from outer space to the inner space of crystals, Gene reveals a remarkable realm of nature in radiant beams, gleaming facades, and expansive auroras. His work brings forth the wisdom of the earth, with it's record of humanity's transformation.

Gene's remarkable photographs have been enjoyed by thousands of viewers, presented to former President Ford, Pope John Paul II, numerous celebrities and displayed at presitgious shows in Paris, New York, Los Angeles, Carmel, Phoenix and many other galleries throughout the world.

This work was selected for it's composite features. Since Gene has completed over 2000 photographs, he was unable to remember the exact crystal. However, this one was selected because it reminded the author of the living cobalt blue light of Lord Michael spilling forth from the Holy Grail. It was selected also for the richness of earth tones. It seemed the perfect merger of Heaven and Earth, coming forth from invisible realms -- an ordinary crystal reflecting the miracles within.

Products

(Please tear out and and mail this form)

Name ______________________________ Date ____________
Street _________________________ City ____________________
State __________________________ Zip ____________________

Miracles and Other Ordinary Things $19.95 [ ]

Audio Tape Series

Entering the Silence (3 audio tapes) $29.95 [ ]

A: Kinesthetic Awareness and Relaxation of the body
B: Brain Body Temple
C: Bioenergetics: Subtle Bodies and Chakra Centers

Guided Meditations adapted from *Miracles and Other Ordinary Things:*

101: Alignment of the Physical Body	$ 9.95	[ ]
102: Entering the Brain Body Temple	$ 9.95	[ ]
103: The Evolutionary Brain	$ 9.95	[ ]
104: Multi-Sensory Tracking	$ 9.95	[ ]
104: Balancing the Chakra Energy	$ 9.95	[ ]
105: Healing the Inner Child	$ 9.95	[ ]
106: Journey into All That Is	$ 9.95	[ ]

Shipping add .15% of total purchases. [ ]
Arizona residents add 7% tax. [ ]

Money Order/Cashier's Checks/Personal check:

Holistic Healing Arts **Total [ ]**
40 W. Cortez, Sedona, AZ 86351

Products

(Please tear out and and mail this form)

Name ______________________________ Date ____________
Street _______________________ City ___________________
State ________________________ Zip ___________________

Miracles and Other Ordinary Things $19.95 [ ]

Audio Tape Series

Entering the Silence (3 audio tapes) $29.95 [ ]

A: Kinesthetic Awareness and Relaxation of the body
B: Brain Body Temple
C: Bioenergetics: Subtle Bodies and Chakra Centers

Guided Meditations adapted from *Miracles and Other Ordinary Things:*

101: Alignment of the Physical Body	$ 9.95	[ ]
102: Entering the Brain Body Temple	$ 9.95	[ ]
103: The Evolutionary Brain	$ 9.95	[ ]
104: Multi–Sensory Tracking	$ 9.95	[ ]
104: Balancing the Chakra Energy	$ 9.95	[ ]
105: Healing the Inner Child	$ 9.95	[ ]
106: Journey into All That Is	$ 9.95	[ ]

Shipping add .15% of total purchases. [ ]
Arizona residents add 7% tax. [ ]

Money Order/Cashier's Checks/Personal check:

Holistic Healing Arts **Total [ ]**
40 W. Cortez, Sedona, AZ 86351